Quisqueya
la Bella

Perspectives on Latin America and the Caribbean

THE CHAINS OF INTERDEPENDENCE
U.S. POLICY TOWARD CENTRAL AMERICA, 1945–1954
Michael L. Krenn

A HOLY ALLIANCE?
THE CHURCH AND THE LEFT
IN COSTA RICA, 1932–1948
Eugene D. Miller

QUISQUEYA LA BELLA
THE DOMINICAN REPUBLIC IN HISTORICAL AND
CULTURAL PERSPECTIVE
Alan Cambeira

REVOLUTION REASSESSED
DEMOCRACY AND THE LEFT IN
CONTEMPORARY CENTRAL AMERICA
Stepehn R. Pelletier

Quisqueya la Bella

THE DOMINICAN REPUBLIC IN HISTORICAL AND CULTURAL PERSPECTIVE

Alan Cambeira

M. E. Sharpe
Armonk, New York
London, England

Library of Congress Cataloging-in-Publication Data

Cambeira, Alan, 1941–
Quisqueya la bella : the Dominican Republic in historical and cultural perspective / Alan Cambeira.
p.   cm. — (Perspectives on Latin America and the Caribbean)
Includes bibliographical references and index.
ISBN 1–56324–935–9 (alk. paper). —
ISBN 1–56324–936–7 (pbk. : alk. paper)
1. Dominican Republic—Civilization.
I. Title.
II. Series.
F1935.C36   1996
972.93—dc20
96–32355
CIP

Printed in the United States of America

The paper used in this publication meets the minimum requirements of American National Standard for Information Sciences— Permanence of Paper for Printed Library Materials, ANSI Z 39.48-1984.

∞

BM (c)   10   9   8   7   6   5   4   3   2   1
BM (p)   10   9   8   7   6   5   4   3   2   1

Quisqueya la bella (Beautiful Quisqueya). In the language of the indigenous Taíno culture, *Quisqueya* meant Mother of All Lands. *Haiti* meant Land of Mountains. These were the alternating names for the island prior to the arrival of the Spaniards, who renamed it *Hispaniola* (Little Spain).

To Julio César Belén,
whose loyalty from the inception of this project
was absolute and unwavering,
and whose skillful assistance to me
in interpreting the Dominican experience was indispensable.

También a mi querida mamá, a mis hijos Lorenzo, Ricky, *y* Carmen,
pero especialmente a mi esposa Angela Vielka.

To the memory of my genius brother, Talib Hakim,
my niece Pam, and my nephew Jon, who loved Quisqueya.

Contents

List of Maps

Acknowledgments

The author is indebted to the National Endowment for the Humanities, the Rockefeller Foundation, and the Council for Basic Education/The Andrew W. Mellon Foundation for fellowship awards that made this undertaking possible. I would like to express my sincerest gratitude to some very special individuals who, in one significant fashion or another, and quite unexpectedly, actually collaborated in the realization of this book. For their unselfish support and wonderful encouragement throughout, for their graciousness and compassion in understanding my intentions, these special individuals are deserving of far more than this humble public acknowledgment. Doña Paulina Lantigua, Jimmy Lantigua, Milagros Holguín, Fela Jaime Abreu, all the dear members of the Guadalupe Belén family (María, Ramón, and Josefina), Teodosia Núñez de la Rosa ("Rosa"), Bernarda Luna, César Román, Eladio Regalado, Ramón Tejada Holguín and Zeneida Severino, Nelson Mella, Julio Félix, "Fifo" Brugal Paiewonsky, Viga Pichardo, and Doña Gudelia are true gems. Thank you for your invaluable assistance. Also, to the many very kind and thoughtful persons from one end of Quisqueya la Bella to the other, who offered me tremendous insights, I thank you. This book certainly would have been impossible without your help. *Muchísimas gracias a todo el pueblo hospitalario dominicano.* Finally, I am enormously grateful to Stephen J. Dalphin, executive editor at M.E. Sharpe, for his unflagging patience, assistance, and faith in the merits of my manuscript; also, I am sincerely appreciative of the technical assistance of Christine Florie, project editor.

Quisqueya la Bella

Introduction

The Caribbean! The mere utterance of the word instantly conjures up the quintessential vision of its sun, sand, and sea. The images are like polished fantasies taken straight from the glossiest travel brochure: luxury cruise ships pulling into sun-drenched ports, duty-free shopping, deluxe resort enclaves, exotic tales of sunken treasure from mighty galleons sailing the Spanish Main, romantic swashbuckling pirates and buccaneers, plantation ruins from centuries past, historic forts, remnants of massive sugarmills, pelicans, sandpipers, flamingos, windsurfing, snorkeling and scuba, miles upon miles of often solitary sand-swept beaches dotted with cozy cays and coves, radiantly warm turquoise seawater washing across coral reefs, gently lapping against beaches with fine, powderlike sand. The shimmering islands of the Caribbean are undeniably among the most beautiful and captivating jewels in the entire world. The Caribbean lands constitute a distinct world of their own, stretching some two thousand miles from the Central American republics east to the arc of the Lesser Antilles—a tropical paradise of celestial beauty.

Many people often mistakenly include the Bahama Islands in the Caribbean group. In a strictly geographical sense, however, the Bahamas are more correctly part of the total West Indies region, while actually lying in the Atlantic Ocean off the southern tip of Florida. The islands of the Caribbean are properly divided into two principal groups. On the north lie the large and prominent Cuba, Jamaica, Hispaniola, which is shared by both Haiti and the Dominican Republic, and Puerto Rico, together forming what are called the Greater Antilles. Circling eastward from Puerto Rico and then south toward Venezuela, spotting the turquoise carpet, are the Lesser Antilles, including Antigua, Guadeloupe, Dominica, Martinique, St. Lucia, St. Vincent and the Grenadines, faraway Barbados, Trinidad/Tobago, Aruba, Curaçao, and Bonaire.

When we look beyond the fantasy of surface imagery, however, a more naked reality, strapped with centuries of riveting history, greets the eye. The Great Encounter that was eventually to remake three different and opposing worlds—the indigenous Americas, Europe, and Africa—began with Columbus's reconnaissance of 1492 and, later, his unheralded return in 1493 with a total of eighteen ships in tow. They disgorged horses, rats, pigs, weeds, fruit trees, and diseases, and more than a thousand men. Infusions of Spaniards bearing pathogens triggered pandemics that ultimately killed millions of indigenous people who had never before seen or even heard of a European. When the Europeans saw their supply of colonial forced labor rapidly dwindle away, they began a feverish campaign to import captives from Africa. The Caribbean would soon house the dominant new settler group in the region—the Black slaves who began arriving in such astonishing numbers from Africa that within a relatively short time they outnumbered and eventually outpowered all other groups combined.

In the centuries following the Encounter, the Caribbean was characterized by an era of intense imperial rivalry (1625–1765). Fascinated by the region's potential wealth and the strategic importance in naval warfare, the nations of Europe became intimately entrenched in Caribbean affairs, with decisive sea battles occurring in the waters of the region. The fleets of Spain, Holland, England, France, even Denmark and Sweden, all were engaged in bitter action in the region. In the 1640s and 1650s, Dutch refugees from the Portuguese territory of Brazil taught the English and French planters how to produce sugar. Estate owners grew rich on the sweat and blood of millions of Africans who suffered under the whips and chains of slavery throughout the entire Caribbean.

The slave-based sugar plantation system built the economies of the Caribbean. Slave uprisings wracked just about every island in the late 1700s. Rebellion succeeded absolutely only in the wealthy French col-

ony of Saint Domingue—the world's richest colony at the time—
where slaves proclaimed themselves free and established the independent nation of Haiti on January 1, 1804. Britain freed its slaves in
1834; France and Denmark followed in 1848. Spain delayed until the
late 1800s, with abolition finally coming to Cuba in 1886. In 1898 the
Spanish-American War erupted. The United States sent troops into
Cuba, and by year's end American-backed Cuban nationalists had won
freedom from Spain. Meanwhile, the United States occupied Puerto
Rico. As suppliers of sugar and other desired tropical products, the
islands of Cuba, Puerto Rico, and the Dominican Republic attracted
heavy North American investment. Americans invested well over a
billion dollars in Cuban sugar alone. In the era of United States military and economic intervention, the Caribbean was nicknamed "The
American Mediterranean." The core of the United States' sphere of
influence extended roughly from the Virgin Islands to Panama and
Nicaragua. During World War II the United States strung lend-lease
military bases along the Antilles to safeguard the major sea gates joining the Atlantic Ocean and the Caribbean Sea. Since 1945 few islands
have enjoyed vigorous economic growth. Some blame their problems
on neocolonialism, which drains out capital and stifles local initiatives.

New Year's Day 1959 marked the end of the long era of a corrupt
and decadent Cuba under the Batista government. The young intellectual and rebel leader Fidel Castro ushered in a new revolutionary Cuba,
turning the island from capitalism and heavy dependence on the United
States to socialism. Successive waves of emigration since have carried
more than a million Cuban exiles to the shores of the Unites States.
Now, some thirty-five years later and plagued with severely crippling
economic difficulties, Cuba is struggling for new direction, Castro
himself for a new role. The surrounding Caribbean lands have become
sufficiently pragmatic to adjust to the new Cuban reality affecting the
entire region.

Contrary to what many people in the United States believe, the
islands of the Caribbean are quite diverse, while still having much in
common. Most are truly small, except for Cuba and Hispaniola. The
largest of all the islands, Cuba is about the size of Virginia. Grenada
has about the same area as the District of Columbia. Jamaica is roughly
the size of the state of Connecticut. None of the islands is entirely
ethnically or culturally heterogeneous. In fact, the major cultural characteristic of the Caribbean is diversity itself. In race, culture, language,

and religion, the element of diversity makes the Caribbean one of the most heterogeneous regions of the world. This stems from the complex population movements that created Caribbean societies: African, Caucasian, Native American, East Indian—with any number of subgroups and admixtures of Middle Eastern, Chinese, and other Asian peoples. Five of the six countries in the world with the highest per-capita rates for migration to the United States in the late 1980s are from the Caribbean. Almost two million Puerto Ricans (who are, of course, United States citizens) have come, as well as over one million Cubans, about one million West Indians, well over half a million Dominicans, and more than 600,000 Haitians. Clearly, the most impressive link between the Caribbean and the United States is this steady stream of Caribbean immigration to the mainland. It is estimated that since World War II, about one out of every seven living individuals born in the islands now has taken up residence in the Unites States. Perhaps as much as 25 percent of legal immigrants to the United States, and an even higher percentage of undocumented aliens, originate in the Caribbean.

There is also extreme diversity in terms of the Caribbean's economic structure: from the tax havens of the Caymans to the mixed economies of socialism and some degree of state-supported privatization in today's Cuba. Haiti, still among the world's poorest countries, due largely to the devastations of previous dictatorial greed and corruption, offers much hope after the restored presidency of Aristide. But overall, Caribbean economies are in the midst of painfully serious difficulties. Two principal Caribbean exports—sugar and bauxite—are facing trouble with their vulnerability to international market fluctuations. The region's lucrative tourism revenues are under strain from rising domestic crime and increasingly unpredictable weather. Agriculture, for the most part, is weak and declining throughout most of the region. Unemployment and underemployment are dangerously high almost everywhere in the Caribbean. We have yet to determine the total effects of newly signed regional and world trade and related commercial agreements initiated by the United States.

Added to the list of problematic questions beyond the facade of sun, sea, and fun is the reality of a growing restlessness during recent years. Most of the Caribbean islands are quite overpopulated, and emigration from all these islands is high, with a steady rise in illegal passage. Regional economic difficulties, for certain, have been a key factor. But underscoring the societal discomfort and anxiety has been the conflict among fundamental, legitimate goals and earnest community and individual frustration about not achieving these goals. Economic growth, improved equity, full employment, genuine political representation and responsiveness, and meaningful national autonomy are frequently the common themes throughout the region. All the islands are to varying degrees dependent on close ties of one kind or another to a metropole requiring a tightly regulated pattern of relationship (but almost never partnership) with a power center located elsewhere. In recent years, that center has been Washington, D.C.

The United States is very closely involved with the entire Caribbean basin—increasingly dominating the trade and investment, even the internal politics of the countries in the region. Whether monitoring, then condemning, national elections in the Dominican Republic, physically escorting Aristide back to his presidential post, physically extraditing Noriega from Panama, or being instrumental in eliminating Grenada's elected president, Maurice Bishop, the United States is finding that its activity (economic assistance or military presence) in the region has multiplied more than tenfold since 1977, even while overall foreign aid amounts have been downscaled. Except for Israel and Egypt, the countries of the Caribbean basin are the largest recipients of United States monetary assistance in the world. Yet, serious social ills remain lurking in full, often inexplicable view. Poverty, disease, illiteracy, and critical housing shortages plague the region still. Viable development strategies apparently have not been very successful. Progress has been elusive and, understandably, mounting frustration has resulted. Escalated United States involvement, along with renewed North American interest in the Caribbean, especially in the areas of crucial diplomatic and demographic matters, has heightened in significance. The islands of the Caribbean hold many votes in the United Nations, the Organization of American States, and other bodies, thus rendering these island nations a valuable ally in supporting United States positions on any number of international issues. In terms of demographics, the United States has a definite stake in regulating the migration flow from the region, thus dispelling local, stateside anxieties and potentially explosive situations in communities from Florida to New York and New Jersey, California, Texas, and other states as well.

Eliminating the possibility for regional conflagration in the Caribbean, keeping accessible and open the vital sea lanes that pass through the Caribbean, and promoting significant economic development and long-term political stability for the ultimate goal of self-sufficiency are thus some of the fundamental concerns of United States involvement in the region. The real challenge for sincere United States commitment to the islands has therefore become a matter of national will and credibility. Perhaps at last the people of the United States have awakened to the reality that their happiness and tranquility, prosperity and growth are vitally interlocked with the well-being of the populations of the Caribbean. Open and honest discussions and helpful information about the region, its history, culture, and people have today become an urgent necessity.

Quisqueya la Bella

We now turn our focus, in prefacing this work, upon one island in particular, which the indigenous Taíno culture called Quisqueya or sometimes Haiti. Quisqueya, Mother of All Lands, is today La República Dominicana. The reasons for an introductory profile of the Dominican Republic are not difficult to fathom. At present the United States is in a seriously tense, and frequently ugly, period of its history that is marred by a resurgence of urgent questions of ethnicity and immigration as a double-edged, major component of its political, social, and economic development. Until recently, this resurgence, especially as it characterizes the Hispanic or Latino as protagonist, was largely ignored by most culturalists, historians, and sociologists. In the last few years, however, the impact of Caribbean immigration— and most pointedly the undocumented arrival of Spanish-speaking and Creole-speaking Antillean groups—on ordinary, everyday life in targeted American cities has been so overwhelming that academicians, policy makers, and numerous social agency personnel have all been suddenly forced to pay attention and recognize that impact.

Seldom are students in most North American schools and universities introduced to Caribbean peoples and their diverse cultures. Even less frequently are these students exposed to the Spanish-speaking Caribbean, which stands somewhat apart from the general Antilles experience. I have noticed from my own personal classroom experiences, for instance, that even in most Spanish language courses, the units on Hispanic culture will invariably present Mexico, mention the region of Central America, then romanticize South America. Any deliberate study of Spain's legacy in the Caribbean is routinely confined to a few brief paragraphs devoted to the islands of Cuba and Puerto Rico, unless, of course, there is a fully structured Puerto Rican Area Studies component at the university level. Both these islands have been closely linked economically and politically to the United States throughout most of the region's modern history (primarily since the early 1860s when Washington contemplated and attempted negotiations to annex the Dominican Republic's Samaná Peninsula). Students need to review thoroughly the long, ugly, and shameful history of North American intervention and occupation in the various nations of the Caribbean basin, as well as the United States' ubiquitous involvement in the internal affairs of these countries.

Although La República Dominicana is a mere two-hour flight from Miami, many students and often their teachers know embarrassingly little about Dominican culture, its history, and its people, who are unquestionably a major source today of immigrants to the United States mainland. With the exception of Puerto Rico, Cuba, and Barbados, more migrants flow from the Dominican Republic than anywhere else in the Caribbean. Current estimates of *dominicanos* living in the States as official resident aliens and/or undocumented immigrants reach more than a half million. So, besides the immediately obvious connection—the volume of trade and tourism with the United States— by far the most significant ties between the States and the island nation known as Quisqueya la Bella actually involve people. The island nation, together with the Caribbean region as a whole, by reason of its proximity to United States shores and of the growing international prominence of some of the region's fascinating and charismatic leaders, has become a kind of litmus test of the attitudes and official policies that Washington will inevitably adopt toward countries of the developing world generally.

From my personal observation to date, there is lamentably a profound scarcity or often a total lack of information written in English about the cultural formation of La República Dominicana. Every Dominican student, however, before completing the rigorous *bachillerato* (secondary-level academic course of studies in Latin America), has had, as absolutely required reading, the island's legendary giants of Dominican history and related social commentary. Included among the most widely read and highly respected historians are Frank Moya Pons, Roberto Cassá, Rubén Silié, Franklyn Franco, Emilio Rodríguez Demorizi, and Emilio Cordero Michel. The truly commendable books monographs published in English about specific aspects of the island—dealing almost exclusively with the subject of the United States military interventions of first 1916 and later 1965—number, to my knowledge, under a dozen. Perhaps the most familiar works include Bruce J. Calder's scholarly *The Impact of Intervention: The Dominican Republic During the U.S. Occupation of 1916–1924;* Theodore Draper's *The Dominican Revolt: A Case Study in American Policy;* and Michael J. Kryzanek's *The Dominican Intervention Revisited: An Attitudinal and Operational Analysis.* The general reader, however, may well find these studies complex and quite frustrating. Moreover, the reader will very likely feel at a loss in arriving at any sensitive appreciation unless first having become sufficiently groomed for La República Dominicana with an introductory cultural overview.

This book aspires to provide precisely that needed overview, as well as to help satisfy the growing demand in the United States for instructional aids and appropriate resource material on La República Dominicana. I seriously hope that the reader, upon completing this preliminary source book, will decide to explore further into the various topics and issues introduced here by consulting the references suggested in the general bibliography. The reader is forewarned that this book is laced with my own personal observations, perspectives, and opinions. Most assuredly, though, these personal views are buttressed solidly by trusted, unselfishly helpful Dominican friends, family, and colleagues, themselves keen observers and faithful commentators, some of whom are professional analysts and seasoned interpreters of Dominican culture and society. Under no circumstances was there ever any broad scheme or personal thesis to prove or sociopolitical agenda to present here. Rather, this book may be regarded as *un manual introductorio* (introductory manual), a kind of basic working tool for those readers with a genuine desire and interest in being formally introduced to Dominican culture. This is not, in the strictest sense, a history text, conceived and structured according to conventional criteria. Instead, it is more an integrated exposition of the sociohistorical evolution of Dominican culture, with primary focus upon those elements of cultural and ethnic diversity that ultimately constitute a collective, national identity. It is this *identidad nacional* that serves as the logical backdrop for that exposition.

My own exploration to find and understand that national identity led me on a four-month-long journey to the island in 1993. Under the auspices of a fellowship award from the National Endowment for the Humanities/Rockefeller Foundation, I was able to investigate at close range the formative ingredients of Dominican culture. Together with a few dedicated travel companions and very encouraging friends—all Dominicans—we set out upon the roads, back roads, paths, and trails of the Republic, crisscrossing the island from one corner to the other, from the northern coast to the southern coast, determined to gather as much information as possible. Traversing nearly all twenty-seven provinces, from the remote Elias Piña at the far western end near the Haitian border to the eastern end at Higüey, we met and talked with all kinds of Dominican citizens. We recorded countless hours of informal, candid conversations and provocative interviews that ran the gamut of socioeconomic groups, political ideologies, and educational backgrounds. As we traveled across the island's different locales, the changing linguistic variants became most striking—a difference in pronunciation, tone, vocabulary, and sometimes in syntax. From taxi drivers and dock workers to palace guards, sugarcane workers, border zone merchants, university academicians, erudite museum directors and curators, town mayors and shoeshine boys in town parks; from elegant banquet halls with the country's top military brass, active and retired generals, to *chimichurri* street vendors; from former United States Ambassador Robert Pastorino to the almost mythical Don Viga Pichardo of Tamboril—visiting places as contrasting as the humble market stalls along Calle Duarte to the stately corridors and receiving room at the National Palace, I was able to gather a most intimate, rare, and unforgettable view of what is exposed in this book, *la cultura dominicana.*

Quisqueya: Hospitalaria Amatoria
(Quisqueya: A Loving Hospitality)

The essence of Dominican culture is embodied in a people who have spent three centuries immersed in an audacious struggle for their freedom, their sovereignty, and their empowerment to forge a national identity and collective purpose. Dominican culture is exemplified in a people whose origins sprang from the fusion of three profoundly rich heritages—the indigenous, the Spanish, the African. The result was *los dominicanos,* a people who early armed themselves with commitment and hope, and who fought long and hard in order that the inalienable right of national integrity and self-determination be forever guaranteed

and secured. Through sustained periods of suffering, misery, and repression, through repeated foreign military intervention and occupation, as well as nefarious local schemes by self-serving Dominicans to
compromise the nation itself, *el pueblo dominicano* has displayed its
unique resolve to survive the often monumental odds. I would certainly
describe the Dominicans' half-century fight for liberty as being the
most protracted and agonizing in the record of the emancipation of
Spanish America.

The nation had been unavoidably caught up in the bloody turmoil of
neighboring Haiti, and had become the prized target of the French,
Spanish, English, and other European powers obsessed with the notion
of acquiring the strategic Caribbean island for purposes of expanded
trade and empire building. Even after independence was won (1844),
los dominicanos were ill equipped to make gains on their hard-won
liberty. Theirs became a dismal record of renewed fighting and suffering for some seventy-three additional years under shamelessly corrupt,
incompetent, and brutally oppressive dictatorships. Anarchy, a swift
succession of short-lived and generally avaricious, self-serving presidents, and unbelievably monstrous foreign debts—perhaps more than
$30 million owed to creditors of France, Belgium, Germany, Italy,
Spain, and the United States, became characteristic of life in the island.
More assassinations, civil wars, and general chaos continued until
1916, when the United States Marines were sent to intervene in the
disorders, beginning an eight-year military occupation and domination.
Still, *el pueblo dominicano* endured.

Throughout the era of Trujillo, the Dominican people survived a
period of unprecedented tyranny. It is said that perhaps no other Latin
American ruler presented a more spectacular record of actual material
achievement—impressive buildings and massive public works—or a
more heinous record of reprehensible human rights atrocities. *El Benefactor de la Patria* had a total of 1,870 monuments to himself in the
capital city alone, many others scattered around the island. Yet still
the people survived. But the grossly tragic upheaval came in April
1965. A most destructive, bloody civil war occurred (some have
called it a revolution), with the subsequent unilateral United States
military invasion—again without the required OAS consultation. This
action evoked a colossal outcry from the whole of Latin America. This
monstrously devastating civil war cost the Republic an estimated five
million Dominican lives! The Dominican crisis of 1965 is still debated

and analyzed to this present day. Perhaps at no other juncture in the nation's history—once North American troops finally left Dominican shores following the elections of 1966—was there a more critical time of agonizing reflection to determine the national direction and its multifaceted implications for the future. Yet, even with the resultant severely divided nation, *los dominicanos* were able to summon up their traditional inner resources and strengths to endure the calamity of a house divided. The people, through their electoral decisions—however laden with serious problems and often ugly controversies the process has been over the years—have ultimately chosen a return to relative normalcy. The people have demanded an end to the disruptive warring factions that had been ripping the country apart; they have wanted long-deferred and much needed economic stability and a favorable business climate for investments. When Antonio Guzmán later assumed the presidency, for instance, La República Dominicana, according to many observers, enjoyed its first peaceful democratic transition in generations of domestic politics. There was widespread hope that the Republic was at last on the sensible, substantial socioeconomic progress in a manner akin to liberal democracy.

Solo el Pueblo Salva al Pueblo
(Only the People Themselves Can Save the People)

How true rings this simple phrase! The country, in most recent years, has been faced with rather grim socioeconomic and political pressures. In the midst of deadly and explosive outbursts of anger, renewed civil unrest, and discontent throughout the country—and to mention only in the most minimal fashion the growing allegations of fraudulent elections—the Dominican people still manage to overwhelm the odds. As a consequence of enduring the harshness of all kinds of vicissitudes, *los dominicanos* have unconsciously realized their long-sought-after, yet elusive *identidad nacional*. The Dominican people, through a genuine and committed strengthening of faith in themselves, fully understand that the national identity is being forged as the nation and the people become one, as the people transform themselves into the legitimate hegemony of their society. *El pueblo* will at last recognize themselves as the logical and the only honorable successors to the collective spirits of Enriquillo, Lemba, Duarte, Luperón, Manolo, and all the other historic champions of liberty. On the occasion of a public rally in the nation's capital during the presidential campaign of 1993, a full year prior to the following year's actual election, candidate Dr. José Francisco Peña Gómez admonished the listeners

> La hora es de unión, de patriotism, y de dominicanidad. Nosotros los caribeños somos una dimensión de la humanidad que ha tenido que batirse y que se bate todavía muy duramente para que hacer que se le respete esa dignidad.

> (The hour is now for union, for patriotism, for Dominicanness. We Caribbean peoples are a dimension of humanity that has had to fight and is still fighting very hard for that dignity to be respected.)

Map 1. The Caribbean Region Showing the Dominican Republic

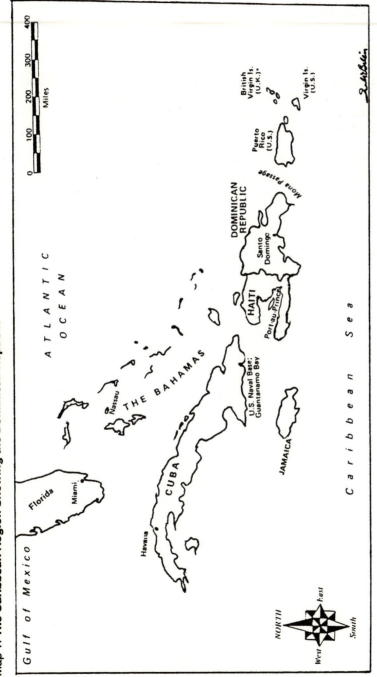

1

Introducing Quisqueya

Beacon of the Caribbean, La República Dominicana should definitely not be confused with the much smaller, English-speaking island of Dominica, located among the farther eastern Caribbean Leeward group. The Dominican Republic, once called Quisqueya,[1] boasts sixty-seven types and three hundred species of orchids found on the island. The national tree is the *caoba,* or mahogany. The national bird is the *cotica* parrot, which is bright green and very talkative, and is a popular pet in many Dominican households. The national dish is *sancocho;* the national dance and music style is the *merengue.* The national sport is unquestionably *béisbol.* More than half of the more than three hundred professional Dominican ballplayers currently active with North American major and minor league ball clubs come from the town of San Pedro de Macorís. This island nation is one of the few countries (if not perhaps the only one) that honors a trio of *Padres de la Patria* (Fathers of the Nation): Juan Pablo Duarte, the writer; Matías Ramón Mella, the soldier; and Francisco del Rosario Sánchez, the lawyer. A high-ranking Catholic clergyman, Padre Fernando Arturo de Meriño, has served as president. Archbishop Adolfo Alejandro Nouel was a short-term interim president. The region's history is reflected even today as witnessed in neighboring Haiti, where a radical, former Catholic priest, Jean-Bertrand Aristide, has also served as president.

La República Dominicana is a country of dramatic contrasts and stark contradictions. At the same time seductive and captivating, it is a

country that also can provoke utter frustration and absolute exaspera-
tion. It is a Caribbean country of puzzling idiosyncrasies and agonizing
surprises. From almost any conceivable vantage point, the Dominican
Republic can readily present a long list of contrasting features that, as
evidenced throughout its lengthy and frequently turbulent historical
and cultural evolution, have had wide-ranging effects to varying degrees upon the society as a whole. The land, the people, their history,
and their identifying national traditions and customs, the social, political, and religious institutions all combine to offer the visitor an immediately friendly and gregarious community. It is a *comunidad*
(community) that can be accurately described as possessing boundless
energies and tremendous richness of spirit, along with genuine warmth
unlike any other island society in the Caribbean. Unmistakable also is
the ready, easy openness and unconditional hospitality of the remarkable Dominican people themselves. But still, the contrast and contradictions remain prominently evident. The paradox that is Quisqueya
looms heavily over this beautiful tropical island.

Azúcar

One paradox worthy of special note is the question of *azúcar* (sugar),
the cultivation of which was begun about 1506 on the island. By about
the year 1520 sugarcane cultivation had become an industry. To say
that sugar historically has been—and still is—extremely important to
the Dominican economy is a gross understatement, even given the
government's efforts in recent years to encourage diversification in the
agricultural sector. Despite the considerable wealth derived from
sugar, which accounted for and sustained the principal cities, and the
entire nation as well, the overwhelming majority of Dominicans
throughout the country's evolution have remained shamefully poor!
This circumstance was a direct result of the fact that many of the
lucrative profits and related benefits of the sugar-based economy made
their way exclusively to the socioeconomic upper echelons of Dominican society and to foreign investors. Moreover, most of the nation's
untapped wealth remained noticeably undeveloped or underdeveloped.

On the subject of sugar quotas, there is another interesting note.
Until 1984, the United States' import quota system, of which La
República Dominicana was the largest beneficiary, provided a prefer-
ential market for over half the country's sugar exports, as well as a

handy safety net to cushion against the slump in sugar prices on the global market. The inevitable switch in United States consumer tastes—going from traditional sugar to high-tech fructose corn syrup—signaled the move by the United States to reduce quotas to a truly devastating level. By 1988, the Dominican Republic's quota had been cut to 25 percent of previous levels. The main economic thrust was now reshaped into three areas that the Dominican government hoped would replace sugar: tourism, agro-industry, and the expansion of foreign-owned manufacturing/assembling operations in what are called *zonas francas* (free-zone operations), strategically located around the country. It is said, however, that the actual selection site for any new *zona franca* is often determined more by political considerations than motivated by any particular economic factors. Of the three, tourism has shown the most spectacular growth. Today it is the largest foreign exchange earner—with nearly twice the combined income from sugar, coffee, and cocoa. Increasingly, La República Dominicana is becoming known internationally for its magnificent beaches. According to recent UNESCO reports, for instance, the Dominican Republic "has some of the best beaches in the world: white sand, coconut palms and many with a profusion of green vegetation. Current annual receipts from tourism are estimated at about U.S.$750 million."[2]

The Dominican Reality

However, no introduction to Quisqueya would be faithful without a studied view of the Dominican reality today, a reality that remains quite grim. This reality is laden with potholes as potentially ruinous as those encountered on most streets of the nation's capital city, Santo Domingo, as well as on the roads of small towns and hamlets throughout the Republic. Continued devaluation of the Dominican peso is steadily eroding purchasing power, and mind-boggling inflation is leaping out of control.[3] The continuing impoverishment is reflected in an alarming exodus of "boat people" to the neighboring island of Puerto Rico. Often the journey is ill fated, as increasing numbers of the crudely built *yolas*[4] (wooden rowboats) capsize, leaving the fate of the occupants to the shark-infested waters of the Mona Passage. The Dominican reality, with the dilemma of its U.S.$4 billion debt, is seen as a warning of the perils of entanglement of governmental policies with the International Monetary Fund (IMF).

Unpopularity of governmental policies (i.e., austerity measures) enacted to satisfy IMF demands is widespread. Still, the Dominican government continues negotiations for new agreements, as poorer *dominicanos* are becoming highly politicized and determined to resist the new pressures. The Dominican reality is a society without easy and quick solutions. No single political force in the country today seems to be offering the definitive alternative program. The three major parties are entering a period of special uncertainty after the tumultuous elections of May 1994. An in-depth analysis and commentary on the election results and consequences most assuredly will be a necessary update in a later edition of this present work. La República Dominicana, as well as all the other island societies in the Caribbean, have a common historical legacy: corsairs, buccaneers and pirates, a plantation society of slavery and indentured labor, exploitative monocultural economies (based primarily on sugarcane) producing what they did not consume and consuming what they did not produce, and perhaps the lengthiest period of external political–economic dependence and domination in any part of the developing world.

About the Land

The island is called Hispaniola, and it is the only Caribbean island shared by two distinct countries. There is one other island that does have an almost similar circumstance. Both France and the Netherlands share possession and governance of the same tiny island called both St. Martin/St. Maarten (French-speaking on one side, Dutch-speaking on the other). It is located in the eastern Caribbean between Anguilla and St. Barthelemy. On Hispaniola, two distinct cultures have developed. La República Dominicana, which is Spanish-speaking, occupies the eastern two-thirds of Hispaniola. It has a total land area of 48,734 square kilometers (or 18,816 square miles). The country sharing the island on the western end is the Kryol- and French-speaking Haiti, with a land area covering about 27,750 square kilometers (or 10,714 square miles). The two countries share a common border of some 375 kilometers (232½ miles). This is a border left mostly without adequate or even constant vigilance by border patrols. It is a border where at certain points along its route a traveler can merely slip off his or her shoes, roll up the pant legs or skirt, and wade across a shallow stream of clear water. Hispaniola is the second largest of the Greater Antilles.

The largest, Cuba, is separated from Hispaniola by the Windward Passage and lies about seventy-seven kilometers northwest. The island of Puerto Rico, across the Mona Passage, lies one hundred kilometers eastward.

Cordilleras

Mountains figure prominently in the geography of Hispaniola. Pico Duarte, at 3,175 meters or 10,417 feet, is the highest mountain on the island and in all the Caribbean. Although mountainous, La República Dominicana is actually less mountainous than its western neighbor, Haiti. The whole of Hispaniola, in fact, consists of an impressive series of three major, parallel, east–west mountain chains (*cordilleras*) with alternating, deep valleys. The breathtaking sweep of Dominican landscape is a contrasting mix of low-lying coastal plains, humid lowlands, arid desertlike zones, abundantly lush intramountainous valleys, and high peaks. This alluring and diverse topography accounts for the country's distinct geographic regions, figuring as it has, very decidedly, in the pattern of divergent socioeconomic and political development. Because the Dominican Republic, like the other island nations in the family of the Greater Antilles group, is part of a submerged mountain chain, the country's configuration rests largely upon the three powerful and majestic *cordilleras:* the Cordillera Central, the Cordillera Septentrional, and the Cordillera Oriental. Water draining from these mountain chains forms the principal rivers and waterways of Quisqueya.

Garden of the Antilles

Situated in the country's wide middle zone, the Cordillera Central is the island's massive backbone. It runs well into Haiti, where it becomes the Massif du Nord. It is composed mainly of a variety of volcanic, metamorphic, and sedimentary rocks. To the north of the Cordillera Central, and between this range and the Cordillera Septentrional, which fronts the Atlantic Ocean on the north coast, lies Hispaniola's largest and most fertile valley: the legendary Cibao. This fiercely independent region has served as the dramatic backdrop for many significant episodes in the country's history. Located here also is the Vega Real (Royal Plain), often called "The Garden of the Antilles."

The Cibao-Vega Real is endowed with exceptionally rich alluvial soils, is watered by the many tributaries flowing from the two *cordilleras,* and is liberally supplied with rainfall. These favorable circumstances amply justify the region's renown for the nation's prime crop harvests. The western portion that penetrates Haitian territory becomes the Plaine du Nord for Haitians. Moving southward, the traveler soon comes upon a series of ridges and valleys flanking the Cordillera Central. These several parallel basins are the most important configurations of this southern region (known as the Massif de la Hotte and the Massif de la Selle in Haiti). These units include the very humid Azua lowlands, the smaller ranges of Sierra de Neiba and Sierra de Bahoruco, situated contrastingly in the arid southwest region, and the Enriquillo basin, where we find the largest lake in the entire Caribbean, Lago Enriquillo.

More Contrasting Topography

There is also the Cordillera Oriental, situated just below the Bay of Samaná. Again in terms of historical turmoil, this particular region, which features the much disputed Península de Samaná, provided an influential scenario for Quisqueya's social evolution. Another diverse topographical configuration of maximum socioeconomic and historical importance is the southeastern coastal plain of Seibo, the product of emergence from the sea and alluvial deposits. It is here that the chief Dominican crop throughout the major part of the country's history— sugarcane—developed its primary center of operation.

So it should not be at all surprising that a region possessing such sharp contrasts and paradoxes of relief within a relatively small area should experience a great diversity of soils, climates, and vegetation cover. Even though La República Dominicana is normally spared the extreme climate conditions usually associated with most tropical sites, the country unfortunately still lies directly in the path of violent, often devastating seasonal hurricanes. Not only are temperatures affected by elevation and shelter from maritime influences, but there are also acute differences in rainfall amounts between exposed coastal regions and deep, cavernous valleys resting leeward of the island's transverse *cordilleras.* Upon this markedly varied physical background, two very contrasting countries and cultures evolved, often with violently conflicting ideologies, national interests, and agendas.

But also there has been an intimate symbiosis that continues even today—often against the ready acknowledgment on both sides of the fragile border. It is absolutely essential that the reader understand the pivotal role that the land executed on the stage of cultural evolution in La República Dominicana. When we inspect at close range the formation of Dominican culture, we quickly see the interconnectedness between the specific contributing human element and physical geography. From the era of the first prehistoric migrations across the Antilles from the South American mainland to Hispaniola in at least 3000 B.C., giving rise to the early Taíno culture, to the unanticipated and purely accidental arrival of the Spanish conquistadors in the late fifteenth century, together with the forced introduction of African captives, the land mass in all its magnificent diversity, all its splendor and provocation, has exerted a wide-ranging, long-lasting impact upon Dominican culture. Today the land features about 13 percent forest and woodland, 31 percent arable land, and 43 percent pasture. Agriculture provides work for about 22 percent of the country's entire labor force, with a comparative figure of 12 percent in manufacturing and 4 percent in construction.

The Rivers

Splendorous also are the many rivers flowing through La República Dominicana. The contrasting and diverse topography and climate greatly determine the character of the country's river network. Despite the relative meagerness of its territory, La República Dominicana holds lengthy and abundant waterways. In the lush Valley of the Cibao, for instance, near the principal city of Santiago de los Caballeros toward the east, flows the Yuna River. It empties into the Bay of Samaná, after traveling across a distance of some three hundred kilometers. The other chief river of the Cibao, and also running past Santiago, is the Yaque del Norte. It rambles through the northwest corridor, passing the towns of Esperanza, Mao, Castañuelas, and Villa Vásquez, before finally emptying into the Bay of Manzanillo, some four hundred kilometers away. A number of smaller tributaries include the Jimenoa, the Jagua, and the Mao, among others. The Yaque del Norte, like the Yuna, brings an extraordinarily rich silt into the alluvial terraces of the Cibao Valley. In the meandering southwesterly Cordillera Central, the Artibonito originates, flowing first southward, forming a visible borderline with Haiti, then later penetrating into Haiti proper. The Dajabón River[5] farther north also shares the border with Haiti. The fourth very prominent river is the Yaque del Sur, which, like the Yaque del Norte, has its origins in the vicinity of the towering Pico Duarte. The river runs in a southerly direction until reaching the sea near Barahona, in the Bay of Neiba. Finally there is the truly historical Ozama, upon whose ancient banks lies the capital city of Santo Domingo. For centuries the single port for the entire country was at its mouth. The Ozama bears wealthy testimony to a series of major events unfolding in rapid succession that reveal much about not only the city's growth and development, but equally so the nation. In later sections there will be ample discussion of such events.

Notes

1. Quisqueya was the name that the pre-Columbian indigenous Taíno people called their island; it meant *Mother of All Lands.* The reader is reminded here that the entire island was variously called *Quisqueya, Bohío, Isla Española, Hayti,* and *Santo Domingo.*

2. James Ferguson, *The Dominican Republic: Beyond the Lighthouse,* pp. 38–41.

3. For instance, during the summer months of 1993, this writer, in traveling throughout the island from Elias Piña to Higüey, found that an eight-ounce bottle of Pepto Bismol in most places cost 105 pesos or U.S.$8.40 (1 peso RD = U.S. 8 cents).

4. The most frequent point of departure in these *yolas* is the Atlantic coastal town of Miches. In fact, in local conversation, it has become almost commonly understood that if someone says, "Carlos has left for Miches," the listener automatically assumes that Carlos is preparing to leave the country—without documents—from Miches!

5. With only about three exceptions—San Juan, Isabela, and El Masacre, which until the seventeenth century was called the Dajabón—all the major rivers in the Republic preserve their indigenous names.

Map 2. The Island of Hispaniola

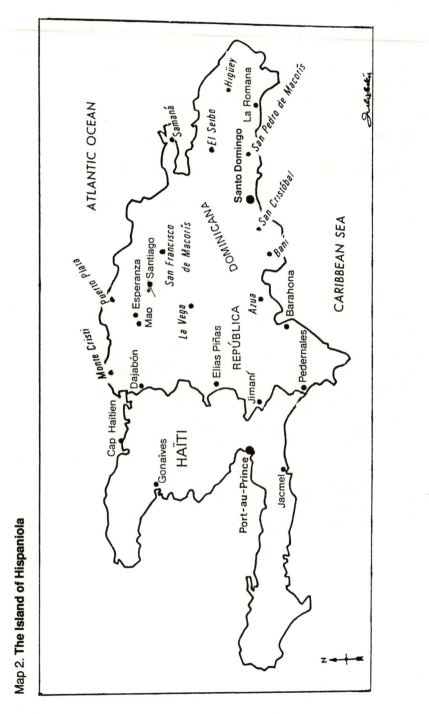

ATLANTIC OCEAN

DOMINICANA

REPÚBLICA

HAÏTI

CARIBBEAN SEA

Samaná

Higüey

El Seibo

La Romana

San Pedro de Macorís

Santo Domingo

San Cristóbal

Bani

Puerto Plata

Esperanza

Santiago

San Francisco
de Macorís

Mao

La Vega

Azua

Barahona

Monte Cristi

Dajabón

Elias Piñas

Pedernales

Jimaní

Cap Haïtien

Gonaïves

Port-au-Prince

Jacmel

N

26

Map 3. The Relief Units of Hispaniola

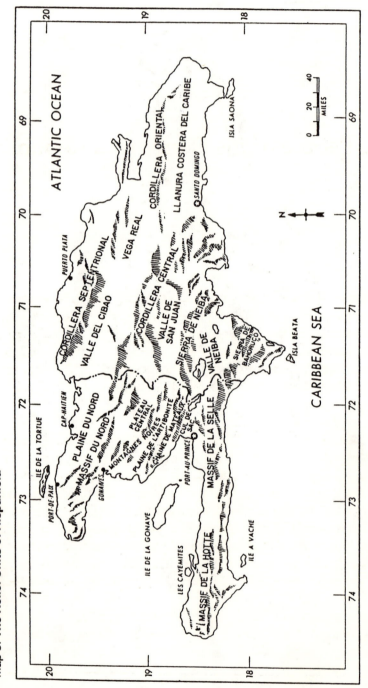

2

The People of the Dominican Republic

The Dominican society of today is the result of an intriguing evolutionary process in terms of both geography and history. At varying stages
in this process, different descriptive names have been employed as
points of reference. These names have evolved in direct correlation
with the society's insular or semi-insular circumstance. Today in some
of the rural zones of the country, for example, the *campesinos* (people
who traditionally live and work in the countryside) refer to the mountains as *haitises*.

The first residents of La República Dominicana, the ethnic Arawak,
called their island by the name Haytí, which meant *Tierra Alta* (Land of
Mountains). The later Taíno culture, arriving about 3000 B.C., called the
island Quisqueya, meaning *Madre de la Tierra* (Earth Mother). With
the arrival in 1492 of the Spanish conquistadors, the island received the
name La Española (Little Spain). This designation, with its English
spelling Hispaniola, was an unmistakable politicohistorical reference to
the territory as a possession of Spain. The name changed to the preferred Santo Domingo, meaning Holy Sunday, during the seventeenth
century.

The name Santo Domingo acquired special significance as a result
of its prominence as the name of the territory's chief city and port
during the whole of the colonial era. Santo Domingo de Guzmán was
founded on the banks of Río Ozama in 1491, but was originally called

27

Nueva Isabela in honor of the Spanish monarch Queen Isabela. The popularity and historical preference of Santo Domingo as the designation was due, in large measure, to the French. It was the French who, upon gaining control of the territory and then establishing a colony in what is today Haiti, called the territory Saint Domingue.[1] The French version, Saint Domingue, was readily popularized in Europe by the eighteenth century and eventually replaced completely the term La Española. When the island formally separated into two distinct societies, and the eastern portion proclaimed its very short-lived independence from Spain in 1821, one of the leaders of the independence movement, José Núñez de Cáceres, designated the name Haití Español (Spanish Haiti) for the Spanish portion of Santo Domingo. Soon afterward, in 1822, Haitian president Jean-Pierre Boyer initiated his ominous invasion of the eastern end of the island, which ultimately resulted in the unquestioned Haitian domination of the total island.[2] The controversy continues today in Dominican society among students and scholars of Dominican history as to the historical validity or appropriateness of acknowledging this crucial period, the proclamation of the *Estado Independiente de Haití Español* (Independent State of Spanish Haiti) of 1822, as the actual beginning of what we now call the Dominican Republic. It has been since only 1844, with the ultimate winning of independence from Haitian occupation and domination, that the country has been officially La República Dominicana.

It perhaps should be pointed out that the term "Dominicana" remains faithful to the name of the country's principal port and city. There is also the speculation that the name was used to honor the religious order of Dominicans (Dominicos). The concept of Dominicano as we conceive it today was employed with greater propriety by Núñez de Cáceres, who, upon drafting the nation's constitution, referred to the citizenry and not to the nation he intended establishing. With Juan Pablo Duarte, one of the Padres de la Patria, the use of the term reached a still greater dimension. It was in 1833 that Duarte conceived the country's independence under the glorious banner *"Dios, Patria y Libertad, República Dominicana."*[3] Since the period of the country's independence, the designation "Dominicana" has taken on the desired political character, as well as the sought-after cultural separation from neighboring Haiti.

Who Are *Los Dominicanos?*

Any attempt to answer the question "Who are the Dominicans?" will automatically begin with a pause for serious reflection. However simply phrased, the question is a source of heated and continuous debate among both Dominicans themselves and sympathetic outside observers and aficionados of Dominican culture. Moreover, the question often elicits startling surprises, puzzlement, controversy, and contradiction among the debaters, who represent quite an array of socioeconomic and educational levels and political ideologies within the community. The arguments became even more emotionally charged during the height of the country's 1994 presidential elections, in which one of the two leading opposition candidates was of alleged Haitian parentage, the other of Lebanese heritage.[4] Almost daily, the rhetoric flared, the editorial commentary sizzled. The question, with a multiplicity of possible answers, persisted: Who are the true Dominicans, *los dominicanos puros?*

The only irrefutable point in the argument is the statistical data. With a total area of about 48,734 square kilometers, about the size of Vermont and New Hampshire combined, La República Dominicana has an estimated 7.5 million inhabitants (1993). The capital city alone, Santo Domingo, has 1.7 million residents. Projected average annual population growth is 1.98 percent (1990–1995); per-capita income averages about U.S.$1,019. Projected infant mortality rate stands at fifty-seven per one thousand births. Literacy is estimated at 83.3 percent, and almost 42 percent of the total population is below the age of fifteen. It is estimated that by the year 2000 La República Dominicana will have a population exceeding ten million.

Although it comprises approximately half the area of the Dominican Republic, neighboring Haiti with 27,750 square kilometers (10,714 square miles) has a noticeably larger population. It had a population of almost 8.5 million in 1993, and the pressure of this human factor alone on Haiti's resources is one staggering feature distinguishing the two republics. For instance, the luxuriant forests that once carpeted Haiti's mountainous terrain are all but gone! As erosion strips away the exposed soil, Haitians—left with no other recourse—continue cutting trees to make and sell charcoal for needed fuel. The human geography of Hispaniola is a conspicuous example of the effects of sometimes contrasting, sometimes similar, but largely paradoxical historical and cultural circumstances on a similar physical background. A more detailed consideration later will attempt to confirm this contrast.

In easily visible contrast to the fairly even spread of the teeming Haitian population, La República Dominicana has two particular regions (described earlier in this work) where densities are much higher than other places in the island. These regions are the Cibao-Vega Real plain of the north, and the southeastern lowland. Because of strenuous efforts on the part of the Dominican government to diversify a traditionally monocrop economy, the result has been a major demographic shift. For the first time, more *dominicanos* are living in urban rather than in rural areas of the country. Two cities especially, which happen to be the island's two largest, are the prime beneficiaries of this population shift. Metropolitan Santo Domingo and Santiago de los Caballeros, the premier city of the Cibao, have both been reluctant recipients of this population shift, if for no other reason than that the augmented numbers have meant pressures of all types upon the limited resources of these two dynamic cities. This dramatic shift in people has exacted unanticipated tolls on practically every zone in the Republic.

However, perhaps hardest hit have been the traditional agricultural zones, *los campos*. The rural sectors throughout the country are fast losing their residents to the more lucrative economic enticements and the general upbeat attractiveness of the urban centers. As for the reduced numbers of rural inhabitants, their places are being filled by often all-too-eager Haitian *braceros* (farmhands), who are more frequently becoming part of a growing illegal trafficking in needed agricultural workers. These Haitian *braceros* are usually undocumented, often illiterate, routinely exploited laborers who have been pressed into grueling service in the sugarcane industry as cane cutters.

Notes

1. The historic Treaty of Ryswick of 1697 officially divided Hispaniola into two separate territories, thus recognizing French sovereignty over the western portion of the island. The important Treaty of Aranjuéz in 1777 assigned the borders between the French and Spanish sides; then with the Treaty of Basilea in 1795, Spain ceded the entirety of its eastern colony to France.
2. The sociopolitical and economic union between the two countries was executed and would last until 1844, the official date of the establishment of an independent and free República Dominicana.

3. *Dios, Patria y Libertad: República Dominicana* (God, Country and Liberty: The Dominican Republic). These words convey the spirit of national sovereignty for the new nation. This was the official slogan of the country's freedom fighters during their struggle for independence.

4. José Francisco Peña Gómez and Jacobo Majluta. The former is frequently said to be of Haitian descent, while the latter is of Lebanese parentage. However, the reader should be aware of the current controversy involving the actual birthplace of Dr. Peña Gómez. According to the prominent biographer of Peña Gómez, Victor Salmador, Peña Gómez was born in Dominican territory, in a place called La Loma del Flaco.

32

Map 4. The River System of La República Dominicana

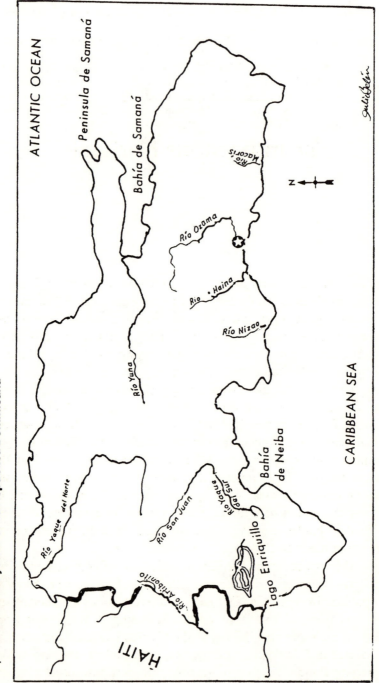

3

The Indigenous Heritage

In this section the primary objective is to delineate the ethnohistorical processes involved in the formation of Dominican culture. Contrary to what many investigators, analysts, and historians would have us believe, the process was quite simple. True enough, the arrival of Cristóbal Colón constituted a very major turning point in the ethnicity of the whole Caribbean region. But equally true is the fact that well prior to the year 1492, there were groups of indigenous peoples living in the region, trying to cope with their environment as skillfully as they knew how. These were people with a history, a culture, a reality—people who had been living for centuries in the Antilles when Columbus first encountered this other reality. Wheels, for instance, existed in the Americas long before Europeans did; ancient American cultures used wheels on children's toys. What arrived after the Great Encounter of 1492 was the notion of utilizing those wheels for purposes of work. The obsidian blades used by Aztec surgeons, in another instance, rivaled even modern steel for precise incision.

This other environmental reality was also one of contrasts and contradictions—seemingly the leitmotiv of what we have come to know as La República Dominicana. The natural topographical splendor of the region was then, as it is now, quite captivating to the visitor from outside. At the same time, however, the hazards remained real, then as now: violent and destructive hurricanes, earthquakes, erupting volcanoes, raging floods, diseases of epidemic proportions, insect plagues.

Despite the persistence of such life-threatening forces, the indigenous peoples confronted the frustrations and hazards with astounding creativity and sophistication. Their world was definitely one with unending problems and transitions. Their history is a combination of myths, beliefs, customs, and philosophies that enabled these early societies to adapt successfully to the prevailing circumstances.

The Original Inhabitants

It has been estimated that the original inhabitants throughout the entire Antilles probably numbered three-quarters of a million at the time of the Spanish invasion. Most substantiated theories seem to suggest that these first residents had migrated into the region from the nearby South American mainland, proceeding from the mouth of the Orinoco River in Venezuela and the Guyana Highlands. Relatively uncomplicated migrations—a considerably long and steady process—were made possible because of the prevalence of quite favorable conditions. Facilitating these intrepid voyages by aboriginal groups were the advantageous winds and ocean currents. Moreover, the distances to be traveled would not have been a major deterrent. Basically, given the geological history of the islands in the region, it becomes clear that autonomous human evolution here is improbable. The islands are simply too young to have allowed for such evolution. It is still not absolutely certain just when human groups first inhabited the island of Haytí, or the other islands forming the Greater Antilles (the larger northern islands of Cuba, Hispaniola, Jamaica, and Puerto Rico). Archaeological evidence does suggest that the presence of humans in Haytí-Quisqueya dates to at least 3000 B.C., perhaps even earlier. Because of its size and location, this particular island may well have been the site of most of the region's aboriginal people. It was probably also the site of the most sophisticated cultural groups, with longer residency as well. From the mainland, one group after another arrived, partially expelling, partially incorporating and absorbing one another. Over a period of time, a certain fluidity, fusion, and merging took place.

The earliest Caribbean societies of the region's inhabitants, and the first element of the Ethnic Trinity of Dominican culture, exerted a profound impact on the future social evolution in the island. By the end of the fifteenth century, three different groups of people were predominant: the Ciboney, probably the oldest cultural community; the Taíno-

Arawak, the least aggressive and most artistically creative; and then the fierce, warlike Caribe, after whom the entire region and the sea itself were named. The eastern Caribbean island of Dominica has the only remaining reservation for Caribs. Other important groups included the Ciguayo and the Macorix. These pre-Columbian cultures together represent the very first acknowledged victims of the consistent and often perplexing transition that characterizes the area's ethnohistorical process. These original communities found themselves in a state of perpetual response and reaction to external circumstances. Eventually, within a relatively short time, the end would come to these societies. Infusions of Spanish conquistadors—either calculating designs to exterminate or inadvertently bearing pathogens that triggered pandemics—ultimately killed millions of aboriginal peoples who never before had seen or even heard of Europeans.

Any examination of the impact of the indigenous heritage begins with certain clear admonitions. First, this uniquely rich, primary heritage cannot be exaggerated. Of necessity and for historical accuracy, attention must be focused within appropriate limitations. Second, there must not be any attempt, however much unintended or unconscious, to romanticize this heritage or its impact. What occurs all too often is an erroneous and sometimes determined effort to overstate the case for the *raza aniquilada* (annihilated race) in order to downplay the more overwhelming impact of the African presence, powerful as it is in the formation of Dominican culture. The simple fact is that the assumed intensive, sustained contact between the Spaniards and Africans with the indigenous groups in the Antilles as a whole did not last much beyond perhaps fifty years! This fact in itself is the prime factor that absolutely limited the total impact that these earlier communities could have had in the evolutionary process. In Hispaniola nearly all the indigenous populations had practically disappeared by the middle of the sixteenth century. Of approximately 300,000 to 400,000 or more original inhabitants on Hispaniola, an estimated five hundred remained by the year 1548.

Thus, in less than sixty years from the year of the initial arrival of those three caravels—La Santa María, La Pinta, La Niña—some 500,000 aboriginal people had perished. The untimely disappearance of the native populations as a cultural entity was near completion. Their material as well as their spiritual world, their level of development, their way of life, were all being torn down and replaced by the ferocious intentions of an imposed social model known as the *encomienda* system,[1] which had replaced an earlier practice known as the *repartimiento*.[2] This large number of human beings disappeared as a consequence of the intricate operational strategies carefully devised by the conquistadors for the single purpose of exploiting the territory's gold. The Europeans had come, as later Spanish chroniclers would affirm, to give light to those in darkness, but also to get rich. But those assets of the Americas not counted in gold and silver only gradually engaged the rest of the globe's attention. The indigenous inhabitants of Española were undoubtedly the first victims of the process of initial accumulation of wealth in the sixteenth century. The process of deculturation was so swift that the subdued cultures hardly had time to acclimate themselves to the newly introduced, or rather, intrusive social modes. The strange and remotely alien systems bore no resemblance whatsoever to any sociocultural values or practices known previously to the original *quisqueyanos*.

The Taíno Culture

The differences between the aboriginal people and the Europeans were readily apparent and quite at odds. In fact, the differences were indeed awesome. The newer arrivals were in marked contradiction to the established traditions that had evolved over a lengthy period in the island. Taíno society was basically communal and egalitarian in nature. There was no notion of private or individually owned property, for instance. Every available resource was the property of the whole community. The primary economic activity was agriculture, a necessary activity in which all members of the community both participated and benefited. The society itself had tremendous internal flexibility and mobility. In addition to agriculture, hunting and fishing were indispensable activities that helped sustain the community. Even by the time of Columbus's arrival, the Taíno were still being nourished by the meat of local rodents such as *jutías, curíes, quemíes,* and *mohíes,* which were in abundant supply. Other common food sources included iguana and various other kinds of reptiles. Fishing, although not regarded as important as crop cultivation, and therefore not a major part of the traditional diet, was nevertheless routine. *Lambí, carey, dajao,* and *menjúa* appear on a long list of local fish still found today in the island's rivers and streams and used as a supplemental food source, especially along the coastal zones of La República Dominicana.

The essential social unit among these highly artistic, nonmilitaristic, cassava-producing agriculturists was a rather large family. This family was monogamous, except in the case of the local *cacique* (chieftain of the village clan), who usually practiced polygamy. A clan might be comprised of anywhere from five to eight families, all related by close blood lines. It is suspected that incest was part of the social norms within the clans. While the social structure was predominantly patriarchal, matrilineal inheritance was also frequently practiced. Taíno houses, traditionally arranged in a circle, were of two classic styles. One featured a conical roof and was round in shape. This kind of dwelling was called a *caney*. The other style was most often associated with the *cacique*'s residence. It was large, roomy, and rectangular in shape. This was the classic *bohío*, the exact term still used today to describe the thatched-roof abode found in many rural zones throughout La República Dominicana. A notable characteristic of Taíno culture was the rather complex level of social interaction among the group members, making for a pivotal element in their group solidarity and identity. One of the main group leisure activities featured a kind of ball game played on an open court called a *batey*.[3]

The broader Taíno society was made up of theocratic chiefdoms. These were extensive political units consisting of many smaller villages, each ruled over by the local *cacique*. Major decisions and most laws governing the larger community were executed by an assembly convened by the Paramount Cacique. In active attendance were the local or territorial, subordinate chiefs. The entire island of Quisqueya was divided into five large administrative territories that were called *cacicazgos*.[4] Together, the five *cacicazgos* formed a rather tightly knit federation, organized and governed with amazing similarity, given the expanse of the total land areas involved. The Paramount Cacique, with ultimate authority and prestige, reigned supreme, designating to the local chiefs all the minor and often purely ceremonial functions. The names of some of the most powerful Paramount Caciques can be found throughout Dominican society today: Behechío, Cayacoa, Coanabo, Enriquillo (a name that has become legendary), Goacanagarí, Mayohanex, and Guarionex.

Abundant evidence seems to support the assertion that Taíno society was the least aggressive of the pre-Columbian societies in the Americas. Even though there was great cultural affiliation among the three migrant groups that entered the Antilles region, especially between the Caribs and the Taíno-Arawak, major differences were nevertheless apparent. The social and political organization, even the religious system, of the Caribs exemplified a more bellicose, deliberately militaristic posturing than any other. The Taíno, by contrast, did not produce the strident militarism and religious fervor readily associated with the much larger continental empires of indigenous peoples in the Andes region, Guatemala and the Yucatán, or the Anáhuac Valley of Central Mexico.

The Taíno Spirit World

Religion played a key role in Taíno culture. The Taíno had a sophisticated, very formalized belief system structured around an intimate relationship between a complete pantheon of gods and humans. As with every other aspect of Taíno traditions, religion was also communal. The village *cacique* was highly respected, sometimes even feared precisely because the villagers considered him the authentic and sole spokesman for the gods, and as such was the only officially authorized agent who could communicate with the sacred spirit world via highly stylized anthropomorphic figurines. These skillfully crafted figurines or icons, most often made of bone, wood, stone, or the more popular ceramic, represented religious spirits called *cemí*. Venerated by the entire community, the *cemí* functioned as the medium of communication between the *cacique* and the particular deity. This extremely sacred ceremony was known as the *Rito de la Cohoba*.[5] As part of the ritual, the participants inhaled a powerful hallucinogenic drug made from natural herbs that had been concocted for the express purpose of inducing a trancelike state, *perder la razón* (to lose reason). Supposedly, only while in this trance could communication directly with the spirit world be possible.

Within the social hierarchy was also a very special order of priests called *behiques,* who were viewed as wise men because of their mystical ability to communicate with the dead as well as with the *cemí.* These priests enjoyed many of the privileges of the village *cacique* and were also vested with the powers to cure the sick. So essential was their position in the hierarchy that certain tasks were assigned to them alone: serving as intermediaries to the gods, maintaining the religious-philosophical system on a level of daily observance, functioning as advisers to the *cacique,* and educating the male offspring of the local chieftain. Much of the surviving, well-known ceramic art, especially the exquisite pottery, of this early Antillean culture is accredited to the *behiques,* since they were also at the same time the principal artisans among the Taíno. In effect, the entire body of customs, traditions, myths, and legends was the exclusive responsibility of these sacred individuals, who were the trusted custodians of Taíno culture.

Moreover, these traditions were systematically passed on orally from one generation to the next by means of sacred songs. These legendary songs, called *areítos,*[6] were carefully metered verses, always sung and danced in the precisely exact manner in order to preserve their purity, and were featured at special festivals in honor of the *cemí.* By the time of the arrival of the Spaniards, the Taíno may well have been formulating definite concepts of monotheism. The idea of worshipping a supreme, omnipotent deity—a principal *cemí* called Yocahu—was in an embryonic stage. Yocahu was seen as the Supreme God of the Skies, perhaps even the god of creation.

The Taíno Legacy

What is agonizingly impossible to ascertain is the kind of ultimate social evolution that might have emerged had the Spanish conquistadors managed somehow to delay their encounter with the indigenous cultures on Quisqueya. True, by the time the Spanish penetrated the region and arrived with unmistakable designs of complete conquest at the island, Taíno culture was already undergoing rather significant and critical internal transformations. However, final surrender and subordination to the Spanish were inevitable in view of the striking differences in technology alone. Even with the formidable campaigns of early resistance by the determined native peoples, the military superiority of the equally determined invaders assured definite conquest of the indigenous inhabitants. Moreover, perhaps yet more potent was the introduction of infectious diseases previously unknown to the Caribbean region. These diseases decimated the indigenous populations more rapidly perhaps than did the invading artillery.

So, what constitutes the legacy of Taíno culture in terms of the ethnic components in the formation of Dominican culture? First of all, the total and complete decimation of the indigenous peoples in Hispaniola, however rapid, during the first century of Spanish colonization did not automatically mean that these cultures had a mere minimal impact upon subsequent social development there. Second, what survived of the island's native heritage would enrich considerably the local demographics resulting from this initial contact of the two vastly differing peoples. It is quite clear that large numbers of the early conquistadors and settlers took the Taíno-Arawak women—whom they perceived as exotic—as concubines and/or wives. The offspring of this unprecedented interracial fusion was to produce a startling new kind of human race that would be forever called *mestizo*.[7] The process of what could be called miscegenation was thus officially launched in La Española with this daring union between the light-complexioned Spanish conquistador and the darker, bronze-toned indigenous woman.

There are most assuredly other visible traces of the Taíno legacy in La República Dominicana today. Surprisingly, certain cultural elements have persisted despite the overall brevity of intimate social interaction between the two dissimilar cultural groups. The Taíno-Arawak, for example, taught the Spanish some rather ingenious techniques in agriculture production, methods still employed by Dominican campesinos today. The common practice of *tumba y quema* (cutting down and burning) involved felling trees, clearing away the brush and weeds, chopping up the stumps, then burning it all in a huge mound. The remaining ashes, rich in nutrients, are left in place to fertilize the soil.

Conucos and Casabe

The pride of many a rural or even suburban home today in the Dominican Republic is the family's *conuco*, an indispensable, almost revered feature of the homesite. The *conuco* is a small plot of cultivated ground traditionally set aside specifically for the family's vegetable garden. Initially the *conuco* was monopolized by the cultivation of tubers such as *yuca, batata, yautia,* and *mapuey*,[8] since these local plants did not require later storage.

Even though the Spaniards imported new crops such as sugarcane, oranges, lemons, and bananas, the aboriginal populations introduced the Europeans to tobacco, potatoes, peanuts, manioc, *maíz* (corn), squash and pumpkins, beans, tomatoes, chili peppers, pineapple, cacao, vanilla, and turkey—among a host of other indigenous good items. Of the myriad crops of the Americas, two in particular—corn and potatoes—spread so extensively throughout the world that these items readily became absolute staples of human survival. In terms of agriculture, which was the chief economic activity among the island's original people, there was undisputable significance for two crops. The first, *casabe* (cassava or manioc), perhaps more than any other crop, has played a pivotal role as a staple in the traditional Taíno diet as well as in that of Dominican society as a whole throughout the development of the island's culture. Quite early, *casabe* became to be regarded as *el pan del país* (the bread of the nation). It was then, and remains so today, an excellent nutritional food source.

The Spanish masters throughout the island expected indigenous laborers to produce a consistently high yield of *casabe*. Some historians even suggest that the subjugated populations at one point attempted sabotage of food-crop cultivation by willfully neglecting their own *conucos* of *casabe* in efforts to force a complete withdrawal of the Spaniards from the island. Unfortunately, as history indicates, the settlers were not driven into starvation. Rather, the indigenous groups may have inadvertently contributed, in however minor a way, to the process of their own annihilation. During the colonial era when Santo Domingo became the primary base of strategic operations for launching further territorial exploration and expansion, huge quantities of *casabe* were an essential part of the cargo onboard the departing vessels for the crews.[9] Today the process of *casabe* production continues being virtually the same as that devised by the inventive Taíno centuries ago.

The second crop of tantamount importance that the Taíno also introduced to the newcomers was *tabaco* (tobacco). It survived Spanish conquest and domination of Quisqueya, reaching the levels of production as a profitable export crop from the late eighteenth to the nineteenth centuries. Still fundamentally an export crop, tobacco is a component of the traditional Antillean trilogy of the sugar-coffee-tobacco culture that is of such vital economic importance today to the annual revenue of the Dominican Republic. Tobacco production and manufactured tobacco products during the early nineteenth century replaced cattle raising altogether as the primary economic base in the Cibao Valley. The geographic factor in this northern zone of the country has always been key. Very favorable climatic and topographical conditions conspire to prove eminently suitable for the region's rich tobacco cultivation. Historically, tobacco was also destined to share center stage with sugar as the drama of the nation's social development unfolded. For the first time, the small farmer—who was primarily responsible for the cultivation of this crop—would begin having a voice in the affairs of the country.

Linguistic Legacy

Adding to the list of very important contributions that the indigenous Taíno culture made to the arsenal for survival of the conquering Spaniards was the wealth of new vocabulary. This strange but very useful and practical lexicon enriched the Spanish language and is very much in use today throughout Quisqueya. Mainly in the form of nouns, these words can be heard quite casually among the people in various parts of the island. The following categorized listing includes those words of indigenous origin that remain both a distinctive and an indelible feature of the Spanish in La República Dominicana: *barbacoa* (barbecue), *bohío* (a rural, palm-thatched house), *canoa* (canoe), *cayuco* (small canoe), *guagua* (public bus), *hamaca* (hammock), *maní* (peanut). The following words are fruits local to the Dominican Republic, but are found throughout the Caribbean: *anon, caimito, chirimoya, guanábana, guayaba, guavaberi, hicaca, jagua, jobo, lechoza* (called papaya elsewhere throughout the Spanish-speaking world), *mamey, mamón, piña.* Local vegetables include these items: *amate, ají, bacoanabo, batata, boniato, catey, cumaná, guacanarí, guaguarey, guajabo, maíz, mapuey, yautía* (manioc root), *yuca.* Most of the fishes found in the waters of Quisqueya retain their original Taíno names: *burgao, carey, carite, conjinúa, dajao, guábina, guatapaná, jurel, lambí, macabí, menjúa, tiburón, zago, zurele.*

Names of mountains or sierras include these: Bahoruco, Biajama, Cabao, Cuao, Guaconejo, Guainamoca, Higua, Pico del Yaque. The names of bays, capes, or ports: Bayahibe, Chavón, Cumayasa, Guayacanes, Güibía, Jina, Maimón, Najayo, Neiba, Ocoa, Samaná, Yuma, Punta Hicacos, Punta Macao, Cabo Macorís, Punta Mangle. The names of towns or regions seem almost endless: Acaya, Azua, Baguá, Bánica, Bayacán, Bayaguana, Bonao, Cabia, Camaguasí, Canabacoa, Cibao, Cuey, Cayuano, Duyey, Guabatico, Guácara, Guajimía, Guanarete, Guaniabanó, Guaragua, Guaraguano, Guarey, Hicayagua, Higüero, Jacagua, Jarabacoa, Jaragua, Los Mameyes, El Maniel, Moca, Nicagua, Samaná, Sosúa, Túbano, Yaguate, Las Yayas. The names of many rivers and streams are at the same time the official name of populated areas: Amino, Arazzao, Artibonito, Azuey, Azuí, Bajabonico, Bao, Básimo, Bayajá, Boyá, Camú, Caraba, Casuesa, Casuí, Ceiba, Cenobi, Comate, Cuaya, Chavón, Chacuey, Dajabón, Dicayagua, Duey, Gabón, Guasí, Guabanimo, Guajabo, Guamira, Guanaiboa, Guárano, Guayayuco, Guayubín, Gurabo, Haina, Higuamo, Jagua, Jamao, Jánico, Jaya, Jima, Jiminoa, Joba, Joca, Libonao, Macorís, Maguá, Maguaca, Maguana, Mao, Neiba, Neibuco, Micayagua, Magua, Nigua, Nisibón, Nizao, Ocoa, Ozama, Payabo, el Seibo, Soco, Tabara, Tosa, Yabacao, Yabón, Yacahueque, Yamasá, Yaque, Yuma, Yuna. The names of animals include: *caguama, catuan, cigua, cocuyo, comején, curí, coquí, guabá, guaraguao, guacamayo, jején, iguana, maye, mime, maco, manatí, mohíe, nigua, hicotea, quemíe.* Finally, these are the names of trees, some of which would be a significant part later in the island's growing lumber industry: *caoba* (mahogany), *cuaba, capá, ceiba, corozo, copei, guano, guayacán, guazábara, guayaba, guázuma, guaconeco, guao, manle, manacla, maguey, majague, balatá, búcara, jobobán, yagrumo, yarey, samo, tuna.*

Notes

1. The *encomienda* (from the Spanish *encomendar,* to trust) was the legal instrument under which the Crown entrusted, or allotted, specific numbers of indigenous people to deserving Spaniards as a reward for personal services rendered to the Crown. The practice also included the actual seizure of native lands. The system was based upon the historical experience with conquered groups (Moslems) in Iberia during the period of the Reconquest, whereupon devoted Spanish soldiers were awarded lands that had been confiscated from Moslems. The arrangement in Hispaniola (begun in about 1503) started out by giving the *encomendero* the right to collect tribute and to demand certain services—usually in the form of manual labor. Very quickly this feudal system enslaved the entire indigenous populations. Native labor and land now came to be demanded as entitlements. The aboriginal people were regarded with the same possessive spirit as private property.

2. The *repartimiento* (from the Spanish *repartir,* to divide up) was the brutally inhuman practice implemented by the earlier conquistadors, whereupon they seized indigenous people at random—usually through village raids—and literally divided them up, or allotted them among the settlers. Then the captives would be forced to work the mines or would be shipped to distant outposts as slave labor.

3. Some investigators tell us that *batey* originally referred to the central plaza of the Taíno community where produce and other goods were exchanged or where festivals were held. Today *batey* is the name given to the usually substan-

dard, squalid living quarters of sugarcane workers in the island, now overwhelmingly Haitian migrants.

4. The five *cacicazgos* throughout Quisqueya at the time of the Spanish invasion were the following: Cacicazgo de Marién, Cacicazgo de Jaragua, Cacicazgo de Maguana, Cacicazgo de Maguá, and Cacicazgo de Higüey.

5. Ritual of the Cohoba. Cohoba is an indigenous herb that has certain medicinal properties that can induce hallucinations.

6. The immensely popular Dominican composer and recording artist of merengues Juan Luis Guerra entitled one of his recent albums *Areíto,* recalling the rich lyrical tradition of the ancient Taíno. The internationally famous *merenguero* (one who plays or sings merengues) frequently incorporates meaningful cultural themes, past and present, into his captivating music.

7. Hugo Tolentino Dipp, *Raza e Historia en Santo Domingo: Los orígines del prejuicio racial en América,* pp. 101–5.

8. *Yuca, batata, yautía,* and *mapuey* are tropical tubers that are commonly grown throughout the Antilles.

9. Bernardo Vega, "La Herencia Indígena en la Cultura Dominicana de Hoy," pp. 31–46.

4

The Spanish Heritage

The phenomenal creation of what came to be known as Spanish America was the result of diverse ethnic, cultural, and racial groups working together under often adverse and even antagonistic circumstances to build a New World, different totally from any other place the world had seen previously. The spilled blood, the broken backbone, and the torn muscle of all the groups contributed to the ultimate marvel of that mammoth undertaking. The Iberian Peninsula, whence those first European adventurers came, was a place deprived of a host of otherwise favorable conditions during the sixteenth century that would have made life quite agreeable and full of bright promise for most inhabitants there. Iberia was aloof from all major currents of European thought; living in a kind of cultural isolation would more properly describe the character of the Iberians at that time.

Geography was overbearingly hostile—both in terms of causing, at least in part, this damaging isolation and of accounting for the area's generally poor soil and climate. The internal pattern of the rivers and mountains to this day separates the peninsula into profoundly exaggerated regionalism that borders upon being nationalistic: the so-called *Patria Chica* (little nation). In fact, a strongly defended regionalism has long characterized the history of the Iberian Peninsula. So Spain was economically languishing, with her poor soil depleted, her hills stripped of trees, and her people generally quite poor, but she was richly proud and forceful in terms of religious conviction, tradition, and history. The paradox of resources would account for the readiness of a nation as a whole to want to take to the seas in search of fortune.

The question of miscegenation—or, as it is called in Spanish, *mestizaje*—is far more controversial, and sometimes even provokes emotionally charged debate, than is the actual process itself. The simple occurrence of two individuals, one of indigenous heritage, the other of European heritage, coming together in conjugal union does not require much in terms of imagination. We have learned that the offspring of this union became known as a *mestizo*. The second ingredient in the cauldron of ethnic diversity that produced the *dominicano* is the Spanish. Even with contemporary discussion of this issue, the precise degree and prominence of this Spanish component and its effect upon the cultural formation of La República Dominicana remain the subject of much serious study and investigation.

National Character

The research is notoriously provocative when it results in the claim that the contributions of Spain seem most significant and of greater and more lasting value than those made by other cultures! What follows are but a few glaring examples of the many observations made, and the personal attitudes expressed by some noted Dominican historians writing about what they call the national character:

> Como dijimos al principio, somos un pueblo mestizo; tenemos el predominio de Africa y América en muchos de nuestros factores somáticos; y el de España, en la básica estructura de nuestro temperamento y de nuestro modo de ser. Si urgamos seranamente en nuestros más caros valores y nuestras cosas más valiosas, nos acercaremos más a nuestra herencia española.[1]

> (As we said at the outset, we are a racially mixed people; we have the predominance of Africa and America in much of our physical presence; and of Spain in the basic structure of our temperament and our very being. If we insist serenely upon our most cherished values and those things most precious, we will more likely approach our Spanish heritage.)

On another occasion, we have this personal commentary on what the author in this case describes as the fundamentals and motivations of the Dominican race:

Las migraciones que llegaron en el siglo xvii sirvieron para rescatar de la barbarie a los pobladores. En cierta forma se logró restaurar una serie de costumbres que hoy en día son fácilmente determinables en diversas poblaciones del país. La inmigración española que llegaba principalmente de las Islas Canarias, sirvió para forjar los fundamentos de una nacionalidad.[2]

(The immigrants who arrived in the seventeenth century served to rescue the settlers from barbarism. In a certain way what was achieved was a restoration of a series of customs that today are easily seen in diverse places in the country. The Spanish immigration that came primarily from the Canary Islands served to lay the foundations of a nationality.)

Some commentators have presented the view that these intrepid men, conquistadors with unrelenting zeal and courage, motivated by their lust for gold and other material riches, and with an uncompromising faith in God, readily symbolized the exemplary spirit of sixteenth-century Europe. As a consequence, the determinants of Spanish culture would, without question, be the paradigm of culture everywhere. Thus, the thinking was that there simply was no other civilization or culture in existence anywhere! In fact, the whole of Western civilization was regarded as the only civilization known to mankind. Anything else was viewed as inferior. As we know, the very first official act of self-aggrandizement on the part of the arriving Spaniards was immediately to superimpose a completely new name upon the territory of Quisqueya. The process of transculturation, a result of a clash of two distinct cultures, was under way. Upon initiating their design for conquest and colonization, the Spanish also set in motion a fight-to-the-death struggle for class and ideological dominance.

A Private Domain

It was determined early, perhaps by about 1508 or 1510, that La Española would be much more than an ordinary Spanish overseas territory. In the most usual sense, such a territory would exist merely to provide the metropolis with both a valued source of raw materials and a profitable market for manufactured goods. However, in this particular instance, La Española was regarded as the absolute private domain of *Los Reyes Católicos* (the Catholic monarchs Fernando and Isabel).

Additionally, the island would function as the Caribbean region's strategic recruitment center for subsequent expeditions of discovery. The island's inhabitants, all of them—arriving Spanish settlers and the already present indigenous groups alike—were automatically made vassals of the Royal Spanish Crown.

The pattern of structural and functional organization of La Española was an uninterrupted continuation of the model found in faraway Spain. It was a microcosm of the society these settlers had left on the other side of the Atlantic. From the very beginning of the occupation of the new territories, the Spaniards were fiercely determined to transplant their way of life, a way of life that for centuries had evolved into a national character in Iberia. Their language, their customs and traditions, religious beliefs and practices, economic and political institutions, even their architectural style, were all adapted to the new environment in the Caribbean. All these established institutions and ideas were intended without question to parallel those of Iberia.

The Spain They Left Behind

A most important sociohistorical occurrence in Western Europe has to be keenly noted in order to try understanding the kind of individual who would venture into dangerously uncharted waters, seeking a better life than that which he was leaving. What were the specific factors that served as a catalyst for the decision to venture so far from home? What kind of Spain did they leave behind? To begin with, in Europe the two centuries prior to the Great Encounter were characterized by the decadence of a widespread, oppressive feudal system. A new type of economic system was gradually emerging to replace the cumbersome and inefficient feudalism. The new form was reinforced with a social interaction conditioned by aggressive trade and commerce, plus the rise of influence and power of an urban populace. Most of Europe was undergoing a dramatic transition from feudalism to capitalism. An increasingly powerful urban economy was beginning to appear. The newly evolved bourgeoisie made possible European expansion to other regions. A most important example was the establishment of the Portuguese *factorias* (trading posts) along the coast of West Africa. These *factorias* would soon become the infamous slave markets for a thriving trade in human flesh.

However, the case with Spain was somewhat different. Prior to A.D.

1500 Spain did not even exist as a consolidated nation. A disconnected array of several independent, scattered, rival kingdoms—each with its own distinct traditions and customs, even different languages, in some instances—was entrenched in an exceedingly lengthy War of Reconquest. This was a struggle begun in A.D. 719 by a rather loose confederation of Christian kings in northern Spain engaged in a fanatical effort to retake the Iberian Peninsula from the Moors.[3] The Reconquest was actually a Christian crusade waged by Spain against the invading Moslems, who occupied Iberia for eight hundred years. This grueling holy war was to last, with devastating national and international ramifications, until decisive victory by Los Reyes Católicos in 1492, when the Islamic forces were ultimately expelled from the peninsula altogether.[4]

The spoils of victory, however, were a truly mixed bag of consequences that were to have a profound impact upon the formation of a national Spanish character. For one thing, an absolute monarchy was installed with consolidation of the very powerful kingdoms of Castile (Queen Isabel) and Aragón (King Fernando). Together, these ambitious Catholic monarchs unified the entire country politically and spiritually, centralizing the seat of authority in Madrid (Castilla). Subsequently, the aristocracy grew in both numbers and influence, accumulating massive land holdings as special concessions from the Crown for their loyalty and devotion. Increasingly, land ownership thus became the base of wealth and the primary symbol of economic power.

The Crusader Spirit

Also, the Catholic church, as an immediate consequence of victory against the perceived infidels, increased its ecclesiastical influences in secular matters. A kind of religious zeal or what might be described as *espiritu de cruzada* (crusader spirit) began to be identified with the church and eventually with all of Spain. Closely related to this spiritual attitude was a particular mind-set that resulted in a permanent state of war posturing. This revitalized notion of militaristic chivalry soon became the desired ideal for the landed gentry. Gentleman arrived at the point of now spurning manual labor—in a country that overwhelmingly and traditionally had always been agrarian in nature! Such attitudes would play a very important part in the man-and-labor relationship later in the Caribbean. The crusader/conquistador psyche began to define the national character of Iberia. The military arts became the envisioned means of upward social, political, and economic mobility for the masses of young men throughout Iberia. These youthful would-be conquistadors converged in droves upon Castile, precisely in time historically to be among the original recruitment pool for undoubtedly one of the most unprecedented voyages ever contemplated by Western man.

There was such an obsessive preoccupation with the new militarism that one of the unforeseen side effects was a weakening of Spain's industrial and commercial growth. On the rise was a class struggle between a potentially powerful urban bourgeoisie and the landed aristocracy—a traditional aristocracy vehemently opposed to ideas of mercantile capitalism. In a very short time this conflict of class interests reached explosive proportions. Because of forceful pressure from allied efforts of the aristocracy and the clergy, the Crown decided to champion the cause of the aristocracy, and thus executed steps to strengthen the traditional feudal system. The most decisive weapon against the bourgeoisie, who were considered a menace to the national interests, was to expel them altogether.

The Double Menace

There is much convincing evidence that the financial and commercial life of Spain for quite a long time had been largely captained by the Jewish sector of the nation's population. Jews, for the most part, had financed the Reconquest against the Islamic forces.[5] Some investigators have presented substantial documentation to suggest that wealthy Jewish moneylenders may have even financed the first expedition of Columbus.[6] With the massive expulsion by royal decree in 1492, Jewish properties and assets were immediately confiscated, thus enriching the already stocked coffers of the privileged Christian aristocracy in the country.

With the simultaneous expulsion of the double menace (Arab and Jews), but also of other considered undesirables or non-pure-blooded people such as gypsies, Protestants, and other groups regarded as non-Catholics, virtually every facet of national life suffered immeasurable stagnation. Such obsession with notions of *pureza de sangre* (pure-bloodedness) was yet another ingrained national attitude on the part of Spaniards that would have significant ramifications later in the world

What are the level of measurement of the type of measurement scale.

- The type of measurement scale

General type of measurement

Qualitative → non-numeric

Categories are discrete / Distance between
categories is not determined

Quantitative → numeric

of the Caribbean. With the wide-reaching expulsions of 1492, Iberia was deprived of essential resources, mainly human and financial, that were needed to spark a developing capitalism. Basically, then, this was the desperate state of affairs of pre-imperial Spain at the time of Columbus's departure, the conditions and circumstances of the world left behind by the adventurous souls who set out for a distant and unknown land.

Not just the strategic island of Hispaniola, but the whole of Spain's holding in the Caribbean and Spanish America must be viewed from the perspective of having been a business venture. However full of risks and frightening uncertainties initially, this venture very quickly paid handsome dividends to the Crown, enriched the merchants of Sevilla and Cádiz, and furnished a profitable livelihood to the Crown's American vassals. Profits came from the abundant gold and silver, the varied agricultural crops, the herds of cattle, the output of the mills, and the uninterrupted flow of lucrative trade. The underlying idea beneath Spain's regulations controlling trade with the American territories was to insure the greatest possible profits for the metropolis. By the end of the seventeenth century, it was clear that the *Consejo de Indias* (the Council of the Indies) managed the imperial political coordination for the vast Spanish overseas empire. Established in 1524, the powerful Consejo was the chief royal agency that controlled all matters relating to the administration of the Caribbean territories, as well as all other areas over which flew the Spanish flag.

Who Were These Strangers?

Who were these Spaniards who initially sailed with Columbus? What kind of newcomers came afterward? On Columbus's maiden voyage in 1492, the greatest number of the first conquistadors was originally from the southern Andalucia region of Spain (the provinces of Cádiz, Córdova, Granada, Málaga, Sevilla, and Huelva were prominently represented). These individuals, much like those from other areas scattered across the entire Iberian Peninsula, felt a kind of magnetic pull toward the spiritual center of the now unified nation. Castilla, a vibrant hub of much commercial activity, along with Sevilla, offered a lucrative measure of opportunity to otherwise hopeless, unskilled, and desperate individuals anxious for a better life than they had known for generations. A great number of these souls came from the depressed towns and villages of places found commonly in the regions of Extremadura and Western Andalucia. This motley crew of restless, yet determined individuals departed from Sevilla with a single outlook—an outlook in absolute conformity with that which described Castilla at that time. That description was that Spanish conquest and dominance were a natural outgrowth of Spanish military prowess now that all of Iberia had been reclaimed from eight centuries of Islamic control. Further, this militarism was coupled with a thoroughly material lust for territory, riches—and for someone else to do the work!

Something Better Awaits

For the most part, these were people whose basic aspirations for any kind of future in their own native land were absent. Therefore, their uncompromising determination was to create in the new territory a quality of life and a sociopolitical as well as an economic environment with a marked superiority to that which they were leaving behind. This group of individuals was obsessed with the idea of bettering their lot wherever the shadow of Spanish military power guaranteed protection of their efforts in this quest. Following the initial wave of conquistadors, *exploradores y aventureros* (explorers and adventurers), there came a clear cross section of Spanish society of that period. Listed among the diversity of opportunists figured clerks, scribes, artisans, priests, merchants, landless farmers, titleless noblemen. They were all seeking something better, which they were certain awaited them in the new territory.

Even given the wide assortment of human types, the prevailing social values of the emigrants were still traditionally Spanish. Most of these persons were illiterate, as were most members of this segment of European society generally. At this time, though, the asset of literacy was not considered a prerequisite for holding political office, for upward social mobility, or for the pursuit and/or the acquisition of material wealth. One peculiar trait of these early *aventureros* who set sail for new opportunities in the Caribbean was the readily apparent disdain for tilling the soil. This one characteristic alone, perhaps well above so many others, would explain the major flaw in the subsequent socioeconomic evolution in Hispaniola.

Settler Attitudes

If there were flaws later in the island's socioeconomic development, there were much earlier defects in the attitudes and sentiments of the

Spanish invaders as they encountered the original inhabitants. Sadly enough, the unassuming openness that the indigenous people presented to the Spanish newcomers brought them not reciprocal kindness and hospitality, but rather bitter deception and ultimate annihilation. From the very start, Columbus and his crew regarded the Taíno people as mere vassals of the Spanish Crown. The *encomienda* system, as we learned, became the official and legal instrument for firmly subjugating the island's native populations to a shameful level of inhuman exploitation. This pattern would hold true for the entire Caribbean region. What followed in time was the establishment of the region's first slave oligarchy.

Spanish colonization meant constructing, among other components of the process, a justification for enslavement of the indigenous societies. The first rationalization was based upon what the Spanish perceived as religious differences. Accordingly, the native peoples were regarded as heathen, idolaters, even cannibals, whose alien way of life was looked upon as offensive and barbarian, whose mentality—it was thought—rendered them incapable of conceptualizing *civilization*.[7] Such basic preconceptions quickly gave rise to notions of inherent biological and racial superiority–inferiority of the opposing groups. Even though the Spanish had absolutely no evidence of cannibalism in Hispaniola, the conjecture alone was sufficient criteria to define the aboriginal societies as naturally inferior to the *civilized* Spaniards. The Europeans systematically dehumanized the Native Americans, therefore allowing for the convenient theory of separating those who by nature should command, and those who should obey.[8]

A Smart Business Investment

We cannot for a moment lose sight of the fact that the process of colonization was primarily a commercial venture, with heavy investment, and certainly not a humanitarian mission. Columbus was above all else a businessman. A faithful product of the European Renaissance, Columbus had his dreams, of course. But his dreams were well grounded in solid reality, to be sure. He realized the handsome commercial benefits and profits to be garnered from *discovering* new trade routes to the Far East. Thus, the concept of colonization was, on one hand, a smart business undertaking; on the other hand, it was clearly an exploratory mission with the supreme objective of exploiting the natural (and human) resources of the conquered territories. Certainly not to be overlooked was the important aim also of fervently proselytizing Christianity. Admiral Columbus, the first governor of Hispaniola, proved a most incompetent administrator, showing nothing substantial for the initial investment. True, some gold was found, but not nearly enough immediately to begin satisfying the greed and hunger of the Crown nor of Columbus and his ravenous companions. But gold would be the decisive factor in the social development during the opening phases of the newly established colony. This tumultuous and uncertain period was marked by constant unrest and rivalry among the conquistadors and the genocide of a whole race of human beings. Even the founding of La Isabela, the first Spanish settlement in the island during Columbus's second voyage in 1493, ended in total failure for the admiral.

Nicolás de Ovando

Anxious for tangible results, Queen Isabela removed the Great Admiral as governor and next sent a supposedly stronger Franciso de Bobadilla in 1500 to serve as her chief administrator in La Hispaniola. But it was the island's third governor who would leave an indelible imprint in the annals of the entire Spanish Antilles, not just in Hispaniola. Nicolás de Ovando in 1502, under whose skillful stewardship the city of Santo Domingo de Guzmán was erected on the banks of the Ozama River, was the new appointee. The Reyes Católicos were now more determined than ever to duplicate in the Caribbean the successful sociopolitical scheme that was operating in the Iberian Peninsula. To this end, the Crown devised a precise structure of governance that they felt would assure greater returns on their extremely risky investment.

Just as the strategy had been in the Arab-held territories of southern Spain at the point of final victory for the warriors of the Reconquest, the same plan was put in place in Hispaniola. The idea was to establish fortified Spanish settlements in the conquered areas of the island— erecting them strategically near already standing (or demolished) indigenous communities and, even more significantly, on the very site of newly discovered gold mines.

For the first time, an authentic Spanish colonial administrative policy was officially inaugurated. With the earlier failure of the La Isabela settlement, at least ten successful replacement sites were founded in the eastern portion of Hispaniola: Santo Domingo, Azuya, San Juan de la Maguana, Buenaventura (San Cristóbal), Higüey, Santa Cruz, Bonao, Concepción de la Vega, Santiago de los Caballeros, and Puerto Plata. By the year 1508, these towns were proudly displaying their respective coats of arms. In the same year, the island's first systematic census was conducted; it was estimated that perhaps sixty thousand indigenous inhabitants were among the total population. By the year 1517, approximately twelve thousand native people were counted. Ovando as governor was expertly efficient in executing the royal mandate. Hispaniola became even more exclusive in terms of just who would be admitted as potential settlers. The governor's instructions were to enforce prohibition against Arabs, Jews, any new converts to Catholicism, any Protestants from areas in Europe, and gypsies. Very few non-Castilians were initially permitted entry into the new colony without special consent directly from the Crown. The territory had the orthodox sanction of the Catholic church, which became more prominent during the period of Ovando's command. Populated mainly by the order of Franciscans, later joined by the order of Dominicans, the church in the island saw its principal role as that of a divine mission to spread the Christian gospel, forcibly converting the native populations to the new religion.

Notes

1. Carlos Dobal, "Herencia Española en la Cultura Dominicana de Hoy," p. 103.

2. F. R. Herrera Miniño, *Raíces, Motivaciones y Fundamentos de la Raza Dominicana,* p. 66.

3. The Berber chieftain Tarik claimed the great rock Gebel-al-Tarik (Tarik's Mountain), known popularly as Gibraltar. The year A.D. 711 marks the initial invasion of Iberia by Tarik, and the subsequent occupation by Moslem groups.

4. The Moors *(los moros)* were Moslems from North Africa, most probably from Morocco. They conquered and occupied most of the Iberian Peninsula, exerting a profound cultural and economic impact upon life in Iberia. They were defeated, then expelled totally from the peninsula in 1492. During the eight centuries of Moslem occupation, successive waves of invaders represented many diverse ethnic Moslem groups. Two very fierce, warlike Islamic groups, also from North Africa, who entered Iberia and absorbed the previously established Moslem kingdoms into their clans were the *Almorávides* and the much feared *Almohades.* The Spanish Christians who lived among the Moslems, sometimes even converting to Islam, were called *mozarades.* Moslems who lived in majority Christian districts were called *mudéjares.*

5. Frank Moya Pons, *Manual de Historia Dominicana,* p. 21.

6. Ibid., pp. 45–46.

7. Hugo Tolentino Dipp, *Raza e Historia en Santo Domingo,* p. 26.

8. In ancient Greek philosophy, the basis of Western European thought, Aristotle formulated such theories. The myth of cannibalism, coupled with this line of erroneous thinking, served to prove the racial inferiority of non-Western societies or so-called primitive peoples. Thus, we have a false justification of enslavement of such inferior groups (e.g., Native Americans and Africans) based on theological rationalizations from a Christian perspective.

5

Voices of Opposition

The perception held by the Spanish toward the indigenous populations increased into arrogant racism. The Spanish viewed the island's original occupants as a primary and necessary source of laborers to work the mines, as well as to provide labor for food-crop cultivation. The Spanish successfully convinced themselves that enslavement of these inferior people, or so they were regarded, was essential for the survival of Hispaniola. They provided a guarantee of a readily available labor pool. The subjugated groups were clearly the important link that connected productive efficiency and resultant material wealth. There was hardly the concern that the dwindling native population might pose a threat to the expected continuity of the colony's economic growth.

Gold and God

The simplistic solution was to replace the loss of laborers with a fresh supply of newly conquered native peoples. Ovando had already rationalized slavery in efforts to lay the foundation for Hispaniola's wealth. The two-pronged objective, therefore, of gold and God (in precisely that priority) became immediately reconciled under the institution of slavery. As early as 1509 Ovando and Diego Columbus—the Great Admiral's son and Ovando's successor as governor—were experienced slave raiders. They both had earlier organized and led raiding expeditions to the neighboring Lucayan Islands (today called the Bahamas). With severely bitter consequences, Spain structured the economy of Hispaniola around a base of exploited forced labor (i.e., slavery). This creation was unique in that the world, ancient or modern, had not previously known this kind of economic system: a slave economy.

Denouncements

As the constraints of the *encomienda* system tightened, thus facilitating even more the enslavement of the indigenous inhabitants of the island, voices of genuine outrage became louder and more adamantly opposed to this form of man's inhumanity to man. Friars of the order of Dominicanos, led first by men like Antonio de Montesinos, and later by Pedro de Córdova and Bartolomé de las Casas, raised strident protests on religious and moral grounds against the cruel and unjust treatment of the indigenous people in the Caribbean territories. These outspoken critics from the clergy were authentic crusaders who, at the risk of possible expulsion from the colony, argued forcibly in defense of this exploited segment of the society.

One of the most daring voices of denouncement was that of Antonio de Montesinos, a member of the first Dominican order in Hispaniola. In 1511 Montesinos, aroused by the abuse and exploitation of the island's indigenous people, denounced from the pulpit his congregation and the whole colony for their immoral and shameful actions toward the native community. In blistering outrage, he attacked the powerful *encomenderos,* arguing in favor of the equality of all human beings. He then made the truly inflammatory assertion that *los indios eran hombres con almas racionales*[1] (the Indians were men with rational souls).

> I am a voice crying in the wilderness; you are in mortal sin for the cruelty and tyranny you use in dealing with these innocent people. Tell me, by what right or justice do you keep these Indians in cruel and horrible servitude? Are these not men? Have they not rational souls, and you not bound to love them as you love yourselves?[2]

The response from the congregation was one of bitter protest. The colonial authorities moved swiftly against Montesinos. After all, the friar was espousing thoughts considered extremely radical and inappropriate, even heretical. The settlers were not about to relinquish their mounting profits, even if earned by means of exploited native labor. On short notice, Friar Montesinos was recalled to Spain, never to be heard from afterward.

In Defense of Indigenous Cultures

It was both Friar Pedro de Córdova and Friar Bartolomé de las Casas, however, who were later appointed by their colleagues to travel to Spain so that the case for the exploited native people might be presented directly before the Spanish Court. The basic argument of de Córdova and de las Casas was that Quisqueya's original inhabitants constituted a "natural circumstance," resulting from the perceived notion on the part of the Spaniards of natural masters and natural slaves. In 1519, before the convened Council of the Indies in Barcelona, Las Casas boldly proposed a colonization plan that would guarantee and protect the right of the remaining indigenous populations in Hispaniola. He reminded the wealthy *encomenderos* how they had become rich—*con las fatigas y sudores de los indios* (with the painstaking work and sweat of the Indians).[3] This well-intentioned Protector of the Indigenous Cultures, as Las Casas became known soon thereafter, may not have saved them from total extinction, but he did succeed in raising the level of consciousness of people generally about the gruesome mistreatment of Hispaniola's original inhabitants. These were the souls who had been reduced to slavery or worse; they were being systematically exterminated.

Some observers suggest that the judgment of history has been particularly harsh on Las Casas for his controversial proposal to save the indigenous groups: the first part of his proposal was to replace this aboriginal group with stepped-up numbers of imported African captives. Later in life, however, he repented this advice. His second plan was designed to be a cure for the heinous aspects of the prevailing *encomienda* system. Spanish farmers were to be organized into structured villages of about forty families each. A government-assisted allotment of indigenous people would be held in sacred trust by each village, instead of by a selected individual, as was commonly the practice on the island. The land would be worked in common under the supervision of the friars. This latter portion of the plan failed because of overwhelming opposition to it from the settlers and civil authorities alike, who continued leading slave raids upon the indigenous communities.

Discouraged by defeat, Padre las Casas retired to the seclusion of a monastery in Santo Domingo, where he devoted the rest of his life to writing a prolific series of spirited polemics in defense of the indigenous cultures and the shameful destruction of their way of life at the butcherous hands of the Spanish colonists. His most bitter critics, including much of the clergy in Hispaniola, could not refute his indictments. Las Casas's prose aroused groups of humanitarians everywhere to renewed energy. On the other hand, the masterful works inflamed the ire of colonists and authorities, hardening their joint determination to defeat the meddlesome priest. Las Casas was despised by most of the Spanish community on the island, and even rejected by most of the clergy. There is still debate as to whether he ultimately aided the cause he cherished so dearly, or assisted in defeating it by rendering more adamant the growing opposition. His absolute courage, however, was never a question of debate.

Encomienda Fortified

The defense of the indigenous populations was not sufficiently decisive to bring an end to the campaign of extermination in Hispaniola. However sincere were the efforts of many heroic individuals to protect the rights of the indigenous cultures, acts of cruelty and barbarism against them accelerated to an even higher intensity.[4] Proposals to free them from exploitation under the *encomienda* failed. The decimated numbers of native peoples were being quickly replaced by government-sanctioned slave raids on native communities in neighboring islands. Hispaniola reached a critical turning point in the process of its socioeconomic formation upon the occasion of the birth of a newer social model that was based on a decidedly greater degree of exploitation of labor. Rather than abolish the *encomienda,* the Spanish settlers actually fortified it.[5] The Caucasian population on the island grew steadily. Their numbers were encouraged by the rapid creation of new settlements throughout the territory. The specific factors in the transition to a radically different social model were (1) the emergence of sugarcane as a major crop for cultivation and (2) the aggressive engagement in the transatlantic slave trade—African captives pressed into slavery ultimately to replace the indigenous slaves who were fast becoming extinct as a race.

It would be a gross mistake to suspect that the Spanish colonists did not face repeated, open hostility, resistance, and insurrection from the indigenous communities. Quite early on, these communities were far from being passive. They did not simply resign themselves to their tragic fate as is often mistakenly believed. Rather, they rebelled at every opportunity possible. For instance, during periods when the Spanish departed for newly established offshore territories, leaving Quisqueya temporarily sparsely populated, bloody uprisings were especially prominent and immediate. Once the indigenous people became intimately knowledgeable about the language, the habits, the patterns of behavior, and the thinking of the Spanish colonists, the rebels' military tactics and strategies altered significantly.

Enriquillo

The Spanish faced one of their fiercest challenges when the great Taíno chieftain Enriquillo rose up in battle against them. This rebellion was virtually a sustained major war (1519–1533). Today, placed in the middle of the main crossroad leading to Lago Enriquillo in the country's southwest, there is an imposing monument in his honor that reads: *Cacique Enriquillo, Primer Héroe de América, Fue Justa Su Rebelión y Grande Su Victoria* (Chieftain Enriquillo, First Hero of America; His Rebellion Was Just and His Victory was Great).

This rebellion was undoubtedly the most important of this era of Spanish colonization. Enriquillo not only demonstrated notably sophisticated military tactics and combat skills, but additionally proved his capacity to organize effectively the indigenous communities scattered throughout the Bahoruco Mountains. He formed a confederation among the Taíno communities. One particularly important historical note is that the impact of these confederations was reinforced by the welcome participation and alliance of runaway African slaves, called *cimmarrones* (to be discussed in detail later). Enriquillo was successful in establishing fortified enclaves and strategically located outposts that provided an advance-warning system. He was also astute in erecting separate, isolated villages for the exclusive security of the community's women, children, and elders. Enriquillo launched incessant guerrilla attacks against Spanish-owned properties in selected settlements in the island's major population areas. Communications and transportation were hampered; the island's economy was severely crippled. Even gold-mining activity in the distant Cibao Mountains was in serious peril. The Spanish would not readily forget Cacique Enriquillo and his bold campaigns to liberate his exploited people.

Notes

1. Hugo Tolentino Dipp, *Raza e Historia en Santo Domingo,* p. 54.
2. Ibid., p. 55.
3. Las Casas had not always been so sympathetic to the cause of the indigenous cultures of Hispaniola. He came to the island as a gentleman soldier of fortune in 1502. He was successful, won lands, and held enslaved indigenous people, all with untroubled conscience. Las Casas was the classic *encomendero.* He even continued his profit-earning schemes after becoming ordained a priest. In fact, he was part of the very congregation that Montesinos had denounced. However, by the age of forty Las Casas suddenly realized his role in perpetuating the iniquity of the *encomienda* system under which he had become wealthy. He then gave up all his private property and for fifty years defended ardently the indigenous cultures throughout the Americas.
4. CEDEE, *Escarbando las Raíces de la Explotación,* p. 5. It was estimated that by the year 1520 a mere four thousand indigenous people were present in Hispaniola!
5. A glossary of terms relative to Spanish colonial government in Hispaniola would include the following:
   (a) *adelantados:* During the early colonial period, these were the private individuals allowed to undertake expeditions of conquest and colonization, but they had to share their discoveries with the Crown.
   (b) *audiencia:* a tribunal that formed the civil government, appointed directly by the Crown. It was the instrument that replaced the conquistadors' earlier martial law.
   (c) *cabildos:* town councils that were molded on the relatively democratic town councils of Spain before the time of Carlos the Fifth. The duty of the *cabildo* was to look after the public works, to exert a degree of judicial authority, and to express the general consensus on certain issues of municipal government.
   (d) Casa de Contratación: House of Trade, established in 1503 at Sevilla. It directed all matters of trade and commerce in the new territory.
   (e) *consulado:* Closely associated with the Casa de Contratación, this was a trade guild of the merchants of various Caribbean colonial settlements, functioning much like today's units of the Chamber of Commerce.
   (f) *hacendados:* used interchangeably with the perhaps more common term *latifundistas,* who were large plantation or estate owners. The hacienda was the chief economic and social unit in many Latin American countries. It represented a little world within the larger nation or colony; it was a self-contained community, even with its own church or chapel on the premises. Particularly in Hispaniola, the hacienda was referred to as the *hato.*
   (g) Other appointees by the Crown as observers or examiners, charged with the duty of watching the governors and responsible for giving an

account to the king of what they observed and considered worthy of the Crown's knowledge, included *pesquisadores:* royal investigators; and *veedores:* visitors, also specially assigned individuals who made official trips to the territories.

(h) *residencia:* a judicial review of the performance of colonial administrators, executed by a judge who was appointed by the Crown.

(i) The Spanish Main: the Caribbean coast of South America from Panamá to the delta of the Orinoco River, a heavily traveled sealane that was pillaged for three centuries by ruthless English, French, and Dutch pirates. The Spanish Main was divided between the free republics of Venezuela and Colombia.

(j) Viceroy: a competent, obedient subordinate appointed to represent the king personally in the new territories. The Viceroyalties, established in 1535, were divided into the following geographical regions: New Spain (Mexico), Peru, New Granada (Colombia), and River Plate (Buenos Aires).

6

The Renegades
Marginal People

Pirates and Buccaneers

Almost everyone is thrilled and intrigued by stories of swashbuckling pirates as portrayed in literature or shown in motion pictures. These romantic tales, always full of imagination, are about buried or sunken treasure, blood-curdling sword fights, torture, plunder, heroism, and dashing gallantry on land and the high seas. However, there is much more to the actual event than mere thrills and excitement, for piracy played an immensely important role in the international economic and political rivalries of the sixteenth and seventeenth centuries. More often than not, these rivalries were played out against the lush tropical backdrop of the Caribbean.

Almost from the very beginning, Spain faced strong and determined competition for control of the profitable trade and riches of the new territories. France, England, and Holland each had their eyes on the seductive prize of New World markets and on the acquisition of the region's precious metals and other natural resources. Sea hawks, as sea pirates were commonly called, quickly discovered the profitability in the well-conceived strategies of lying in ambush at several selected vantage points throughout the Caribbean in order to pounce on the rich gold and silver fleets of Spain and Portugal. The question at issue with these marauders was the trade of the world, and they proved in short measure that they could wrest some of it from Spain. They also showed how lucrative piracy could be as a steady occupation, and so attracted many diverse individuals to it.

The Caribbean soon witnessed unprecedented sea travel during this period. Marauding bands of pirates, buccaneers, corsairs, filibusters, privateers—they were known by any of several different names, which essentially engaged in the same activity—for nearly two hundred years made life miserable for the Spanish galleons trying to deliver their precious cargo back to Sevilla and Cádiz. Quite frequently, these French, English, and Dutch privateers conducted their activities with the sanction of their respective royal governments, sometimes even being in their actual employ.[1] In fact, piracy, at least among Spain's bitter rivals, was considered quite a respectable occupation and undertaking. After all, it was a significant part of the war effort, and these countries were clearly at war against Spain and her restrictive, monopolistic mercantile policy. Thus, the plundering of Spanish galleons, the murdering of Spanish seamen, the kidnapping of Spanish passengers, and the ravaging of Spanish coasts were all activities accorded high esteem by most of Europe's other royal households. The island of Hispaniola found itself at center stage in this high drama and intrigue.

Exactly who were these *piratas, bucaneros,* and *filibusteros*?[2] What precise role did they play in the cultural formation of La República Dominicana? The Spanish Crown's absolute rigidity on economic policy for the island and the other territories—monopoly and isolation—provided some important explanations for the surfacing of a prominent buccaneer society within the larger island society of Hispaniola. The origins of buccaneering are associated first with the tiny island of Tortuga, lying just six miles off the northwestern coast of Hispaniola, and with Hispaniola itself, whose northern and western zones Spain had abandoned altogether before the end of the first quarter of the seventeenth century. At about that time deserters from cargo ships, fugitives from justice, survivors from wrecked vessels, and marooned types began to gather at these sites. These individuals lived mainly by hunting in the forests and savannahs the great herds of wild hogs and free-roaming cattle that had multiplied from those stocks first introduced by the early Spanish settlers. These pirates and buccaneers were therefore originally hunters before they became sea hawks, roving and plundering the open seas.

Oral tradition on many of the islands, including Hispaniola, suggests that individuals of diverse nationalities, races, and ethnicities took to pirating and buccaneering because of massive unemployment. Great numbers of seamen were turned adrift at the conclusion of war campaigns that took place throughout the Caribbean. Also significant was the imagined difficulty of settling down quickly and profitably in a new place. There was a tendency for the colonists to wander from one island to another, island-hopping, trying to find their fortune. Furthermore, there was no enforceable international law governing the seas. Also, as had been tested and proved, buccaneering could be very lucrative. More important still was the overt encouragement provided to privateers by European sovereigns. The famous Cardinal Richelieu, for example, in connection with his personal aim to establish a French colonial empire in the West, actually offered his blessings—and considerable financial assistance—to pirate attacks on Spanish properties in the Caribbean, especially on Hispaniola. The French, mainly corsair types, and the English had footholds in Tortuga at different periods in the region's history, with the French gaining the upper hand in about 1659. From Tortuga they reached out to the northern zones of Hispaniola, thus founding the very important colony of Saint Domingue, about which more will be said later.

Individuals Without a Country

The newly formed buccaneer society, more than anywhere else, anchored itself in Hispaniola. Geographical as well as demographical factors contributed appreciably to the island's becoming one of the most preferred bases of operations for pirating and smuggling activities. For the most part, Hispaniola's insularity and the pivotal factor of having extensive, unprotected coasts (unobstructed by natural barriers in contrast to many other islands throughout the Antilles), along with its strategic location in the Caribbean, combined to offer tremendous advantages for a motley band of individuals whose sole mission soon became that of plunder. These were individuals without a country, stateless souls, homeless brethren of the coasts, in many instances wandering aimlessly across the Caribbean except when they waylaid a hapless vessel. These individuals pledged allegiance to no flag but their own, ignoring completely the sovereignty of any and all territories in the region. This was an international assortment of souls.

Among the crews were men as well as women who had early decided they wanted no part of a rigid, extremely regimented social order as found in the sugar-plantation societies throughout the Caribbean. The group's ranks swelled quickly as more and more recruits were seduced by titillating accounts of enormous profits garnered from Spanish galleons laden with cargoes of gold and silver. These recruits were drawn from the lot of pure adventurers and opportunists in search of personal fortune, dissidents and deserts from conventional sailing crews. Often noted among the filibusters (or corsairs, as the French called them) were the faces of Africa and Asia, alongside those of Europe, all mingling together with the same intensity of greed and ruthlessness.[3] This was truly an odd assortment of human types. Hispaniola lay conveniently in the path of vague, hard-to-enforce international statutes. Moreover, there were easily believed rumors circulating throughout the entire region and beyond that the bulky galleons were regularly carrying a cargo of mind-boggling quantities of treasure destined for far-off ports in Spain. There were bands of marauding individuals who would soon become both infamous and dreaded because of their masterful butchery on the high seas. Theirs was a total repudiation of any semblance of law and a relentless pursuit of two things only: loot and liberty. These roving bands were obsessed with the idea of unconditional freedom from the maddening confinement of an orderly society. They were likewise exceedingly desirous of easily won riches. But this was not always the case.

Buccaneers were men who initially earned their living by dealing in hides of cattle, horses, and hogs, which were sold to Dutch smugglers. These animals, roaming wild, were hunted down and slaughtered, then the meat was preserved for later sales to passing vessels. It was the unique method of preserving this meat that lent its name to this group of renegades. The ancient Taíno used the word *boucán* to describe the process of smoking meat. The Taíno tradition involved driving four sticks into the ground, their upper ends forked to support other sticks laid horizontally so as to make an open platform. On this were laid the strips of meat. A fire burned below and the meat was both cooked and smoked. Treated in this manner, the smoked meat could be preserved for weeks in excellent condition. These resourceful individuals planted themselves quite firmly on the western side of Hispaniola, operating all but unhampered by the authorities. Throughout the period of the 1530s, isolated pockets of these buccaneer communities were established primarily in this western zone of the island. These renegade communities soon proved themselves extremely capable of challenging Spanish supremacy in the entire Antilles. Present-day Haiti, where the rapidly increasing African population ultimately erased the dominance of Caucasians, is the result.

Tortuga and Sanctuary

The loosely organized settlements of renegades counted on an economic base primarily constituting the sale of hide and *boucán*. Ever increasingly, inhabitants of these communities expanded their economic activity by daring to pillage the very ships with which they had only recently negotiated commerce. As this shift in commerce proved more lucrative, so too did it prove advantageous to shift the base of this now perilous operation from the mainland of Hispaniola to the smaller offshore island of Tortuga. Tortuga, small as it is, was to continue playing a considerable role in the social development of Hispaniola. *Tortuga era un castillo edificado por la naturaleza* (Tortuga was a castle built by nature). This was an apt description of this tiny island: about twenty-three miles or thirty-seven kilometers long from east to west and maybe four or five miles (six to eight kilometers) across. Tortuga, lying off the northwestern coast of Hispaniola, and today a part of Haiti, is just five miles north of the Haitian town of Port-de-Paix. The island is perhaps best remembered as the most famous haunt of buccaneers and pirates during the mid-seventeenth century. The French buccaneers who gathered there were largely responsible for launching the French conquest of Spanish-held eastern and northern Hispaniola. The terrain is unusually rugged for the tropics. It was found to be easily defensible from outside attack and thus very much out of reach of the sporadic retaliatory strikes by Spanish garrisons on nearby Hispaniola.

At the same time, from their tiny island stronghold, the now-entrenched buccaneer society found itself still quite close to its original source of income, the roaming herds of cattle in the northwestern corner of Hispaniola. So, Tortuga became the commercial capital, the pulse, and home base for the region's newest community of settlers, the *bucaneros*. Interestingly enough, according to one noted Dominican historian, Tortuga witnessed a unique coexistence of both *bucaneros* and *piratas*—a cohabitation that very frequently confuses observers:

La pequeña isla adyacente de la de Santo Domingo fue plaza comercial de los bucaneros y de los piratas a la vez, y cuartel general de los segundos, y esa coexistencia de bucaneros y piratas en un mismo lugar ha confundido a los historiadores.[4]

(The small island next to Santo Domingo was the commercial market square of the buccaneers and the pirates at the same time, and also a fortress and general headquarters for pirates; that coexistence of buccaneers and pirates in the same place has confused historians.)

Both buccaneers and pirates alike, many of them renegades from indentured servitude on the various sugar plantations around the Caribbean, found virtual sanctuary on Tortuga. Particularly harsh circumstances had made these independent-minded individuals quite tough and rugged. One such individual was Bertrand de Ogerón, who had been a buccaneer before rising to the rank of governor of Tortuga in 1665. But because his plans to unify the tiny offshore island failed, de Ogerón became a foe of all buccaneers and thus waged a bloody personal campaign to exterminate this band of rogues from the Caribbean.[5] Perhaps one of the most nefarious pirates to roam the waters of the Caribbean during this period was an individual known as El Olonés. Feared mainly for his merciless cruelty and butchery, El Olonés also managed to reach the rank of governor of Tortuga![6]

Smuggling: A Serious Economic Threat

Recalling the crippling economic hamstrings that the Spanish Crown placed on all its overseas territories, especially regarding Hispaniola's trade, it becomes somewhat easy to understand why the *bucaneros* themselves would ultimately resort to overt piracy as a steady profession. Operating hand-in-glove with piracy was its natural accomplice, smuggling. This clandestine commercial activity, trafficking in contraband, began to appear with a noted degree of frequency and importance throughout the Caribbean about 1565. Within a relatively short time, trade in contraband became the single most important and indeed the most profitable enterprise in Hispaniola. Figuring among the hubs of smuggling activity were towns like Yaguana, Bayaga, Monti Cristi, and Puerto Plata in the northwestern corner. Also listed among centers of aggressive contraband activity were San Juan, Azua, La Vega, and

Santiago, all turning their eyes in the direction not of the major port city on the banks of the Ozama, but toward officially off-limits foreign ports instead. Smuggling rapidly increased to the point of becoming an undisputed menace to the island's economic lifeline. Illicit trade quite naturally undercut the local merchants, subsequently depressing the local economy altogether.

This, then, was another significant component in the ever more intriguing mosaic of dynamics in the formation of the island's culture. Another element is added to Hispaniola's cultural mix. The ethnic interplay that occurred as a result of the arrival and occupancy of these buccaneers and pirates represented quite dramatically the emerging pattern of widening ethnic diversity among the inhabitants of Hispaniola. The buccaneer society originated, grew, and died all within a period of about fifty years. It never subjected itself to the absolute governance of the dominant forces in the island. This society within a society was brought to an end because its original economic base had come to a decided end. The wild cattle herds of Hispaniola that had given this vital cultural enclave its life had now disappeared.

Notes

1. The English pirate Francis Drake, during the 1560s, was one of the first infamous buccaneers in the service of the English Crown. Both Drake and his compatriot John Hawkins were later knighted for their daring feats against England's rival, Spain. Other notorious heretical sea dogs (as the Spanish called them) included Walter Raleigh, Harry Morgan, the Dutchmen Pret Heyn and Edward Mansveldt, and the Frenchman known as L'Ollonais.

2. The English expression filibuster, which means a military adventurer, also refers to the use of delaying tactics by a legislator to prevent or stall a vote on a bill; or a lengthy, often rambling speech delivered for such purpose.

3. A flibustier was a freebooter, a buccaneer. The word flibustier resembles the word flyboat only accidentally, although the buccaneers used the flyboat for coastal journeys. This was a vessel of Dutch type with a flat bottom and a high stern, capable of drawing perhaps four hundred to six hundred tons. Homeless brethren of the coast is still another term for buccaneers. The filibusters were actually distinguished from other pirates in that the former sometimes stole their own ships as they engaged in their activities. It should be noted that in the English language buccaneers and pirates were equivalent terms, mainly because of the later activities of the two groups. Both groups eventually engaged in sea piracy, buccaneers having abandoned completely their original occupation of selling hides and cooked meat to seafaring smugglers in the region.

4. Juan Bosch, *Composición Social Dominicana: Historia e Interpretación,* p. 85.

5. *Bucaneros* had earlier rejected all conventional forms of domination and adherence to rules of law, and so they were not compliant with de Ogerón's scheme.

6. Some noted historians of the Caribbean, like Sir Philip Sherlock of Jamaica, believe the bloodiest pirate of all by far was the Frenchman known as L'Ollonais (called El Olonés in Spanish). L'Ollonais started his buccaneer activities in 1650 and led a more than twenty-year reign of hell throughout the entire Caribbean. According to legend, he pulled out tongues and carved his prisoners into small pieces before roasting the body parts in boiling oil. The merest whisper of his name sent inhabitants scurrying from the villages all along the Spanish Main (Sir Philip Sherlock, *A History of the West Indies,* p. 52).

7

Los Cimarrones
Another Transfrontier Culture

While a more comprehensive treatment of the African legacy in the formation of Dominican culture will appear in later chapters, this present focus continues the exploration of the second of the two basic transfrontier cultural groups—the renegades or marginal people. These, of course, are the groups that, in a most determined fashion, elected to function well outside the ordinary confines of regulated colonial society in Hispaniola. Like the buccaneers and pirates, this second important group, called maroons (or *cimarrones* in Spanish), also symbolized an alternative to the rigidity of Spanish colonial authority. The *cimarrones* were escaped runaway slaves, yes. But at the same time, they were much more than mere slaves who had managed ingeniously to escape from the shackles of plantation oppression.

Early Resistance

Perhaps it is accurate to state, as some historical accounts do, that Spanish authorities first recorded the incidence of fugitive *ladino* slaves in 1503 when these runaways escaped into the remote mountains.[1] The truth of the matter, though, is that given the nature of these individuals who were pressed into human bondage and given the structure of the early colonial system itself, it should come as no great surprise that *cimarrón* activity had existed since the very inception of the idea to enslave African captives. Whether originally undertaken by courageous souls acting alone, or later by small bands of individuals sworn to collective secrecy and absolute commitment, the numbers of active participants in these escapes and the frequency of occurrence grew in a very short time.

Among the earlier experiences of the runaways in executing a full-fledged uprising against enslavement was the rebellion commanded by the legendary Taíno *cacique* Enriquillo (1519–1533). Readily counted among Enriquillo's rebels were impressive numbers of *cimarrones* as well as indigenous peoples. Upon the final suppression of Enriquillo's rebellion, many of the surviving *cimarrones* formed a militia comprised almost exclusively of Africans. By the year 1537 the *cimarrones* of Bahoruco were a well-organized, intricately structured society under the disciplined and skilled leadership of an individual called Juan Vaquero, his original African name having been Hispanicized under the *encomienda* system. Vaquero and his band of runaways struck terror in the minds of the Spanish settlers. Uprisings continued throughout the years following 1537, from the region of Cabo de San Nicolás (lying between the San Juan and the Nagua Rivers) and Samaná Point to Cabo de Higüey. It is estimated that the total number of participants in the scattered uprisings around the island reached anywhere from three thousand to seven thousand insurrectionists. These figures considerably augmented the population count in the various *cimarrón* communities.

The Spanish settlers of Hispaniola felt an immediate sense of fear as they reflected upon the steadily increasing numbers of runaway slaves populating these tactically fortified *cimarrón* enclaves. There was the unimagined fear, for instance, that owing to the superior numbers of these individuals, it would not be very long into the future that the entire island of Hispaniola would be overrun by *cimarrones*. Among the most renowned leaders of the fugitive slave communities, and especially noted as much for their ferocity in military strategy as for their sophisticated leadership and organizational skills, were such men as Diego Guzmán, Diego de Ocampo, Juan Vaquero, and without question the most heroic figure of all *cimarrón* leaders in Hispaniola, the great Lemba. It was Lemba alone who plagued Spanish settlements for some fifteen years in the region of Higüey. These bands of runaways were determined to destroy totally the system that had enslaved and exploited them—thus posing a real threat to the very survival of the colony. These leaders—Guzmán, Ocampo, Vaquero, and Lemba—dedicated completely their efforts and energies to forcibly wrecking the instruments of oppression: the sugarmills, the farms, the masters themselves. However, there is the exact opposite aspect of this feared maroonage offensive, that of simply fleeing into the inaccessible mountains in order to establish unmolested havens of safety, patterned after the model of the traditional African village society that had once been an inextricable cultural element in the past of the African captive who came to American shores. Exactly who were the maroons? What was a *maniel?* The word maroon is actually the Anglicized term of the Spanish word *cimarrón,* which initially referred to the herds of range cattle that had become wild, undomesticated. The French version was similarly *marron.* The term was also used to designate horses that roamed unharnessed or wild. During the earlier periods of island settlement by the Europeans, the term was applied to indigenous peoples who had escaped from the Spanish compounds. Within the colonial society, the runaway was a individual who suffered a double-pronged assault from the European colonizer. First as a slave, the runaway was a victim of oppression, exploitation, and plain barbarity. Then later as a fugitive, this same individual was a target of even more intense hatred, prejudice, and terror. He or she was constantly in hiding, in flight, forever confronting the charge of being uncivilized and wild.

Fugitive Slave Communities

How ironic, though, that the designation *cimarrón* was so ill suited and most certainly did not reflect with any measure of accuracy the precise nature of either the runaways or their unique community. Quite the contrary, the *cimarrón* communities were paradigms of often uncompromising order and stability. These communities were highly structured, well-organized societies with a deep reverence for tradition. *Cimarrón* society was purposely molded to replicate the ancestral communes and villages of an Africa prior to the transatlantic slave trade. The residents of the alternative community—a society within a hostile and noninclusive larger society—were attempting to reconstruct the values and patterns of their forebears, who had come from a number of different African ethnicities.

Manieles: Fugitive Slave Communities

The term *maniel* is uniquely Dominican. The Spanish used the generic name *maniel* to refer specifically to the mountains located to the north of the Neiba Valley. Situated to the south of Lake Enriquillo is the Sierra de Bahoruco. On the entire island of Hispaniola, perhaps of the most preferred hideaway sites that fugitive slaves used for establishing their communities, or *manieles,* was the strategically impressive mountain range of the Bahoruco. *Cimarrón* activity had actually begun as early as the 1520s in Hispaniola, then in Panama, where fugitive slaves fled the brutal whips and chains and the forced labor imposed by their Spanish masters. These resourceful runaways quickly realized the advantage in organizing small, extremely disciplined, and well-armed militia in order to launch assaults upon Spanish overland commerce. The daring and determined *cimarrones* came to be pivotal actors in Anglo-Spanish competition for local hegemony in the Caribbean. Between about 1540 and 1580 the *cimarrones* in Panama, for instance, allied themselves with English buccaneers. The depredations of this *cimarrón-bucanero* alliance were a crushing blow to Spanish shipments of goods across the Isthmus of Panama. The Spanish settlers complained to Madrid that they feared the *cimarrones* more than they did the English. Under superb leadership, many of these runaways had been trained previously as hunters of wild cattle, horses, and hogs for the settlers. Maroon power and the mounting reputation for ferocity increased as the *cimarrones* themselves abducted slaves from nearby European settlements and also as other runaways willfully joined the fast-swelling ranks of these early freedom fighters.

Slave Insurrections

Slave insurrections and rebellions were actually quite common, rather frequent, and greatly feared by the Spaniards on the island. A mere eleven years after the first Spanish conquistadores arrived in Quisqueya in 1503, when Nicolás de Ovando was governor, he wrote to the Spanish monarchs, asking them

> que no enviaron esclavos negros a la isla, porque muchos huían a los montes y no podían ser detenidos y los negros se refugiaban entre los indios y les enseñaban malas costumbres.[2]

(not to send Black slaves to the island, because many of them fled to the mountains and could not be caught; and the Blacks sought refuge among the Indians and taught them bad habits.)

Could Ovando have intended to report that the Blacks were teaching the native populations to stop allowing the Spaniards to exploit them? The fires of Black revolt and resistance across the Caribbean grew more inflamed as the years of harshness increased. In the instance of Jamaica, for example, the rebellions culminated in the famous slave uprising of 1831, which involved some twenty thousand African slaves. This portentous event led directly to the demise of slavery as an institution in the whole of the British Caribbean.

Latin America's first full-scale slave insurrection was launched in Hispaniola in 1522 and was executed with total success. More than twenty African slaves, at a sugar plantation located on the banks of the Río Isabela, destroyed everything in existence. Some twenty other Africans from various surrounding colonial settlements quickly joined this band of fiercely bold insurrectionists, and were soon en route to the town of Azua where they destroyed other plantations. Pressing onward from Ocoa to Nizao, the wrathful insurrectionists burned and looted every farm and sugarmill lying in their determined path.

Basically the African slaves rebelled against their enslavement by frequently electing one of three different formulas: One was by simply running off and hiding for a few days or more—often near the plantation, until caught or sometimes returning on their own volition. Another tactic was by fleeing to a designated hiding site and becoming a declared member of an organized fugitive commune. Finally, there was the objective of fleeing directly into the remote mountains. There the runaway became a kind of guerrilla fighter along with numerous other similarly minded individuals in order to form a decisive band of armed military insurgents. These individuals would be devoted wholly to waging combat against all the island's slaveholders.

This latter strategy, to a large extent, was what characterized the *manieles* of Hispaniola. By the year 1545 it was estimated that some seven thousand runaway slaves were living in such communities. The more significant *manieles* in terms of military strength, duration of existence, and power of resistance, located throughout the island, included the following sites: in the southern zone, in San Juan de la Maguana, and most especially in the Sierra de Bahoruco. *Manieles* were also established in Azua. In the island's northern zone, Puerto Plata and La Vega presented rather formidable strongholds. Higüey in the eastern zone featured some of these slave communities of considerable historical and cultural note. During the height of the *maniel* campaigns, in the region that embraces the Río San Juan and Nagua-Samaná there were an estimated two to three thousand escaped Africans living in skillfully organized and tightly administered enclaves that were absolutely free from the prospect of re-enslavement and exploitation.

Symbol of Resistance

The *maniel* in essence symbolized a classic form of resistance to enslavement and oppression. The site, in practically every aspect of collective resistance, epitomized an unmistakably intelligent strategy to establish completely autonomous societies. These communities were genuinely tailored to be socially and politically independent of the surrounding repressive European colonial unit. The *manieles,* scattered as they were throughout what is today the entire southwestern province of Bahoruco, were bitterly detested and opposed, and feared as well, by the slaveholders and other colonists, and justifiably so. The bold existence of the arrogantly self-confident *manieles* was regarded as a daring affront to the supposedly superior might of the otherwise beleaguered colonial administration. The lengthy survival of the *maniel* societies vexed the will of the Spanish, as well as attested to the ingenuity of the determined-to-be-free residents there. Having acquired a notoriously fearsome reputation, the *manieles* experienced frequent search-and-destroy-type campaigns by the Spanish authorities. These military expeditions met fierce counterattacks by the young able-bodied members, men and women alike, of the communes.

Another important element in the resistance arsenal was the geographical location of these communities. The site of most of the *manieles* featured a terrain that was exceptionally difficult, inhospitable, and practically inaccessible to the invading Spanish garrisons, who were completely unfamiliar with these remote mountainous areas. Almost an impregnable fortress for *cimarrones* from both the Spanish- and French-held territories of Hispaniola for nearly a whole century, the Neiba *maniel,* as a case in point, was suspected of not having been visited or discovered by the first European until about 1590! One rather fascinating cultural note on the *maniel* of Neiba concerns the language used by the residents. Because of the ethnic composition of the *cimarrones* there, the medium of communication—in addition to Spanish—evolved into a distinct jargon employing some French, some Portuguese, and a mixture of Guinea Coast languages of West Africa.[3] This rich and varied linguistic combination gave rise to what we now know as Haitian Kyrol that is spoken by the vast majority of Haitians today.

In these present times, Los Naranjos is a small residential zone near the village of Cabral, located in the province of Barahona. Practically the entire population in the area is composed of the descendants of *cimarrones* from the historic *manieles* of Neiba. The *cimarrones* as marginal people throughout the Caribbean had their very own reality etched meticulously out of their own unique cultural history and special circumstances. The cultural formation of La República Dominicana experienced yet another significant human dimension among the diverse cultural components and historical occurrences that would give completeness and meaning to the true social evolution in this unique island.

Notes

1. *Ladinos* were Spanish- or Portuguese-speaking African slaves who had become Christianized and acculturated to Iberian society. Many *ladinos* accompanied Spaniards to the Caribbean on initial voyages and thereafter. Those African slaves whom the Iberians considered not to have become acculturated were called *bozales,* or uncivilized.

2. CEDEE, *Escarbando las Raíces de la Explotación,* p. 10.

3. For the most part the ethnicity was quite diverse, comprising several distinct Guinea Coast (West Africa) cultural groups: Ewe, Fon, Yoruba, Ga, and Biafra.

8

The Africans
An Early Presence

The earliest African population nucleus in the Spanish colonies of the Americas was made up of groups referred to as *negros ladinos*. They were so named because of their partial, or perhaps in most cases total, linguistic and cultural assimilation and acculturation of Iberia. These *negros ladinos* were the Africans—some of whom were born in Lisbon, Coimbra, Madrid, Sevilla, and other major cities of the Iberian Peninsula—who would later accompany numerous Spanish explorers and adventurers on their expeditions to the new territories. We know, for example, that perhaps one of the very first African *ladinos* in America had piloted one of Columbus's ships, La Niña, during the historic 1492 voyage. He was Pedro Alonso Niño. Other such Africans of renown included Nuflo de Olano, who sailed with Balboa to Panama and sighted the Pacific Ocean. Estebánico journeyed with Coronado through territory of the United States Southwest. Juan Garrido was alongside Ponce de León in Puerto Rico and Florida. Pedro Mejía was the personal servant to Ovando when he arrived to govern Hispaniola. *Ladinos* were with Hernán Cortés during the conquest of Mexico, with Juan de Esquivel when he settled Jamaica, with Diego de Velásquez when he established a colony in Cuba, with Pedro de Alvarado in Central America, and with Pizarro in Peru. From the very beginning, then, the African presence in the Americas was a definite reality. However, the story of that presence begins well before *ladinos* found themselves in significant roles as they accompanied European adventurers across the Atlantic on those initial voyages.

Introduction to the African Past

It is still true that there are many Western historians, and consequently many students, who have yet to accept the existence of an African history to be explored and the findings disseminated. These individuals do not accept very readily the view that this documented African past predates the emergence of Europe by many thousands of years. It is also often denied or ignored completely that European civilization surfaced and began extending itself into the broader global arenas of Africa and Asia during the fifteenth and sixteenth centuries. Colonization of most of mankind was the supreme objective. In due course, these same aggressive colonizers would move toward dominating world scholarship; that is, they would dominate the manner in which history would be recorded. The resultant distortions were, and frequently still are, horrendously damaging through the implication that Europeans were the single creators of something we call "civilization." However, the other side of this issue is considerably more positive. Increasingly today, many students exploring and attempting to understand world cultures are beginning to reconcile themselves to the fact that, indeed, civilization did not have its origins in Europe, while the rest of the so-called primitive, uncivilized world crouched feebly in wait for the arrival of the enlightened Europeans to lift these unfortunate souls out of the heart of darkness. Most of us now accept the prevailing and conclusive evidence that for more than a thousand years various African cultures had been giving rise to one glorious empire after another on the African continent. Recent finds of archaeology and documented accounts of early Arab travelers to Africa now reveal that some of these magnificent African kingdoms, comprising extensive land areas, existed while Europe was experiencing its period of the Dark Ages. These early African kingdoms were administered with an incredibly sophisticated level of managerial skill.

Controversial Discoveries

Remarkable discoveries in the last decade are fast dispelling many long-standing myths, stereotypes, and completely false information about the vast African continent and its diverse ethnicities and cultures. Among the numerous and oftentimes astonishing findings include the discovery, for example, of African steel smelting in Tanzania some fifteen hundred to two thousand years ago. Seemingly, the Haya people had produced carbon steel in preheated forced-draft furnaces, a method that was technologically more advanced than any developed in Europe until sometime during the mid-nineteenth century.[1] The Dogon people of Mali, also the Bambara of the same region, some seven hundred years ago plotted the orbits of stars that circle Sirius. An astronomical observatory uncovered in Kenya that dates to about 300 B.C. suggests that a prehistoric calendar based on detailed astronomical knowledge was in common use in sub-Saharan Africa. Other revelations include the cultivation of cereals and other crops by Africans in the Nile Valley some seven thousand years before any other civilization; and the domestication of cattle in Kenya about fifteen thousand years ago. Among the earliest evidence of the use of numbers is a specific find in Zaire. Markings on a bone eight thousand years old (the famous Ishango bone) seem to indicate without reservation a numeration system—probably used as a lunar calendar. Contrary to popular myth, these African peoples devised a number system that is undoubtedly among the first in the world.

Early African Sophistication: Modern Benefits

Also being unearthed is a startling African background in the medical sciences. It has been proved that traditional African physicians developed effective and quite sophisticated diagnostic and therapeutic modalities in medicine. African herbal medicine, for instance, was far more advanced in its development than any in the world prior to the disruption of traditional African cultures. Even now, the Zulu of South Africa know the medicinal uses of more than seven hundred plants. The Dogon of Mali continue using today—having discovered it thousands of years ago—a certain plant known to cure diarrhea. The plant is called kaolin, the active ingredient in today's widely used commercial product called Kaopectate. For thousands of years, the Mende people of Sierra Leone took the bark of a certain local tree for use in the treatment of musculoskeletal pains. Further, there is substantial evidence that autopsies were being performed hundreds of years ago among the Banyoro people of Uganda and the Likunda of Central

Africa. The Mano of Liberia developed a smallpox vaccine centuries before the famous Dr. Jenner *discovered* the basic principles of the vaccine. Not only did African surgeons demonstrate an understanding of the sophisticated concepts of anesthesia and antisepsis, but these Africans displayed advanced surgical techniques. In 1879 a certain Dr. Felkin from Edinburgh Medical College in Scotland witnessed and even sketched a Caesarean operation executed by Banyuoro surgeons in East Africa. Such are a few of the startling examples of a remarkable historical and cultural circumstance from whence came the Africans who were later to involuntarily populate the island of Hispaniola and the whole of the Caribbean.

African Presence in Ancient America

Perhaps one of the most controversial theories connected with the technological sophistication of African culture concerns the question of navigation. However, once the student looks keenly into the historical circumstances of West Africa in particular, there remains very little doubt about the capacity and potential of Africans to undertake extensive journeys on the open seas. Various African peoples of West and Central Africa crafted an array of powerful seagoing vessels. That unique region once formed part of a massive interlocking trade route stretching from the Mediterranean Sea to the Gulf of Guinea, and from the West Coast to Lake Chad. Western Africa was literally crisscrossed with an intricate network of commercial trading routes leading into the continent's interior zones. These connecting links between the West Coast and the River Niger—a total distance of some twenty-six hundred miles—existed for many centuries prior to the arrival of the first Europeans to the African coasts.

The Chinese, both in literary images and in paintings, graphically record Africans arriving with elephants at the Imperial Court of China in large draught vessels. Such vessels had a capacity to haul ten tons or more of shifting cargo. This was as early as the thirteenth century, two hundred years before Columbus wandered into the Caribbean. Ancient African camel caravans traversing the Sahara certainly must have employed some manner of highly sophisticated nautical science to navigate these treacherous voyages. After all, the trans-Sahara journey is twice as long and twice as hazardous as a similar one across the high seas from the West African coast to the Caribbean—a distance of fifteen hundred miles. There now is convincing evidence that Africans did indeed make such a journey.

Van Sertima's Theories

Noted anthropologist Ivan Van Sertima presents rather forceful evidence of a linguistic, cultural, botanical, social, and scientific nature that Africans were present in the Americas (in Meso-America) as early as the twelfth century. The very idea of an African presence in the Americas prior to the arrival of Columbus is quite difficult for many people to accept, despite overwhelming documentation to support the fact. After careful scrutiny of much evidence of an African presence in pre-Columbian America, in a scholarly monograph entitled "African Explorers of the New World" investigator Harold G. Lawrence reported that from the Mali and Songhay empires, the Mandingo ethnic group, along with other Africans, crossed the Atlantic in order to conduct trade with the indigenous groups of the Western Hemisphere and even established community units throughout the Americas.[2]

It is a fact that the first Spanish and Portuguese explorers stumbled upon communities of unmistakably black men on the eastern coasts of South and Central America, and in Yucatán and Nicaragua. A certain Spanish Friar Román, one of the earliest Catholic missionaries to arrive in Hispaniola, chronicles that a colony of Blacks came from the south and landed in Hispaniola, armed with darts of *guanin* (an alloy of gold, silver, and copper). These individuals were called the Black Guaninis.[3]

Finally, regarding the controversial African presence in pre-Columbian America, there is the additional piece of evidence in the form of those spectacular, colossal stone heads, each one weighing tons, displaying an undisputable African physiognomy, which have been excavated in southern Mexico by several different archaeological teams over the years. Deciphering the pictographs on the base of these monumental stone heads, scientists have translated the date into the equivalent of our contemporary calendar to be November 4, 291 B.C. In various sites—Tres Zapotes, La Venta, southeastern Veracruz—more and more of these gigantic masterpieces, one with a circumference of twenty-two feet and six feet in height and estimated to weigh between twenty and thirty tons, are being unearthed, and all the heads with clearly distinguishable African facial features. Could these pre-Columbian people, the ancient Olmeca—whose culture preceded that of even the Tolteca—have come from the East in seafaring vessels in order to settle in the Nuevo Mundo? Had these immigrants sailed from the African continent?

The Africans Who Came

Who were these Africans who arrived in the Caribbean and populated Hispaniola in such great numbers? What kind of distant land had they left behind? And what were the circumstances under which they came? To begin with, the region of the cultural homeland from which most of the Antilles-bound Africans came, coastal West Africa, has a history dating back to a distant antiquity. Flourishing on the banks of the River Niger were important centers of aggressive commerce and highly advanced learning centers such as Gao, Jenne, and Timbuctu. A virtual Golden Age of West African culture spread across an impressively lengthy period from the opening of the eighth century to the close of the eighteenth century. Four great commercial empires that were prominently conducting their affairs of state during this period of recorded history were Ghana (A.D. 700–1200), which was the first spectacular empire of the Western Sudan; Mali (A.D. 1200–1500), which later absorbed the empire of Ghana, expanding it further westward; Songhay (A.D. 1350–1600), which ultimately overran Mali; and finally Kanen-Bornu, which developed separately and in an eastward direction into the Sudan. Quite earlier still, in and around the Bauchi plateau in what is now northern Nigeria, archaeologists have discovered the existence of a totally developed culture of exquisite beauty in its craftsmanship of fine terra cotta sculptures, the Nok culture. This civilization, advanced by any standard, with conclusive evidence to prove that it is the ancestor of more than a few regional kingdoms and ethnicities, turned to the use of iron from about 800 B.C. to perhaps A.D. 200.

African Antiquity

Ancient Ghana was truly impressive in many respects. It had originated in the Western Sudan, northwest of the Senegal River and northwest of the River Niger. At the height of its predominance, its territory extended over an area that today would encompass portions of Guinea, Senegal, Mali, and Mauritania. It was strategically located at the crossroads of a lucrative trans-Saharan trade route. The empire derived its prosperity and power from its absolute control of the flow of West African exports—mainly gold—to North Africa, and the valuable, highly desirable salt and other commodities from North Africa. By the middle of the eleventh century the empire of Ghana reached its peak, then began to decline. Its destruction came from the more powerful and dreaded Almoravides, an Islamic sect from Northern Africa that would later invade all of Iberia.

With Ghana's collapse, an Islamic chieftain, Sundiata, ascended the throne of the neighboring Mali and expanded his kingdom into an empire. Sundiata and his successors assumed ancient Ghana's role in developing and controlling the salt and gold trade. One successor in particular, Mansa Musa, turned Mali into a household word not only in Africa, but in the Middle East and Europe as well, where his fame was almost mythical. By the beginning of the fifteenth century, the central power of the Mali empire was weakening, then finally collapsed. Now it was the Songhai people who were to dominate the region of the Western Sudan. Since the remotest time, the Songhai (sometimes spelled Songhay) have lived along the banks of the River Niger, between the great bend and the middle section of this mighty river system. Earliest oral accounts indicate that Mali was completely dependent upon the Songhai boatmen for Mali's vital links of communication along the river to the trans-Saharan trade routes. By about 1464 a forceful leader, Sonni Ali, rose to supreme chieftaincy, gaining control of the three major trading centers of the old empire: Timbuctu, Jenne, and Gao—the Songhai capital.

The greatest successor to the Songhai throne was undoubtedly Askia Mohammed, under whom the empire displayed an exceptionally advanced level of intellectual and cultural achievement. Surgeons in Jenne, for instance, were performing successful cataract removal. Universities were offering courses in mathematics, astronomy, philosophy, logic, and medicine. In time, as in the case of West Africa's other impressive empires, internal strife and divisions weakened the Songhai empire, bringing a definite end to its dominance in the region. With the demise of Songhai, West Sudanic civilization moved eastward to Kanen-Bornu, in the vicinity of Lake Chad, and the Hausa states, in the area of present-day northern Nigeria. However, these later nations did not achieve the grandeur or the might of Ghana, Mali, or Songhai.

Europe Awakens

By the fifteenth and sixteenth centuries, all the great empires of Western Africa had risen and begun to decline. Remember, too, that Europe was beginning its ascendancy from the slumber of the Middle Ages, awakening rapidly to the demands of a more expansive world. European merchants, mainly Venetians and their Genoese rivals, were trading with North Africa. The adventurous Genoese, perhaps more than anyone else among the Europeans, from their paid sailors and geographers learned about the trans-Saharan trade with the Sudan and the abundantly supplied gold lands of West Africa. They knew, further, that with suitably powerful sailing vessels and finely honed navigation skills, they might gain access by sea not only to West Africa, but also, by circumnavigating the African continent, to the richer trade of the Indian Ocean. However, by the fourteenth century Genoa's power and influence were diminishing, making it increasingly difficult for the once prosperous Italian city-state to continue sponsoring such lucrative ventures. As a result, unemployed sailors and geographers from Genoa and elsewhere around the Italian peninsula took their easily marketable skills to the anxiously awaiting, now unified Christian realms of Iberia under Los Reyes Católicos.

Africans Populate the Caribbean

In the campaign for the Reconquista of previously held Muslim territories in Iberia, the ultimate Christian aim was to carry the crusade against Islam across to Africa itself. This sweeping anti-Islamic fervor led to the European desire to acquire knowledge of the West African lands lying on the other side of the Sahara with which Morocco traded. Prince Henry, soon to earn the title Henry the Navigator, devoted great energies to organizing systematic explorations of Africa's western coastline.[4] The Portuguese objective in undertaking these adventures was twofold: first, to direct trade of West Africa and then of the Indian Ocean into areas not under Muslim control, thus bringing this commerce immediately into Portuguese coffers; second, to create Christian allies in Africa in order to build a joint offensive against Islam.

Persistent explorations enabled the Portuguese to reach Madeira in 1418, and the mouth of the Senegal River and the Cape Verde Islands by 1444—which by the 1460s were set up as a base for slave trading.

By 1475 Portuguese ships had reached Fernando Po and crossed the equator. Prince Henry's adventurers, in capturing a few Africans and taking them back to Portugal, found that they could earn handsome profits by expanding this venture: capture the Africans, return to Lisbon with them, then sell them for the purpose of working as slaves in the thinly populated southern agricultural districts of the country, which had only recently been reconquered from the Moors. Thus, one of the first major commercial results of an enterprise that had as one of its prime objectives the conversion of the African to Christianity was actually the evolution of a trade that sold human beings into servitude for the benefit of other human beings. By 1492 the Portuguese had secured a permanent base on the African mainland, calling it *A Mina* (the Mine). Later Europeans would call it the Gold Coast. A fortified garrison, warehouse, and official headquarters of the royal governor, Elmina Castle would eventually come to symbolize the definitive foothold on the African continent.

Portugal vs. Spain

Intense rivalry between the two Iberian monarchies, especially involving individual Castilian and Portuguese merchants for dominance of West African, continued until about 1492, when Columbus's arrival in the Caribbean signaled a decided Castilian monopoly. Finally with the Treaty of Tordesillas (1494) between Castile and Portugal, and the earlier papal bulls of 1493, it was proclaimed that Castile would have a monopoly of the European exploitation of the Nuevo Mundo (excluding Brazil), and that Portugal would take Africa and Asia. By the close of the sixteenth century, the Portuguese were no longer the only Europeans who were anxious to establish lasting contact with West Africa. First the Dutch, then the English and French were aggressive in their aim of challenging Portugal's dominance and putting into place their own trading stations along the coasts of West Africa. The opening of a riveting new era began as these Western Europeans quickly regarded West Africa primarily as an extremely profitable source of slave labor for the growing number of plantations springing up throughout the Caribbean. Thus began a bitter and intensive competition among the Europeans for this new kind of trade, a trade in human flesh.

Portuguese navigators had by now established their long-desired sea route to Asia via the Cape of Good Hope, claiming exclusive domain over territories reached along the way. Spain very boldly claimed all the explored territories in the Caribbean and on the mainland of the Americas. Even though the Catholic monarchs now had within their grasp the means to render Castile the richest and most powerful kingdom in all Europe, these conquests were meaningless if an adequate supply of dependable, permanent labor could not be guaranteed. This labor pool was of absolute necessity to work the mines as well as to replenish the decimated indigenous populations of the islands. The Spaniards therefore turned to West Africa for its indispensable labor source. By the year 1511, Spain was granting permission for captives to be officially imported into Hispaniola directly from Africa.

Ladinos and Asientos

At first, by royal decree, the only Blacks permitted into colonial Hispaniola were the *ladinos,* mainly because they had been both Christianized and acculturated during their residence in Spain. The rationale was that the so-called pagan Africans *(bozales)* might easily corrupt or undermine the Christianization process of the indigenous populations of the island. Likewise, Jewish and Muslim slaves were barred from the new territories. Deported criminals were considered a bad risk and not a very dependable labor source. Under pressure from Spanish settlers who wanted to expand sugar operations, and with advice from Padre Las Casas, who wanted to save the remaining Taíno culture, the Spanish Crown relented and allowed the colonists to import Africans directly from their ancestral homeland.

The number of African captives imported into Quisqueya was strictly regulated by the authorities in Madrid. Since Spain had no trading bases or territory in West Africa, the trade in captives was executed by means of contract with other European countries for its slaves. This contract arrangement was known as the *asiento,* an official agreement to supply four thousand Africans a year to the Americas. With few minor exceptions, of which the slave-trading voyages of the English buccaneer John Hawkins between 1562 and 1568 are perhaps the best remembered, the supply of African captives to the Caribbean in the sixteenth century was entirely under Portuguese monopoly. However, slaves were not the only subject of such agreement. Slave ships under the *asiento* contract often carried merchandise for which they had no license. The best estimates available suggest that the total number of African captives arriving in the Caribbean during the sixteenth century was about 150,000. This is a relatively small figure when it is considered that the tiny island of São Tomé, situated off the coast of Equatorial Africa in the Gulf of Guinea, may have absorbed some sixty thousand African souls during the same period, and a small fraction also in relation to the total numbers of later centuries. Incredibly larger numbers of Africans crossed the Middle Passage during the late seventeenth and eighteenth centuries, when the transatlantic slave trade was at its dramatic zenith. There is no question that the massive introduction and settlement of Africans, and the subsequent implementation of a barbaric, inhuman slave system as the primary form of labor organization, reflected a monumental sociopolitical and psychological alteration in the demographics of the entire Caribbean region. Hispaniola, naturally, provided the initial model that was to serve as the focal point for the nefarious traffic and the New Territories.

Inherited Racial Attitudes

In the Iberian setting there were already well-established tendencies toward racial prejudice that became even more elaborate and entrenched once exported to the Caribbean. Although both countries shared the Iberian Peninsula, Spain and Portugal each reflected markedly different attitudes toward African peoples and people of African descent. During their excursions into the African continent and eventually in their establishing the enormous colony of Brazil, for instance, the Portuguese revealed decided aesthetic prejudices against the African physical type, but not against dark color itself. By about the year 1500, more than ten thousand Africans and their descendants were living in the Portuguese capital, Lisbon. These Africans were divided into two basic groups with differing customs and subjected to differential treatment by the Portuguese.

Ladinos and *Bozales*

One group was comprised of what were referred to as *ladinos,* families of Africans and their descendants. This group, over a period of time, had become fully assimilated into the Iberian sociocultural milieu. Gradually many of this group became absorbed into the general population through intermarriage with the Portuguese. By contrast, the other group of Africans firmly maintained their fiercely proud African traditions and customs, married only other Africans, and remained for the most part unacculturated. Often these *bozales,* as they were called, were the more recent arrivals—imported directly from the African continent. With the Portuguese, generally speaking, nowhere was race or color exclusively a barrier against miscegenation. However, marriage with Africans was not readily encouraged in colonial areas where a slave hierarchy was fundamentally crucial to the colony's economy. Such unions occurred frequently at home in Portugal without much voiced opposition.

Pure-Bloodedness

In affirming and reinforcing their absolute control in Hispaniola, the Spanish attempted to superimpose upon the newly evolving society all those social and philosophical ideas and practices then prevalent in medieval Spain. One central concept was the principle of something called *limpieza de sangre* (cleanliness of the blood, or purity). Essentially, the nobility and all those other individuals in Spanish society who could positively claim to have had purely Christian ancestry were assumed to have exemplary moral character. This prized attribute was passed down through inheritance. Therefore, operating under such thinking, the Spanish regarded all Moors, who were naturally of the Islamic faith, other sub-Saharan Africans, Jews, gypsies, and any other so-called Christian *conversos* (converts), as suffering from a distinct moral disability.[5]

In the new environment of the Caribbean, the concept of *limpieza de sangre* underwent a very major change. Skin color became not only quite relevant, but it was also converted into an essential determinant. Mixed blood came to be viewed as conclusive evidence of what was described as moral deficiency and intellectual inferiority. The Spanish authorities, in terms of social and political status, placed all the mixed-blood individuals within the same ethnic category. Thus was created the color-coding system in Hispaniola that determined a person's socioeconomic hierarchal position: that particular status was based on the degree of Caucasian blood that an individual supposedly possessed. The effect of these socioracial categorizations was vital for enforcing notions of White supremacy, while at the same time propagating the belief that African heritage was somehow insignificant, even negative, shameful, and undesirable. After the Portuguese had established the African slave trade, the determining and dominant fact of existence for an African in either Spain or Portugal was that he or she existed not so much as a Black person, but rather as a slave.

The Question of Miscegenation

In the Caribbean, the Spanish colonists quite early in the social evolution of Hispaniola created major and very lasting divisions or categories among Blacks and mulattos in accordance with the regarded purity of their blood. At times the elaboration of terminology for the degrees of mixtures and/or physical types became so all-encompassing as to suggest an obsession with the question altogether. This tendency was especially striking in Brazil. In large measure, the Spanish Crown opposed notions of intermarriage between Europeans and Africans. One of the reasons for this attitude was that slaves were to be prevented from ever obtaining freedom for their children or even for themselves in this way—marriage with a free Caucasian. Although intermarriage with Africans was discouraged in Spain in a policy opposite to that in neighboring Portugal, having offspring by African concubines was not regarded as taboo either in Spain itself or in Hispaniola, or in other Spanish territories in the Nuevo Mundo.

It could be speculated that in both instances, Spain and Portugal, and in their peripheral subcultures, the attitude toward unmixed Africans was more similar to that practiced in the Islamic world than to that of medieval Christiandom. Often what resulted, as was the case in Haiti, for example, was a demographic circumstance in which Africans outnumbered Caucasians and the *mestizos,* or mixed blood, and mulattos. Clearly such overwhelming numbers tipped the balance away from the universalism of both Christian and Islamic values toward that particular set of values and practices deemed vital for protecting the prevailing socioeconomic system and the privileged sector within that system.

The transfer of the sugar-producing complex from the African offshore islands of Cape Verde, Las Canarias, and São Tomé to the Caribbean emphasized such tendencies toward a clearly distinct racial slavery, tendencies that were not exactly typical of slavery in Iberia. Perhaps because of the appreciable presence of *ladinos* in the system in the European setting, Christianized and acculturated and not all slaves, as well as some Caucasian slaves, color prejudice was tempered. Actually, values associated with slavery in Iberia made it difficult for a Latin American system to reduce Africans to a completely degraded, subhuman status. It has often been argued that the opposite was the case historically under the North American slave system. In fact, from quite early on, some *ladinos* in Hispaniola were accorded a treatment that could be characterized by a considerable degree of genuine trust and respect. Undoubtedly, the supreme example of such trust may well be the case of Pedro Alonso Niño, who piloted one of the ships of the Gran Almirante Columbus on that first voyage to the New Territories. The registers of the Casa de Contratación indicate that many African freedmen crossed the ocean, sailing from Sevilla, and reached the island of Hispaniola during the sixteenth century. Most of the African emigrants were single men and women with young children and family groups. If it was difficult for freedom to improve their status in Sevilla, they seized the opportunity to resettle in Hispaniola. In Iberia, Sevilla seemed to have had the largest African population of all the major Spanish cities where Africans were counted among the residents.

Notes

1. Ivan Van Sertima, pp. 7–12.
2. Harold G. Lawrence, "African Explorers of the New World," p. 84.
3. Ibid., p. 96.
4. The Portuguese initially sought to conquer Morocco, but overtook Ceuta instead. Prince Henry, a young son of the Portuguese monarch, in 1415 was named Ceuta's governor.
5. Hugo Tolentino Dipp, *Raza e Historia en Santo Domingo,* p. 102.

9

Azúcar

The Advent and Decline of Sugar

In terms of the primary sociopolitical and economic factors that shared a major role in the cultural evolution of Hispaniola, it was *azúcar* (sugar) that was the unquestioned protagonist. There is very little doubt that sugar and sugar byproducts became the actual backbone of the island's economy, serving in time as an accurate gauge of the colony's continued viability or ruin. No discussion of sugar could possibly be complete without the intricately interwoven topic of slavery. Slavery penetrated deeply and sustained sugar production to the degree that cultivation of this crop soon blossomed into the sugar industry. What resulted was an entirely new subculture, the slave-plantation complex. A truly symbiotic relationship developed since the large-scale sugar industry depended exclusively upon a constant and very heavy supply of slave labor. Sugar managed to create its own distinct form of society whose imprint still is very visible today in the cultural patterns of La República Dominicana.

Sugar and slavery have shared a common history in the long process of European territorial conquest, expanding ever westward. In all probability, sugarcane has its site of origin in the lush valleys of northeastern India. Various botanical factors, and ancient literary and etymological references, provide convincing evidence for India's claims. From India, sometime between 1800 and 1700 B.C. sugarcane cultivation spread to China. Once the cane was established there, island navigators undoubtedly carried it to the region of the Philippines, Java, and Hawaii. When Spanish adventurers arrived in the Pacific hundreds of years later, cane was already growing wild on many of the Pacific islands. The Arab conquest, sweeping from the Near East across Northern Africa and into Spain from the seventh to the ninth century, introduced sugar cultivation throughout the Mediterranean zone.

Sugar Comes to Hispaniola

By the fifteenth century the sugar industry had become extremely profitable in the eastern end of the Mediterranean. With heavy financial backing by Venetian and Genoese capital, the industry had to be moved out of this region altogether as the Ottoman Turks and the Islamic rulers of North Africa encroached, then eventually occupied the entire area. The Crusaders had initiated sugar cultivation in the conquered territories of Syria and Palestine, using Arab methods and slave labor. When the Crusaders were expelled from these lands after the twelfth century, they moved their sugar operations to such islands as Crete, Cyprus, and Sicily. As pressures from the advancing Turks in the eastern Mediterranean increased, the industry continued still westward, first to the Iberian Peninsula, where some cultivation had already been introduced earlier by the Muslim occupation, and then to newly sighted and conquered islands in the Atlantic, off the African coast.

Investors soon moved the entire industry and its operations to the offshore islands of Madeira, the Canaries, Cape Verde, and ultimately to Fernando Po and São Tomé. On his second voyage to the Caribbean, Admiral Columbus brought sugarcane to Hispaniola. The crop, in time, became the most profitable among all the New Territories' exports. With justification, the Antilles region was given the name the Sugar Islands. As more and more Northern Europeans discovered the gastronomical delights of this new crop, *azúcar,* a rising demand for sugar increased the importance of Caribbean-grown sugar. The demand grew even greater after the victory of the Ottoman Turks over the Byzantine Christian Empire, which included the capture of Constantinople in

1453. The conquerors immediately began discouraging sugar production in their newly acquired Mediterranean domain.

Sugar and Los Jerónimos

The opening phases of the sugar industry in Hispaniola were closely linked to the dwindling supply and ultimate decline of gold as the island's economic base. Gold had been in serious economic crisis since about 1515. Equally central as a factor in gold's decline was the quickening extermination of the island's indigenous populations—the prime labor source under the old *encomienda* system. By 1516 the religious order of St. Jerome (Los Padres Jerónimos) were in a uniquely influential position in Hispaniola. This particular order of friars had been appointed to govern the colony as chief administrators by the regent of Spain, the very powerful Cardinal Cisneros. Thus, Los Padres Jerónimos were fully instrumental in convincing the reigning cardinal of Spain to invest financially in sugar production.[1] These astute clerics were also quite successful in winning the support of the Spanish colonists to petition the Royal Spanish Court to admit African captives into Hispaniola as needed replacement labor for the decimated indigenous-based *encomienda*. Sugar production finally gained the protective support and alliance of the authorities in Madrid.

Although the first recorded instance of sugarcane cultivation in Hispaniola occurred during the year 1506 (in the area of Concepción de la Vega), the first successfully operating and productive *ingenios* (sugarmills) were in high gear sometime between the years 1520 and 1527.[2] Many innovative cooperatives and partnerships developed, merging an assortment of government officials and independent planters in an attempt to duplicate the economic successes of the earlier sugar estates in southern Iberia and the Canary and Madeira Islands. Even Diego Columbus, with the assistance of more than thirty African captives, had a sizable sugar estate outside the city limits of Santo Domingo. As early as perhaps 1522, his estate was producing sugar for export. Also, the hemisphere's first university (La Universidad Autónoma de Santo Domingo), which began as a secondary school—Colegio de Santo Tomás de Aquino—was built with sugar profits earned by successful planter Hernando Gorjón of the town of Azua.

Sugar and Slaves

Integrated financial resources were quite practical because an *ingenio* required both a large amount of operating capital and a considerable supply of the crop itself. Both components, especially for the majority of the early planters on Hispaniola, were well removed from any single productive capability. Moreover, there was the consistently high volume of forced slave labor, a need that absolutely had to be filled if the industry were to survive at all. As sugar cultivation continued its rapid expansion, the industry demanded additional manual labor—literally hands—to gather the cane and work the crude machinery. With the near total elimination of the native Taíno, the *encomienda* was replaced outright by a slave system with complete dependence upon African captives. During these opening years of the island's sugar production, the undertaking was rather ambitious, offering promise of substantial economic wealth for the untiring planter. At first, cane grinders were a basic manual wooden press operated by rotary animal traction (oxen or horses). This type of primitive sugarmill was known as a *trapiche*. Gradually, in those areas favored by the trade winds, stone windmills replaced these less efficient methods. The higher-efficiency mill, with initial export capacity of approximately three thousand *arrobas* (about thirty-eight short tons), was operated by hydraulic energy. By the year 1526, there were a reported nineteen *ingenios,* requiring the importation of about five hundred African slaves annually, operating in Hispaniola.[3]

The hydraulic mills experienced impressive technological advances as the Spanish Crown, naturally desirous of high yields, tended to underwrite the new industry. Because of its sophistication, the technology was brought into the Caribbean from Western Europe, mainly from Italy and Holland. In terms of further offshore dependency, the refining process took place in the sugar refineries, also located in Europe. Even today, such processing is often completed elsewhere than on the island. Production on the whole—even with the new technology—remained relatively simple. After crushing the raw cane and purifying the resultant liquid with lime, clay, or ashes, evaporation occurred in massive iron pans directly over constantly burning wood fires. Refinement consisted of melting the crystals, boiling the mixture, and then recrystallizing the sugar particles.

Sugar and Colonial Politics

The *ingenios* soon became unquestionably important and influential socioeconomic enclaves for the evolving Spanish settlement. The relative political clout of the island's towns was conditioned proportionately by the incidence of established sugarmills in the area. The mills were not merely centers of production, but were the hubs of communication and necessary social interaction as well. There were also strategically located official military units, garrisons, which guaranteed protection of the colony's economic interests. These military installations factored heavily in the mill's importance. Even today in La República Dominicana, the location of such units adheres to the traditional pattern of juxtaposing these two strategic components.

These mills would thus be transformed into a fortified defense against insurgency—uprisings by native groups, attacks from runaway slave bands, raids by pirates. Such unwelcome activity was gaining in frequency and intensity during this period. Overall sugar production remained appreciably high until about 1580, even given the serious disruptions by slave rebellions and major crop failures in the intervening years. Documented reports indicate that between eighty-six thousand and 100,000 *arrobas* were being exported to Sevilla by the time of the final phase of the flourishing sugar industry.[4] Without question, Hispaniola depended upon the profitable sugar industry as its chief source of wealth. By the mid-seventeenth century, Saint Domingue and Brazil had emerged as the main sugar producers of the entire world.

Sugar's Decline

The decline of *azúcar* as the supreme economic base during this early period in the cultural development of the island was attributed to several key factors. In our previous discussions about the components of Hispaniola's cultural formation, we mentioned the flaw of an economy built exclusively upon forced slave labor, producing ruinous long-term consequences. Additionally, a prosperity founded and consistently dependent upon crop export would prove temporary. Another equally important circumstance was the rigid character of Spanish colonialism. Spain, despite its imperial status at the time, was really quite provincial in its concepts of the mercantile system, and lacked altogether an influential, well-organized bourgeoisie such as that which existed in England, France, or Holland—European countries that would prove later to be formidable economic and territorial rivals in the Caribbean. Consequently, even though Flanders and the Low Countries (Belgium and Holland), during the pending decline of Hispaniola's early sugar industry, were also part of Spain's imperial realm, Spain did not allow these territories to sell sugar and sugar byproducts to other European countries. Holland was actually trading aggressively with the whole of Northern Europe and could very readily have sold sugar from Hispaniola to this European region. However, the Spanish Crown had the rule that

> ningún territorio español de América podía comerciar directamente con otro país, aunque se tratara de uno que era parte del imperio español.[5]

> (no Spanish territory in the Americas could trade directly with another country, even though it—such trade—involved one that was part of the Spanish Empire.)

So, whereas Hispaniola could have had a ready and open market for its sugar and its sugar byproducts, it did not because of this royal edict restricting both navigation rights and export sales beyond Spain itself. American commerce was severely monopolized by Sevilla's Merchant Guild, or Casa de Contratación. Failure to secure a lucrative outside market delivered a crippling blow to the island's sugar oligarchy, which was fast developing as the focal point of the society's sociopolitical response to Hispaniola's colonial status. Being able to engage in international trade, expanding import–export commerce, and affecting cultural exchanges would have signaled the clear emergence of a firmly based local nucleus of individuals with powerful and strategic ties to potential allies in Europe.

Looming Threats

As it was, a local power base formed nevertheless, with somewhat awesome prestige and influence. From those rudimentary stages of limited sugar production in La Vega, the industry in time expanded with hurricane-force velocity throughout most areas of Hispaniola. *Ingenios* were operating successfully in San Juan de Maguana, Azua,

Ocoa (today known as San Cristóbal), Higüey, Bonao, Puerto Plata, and of course on the outskirts of the capital city Santo Domingo. The tendency developed early to concentrate the establishment of sug-armills in a special zone located between Santo Domingo and Azua. Such concentration, the bulk of which was constructed during the six-teenth and early seventeenth centuries, placed the mill within easy reach of the main port, Santo Domingo, for shipment to Spain. These operations were built on the banks of the Rivers Ozama, Haina, Nizao, Nigua, Ocoa, and Yaque del Sur. The seat of social authority in His-paniola would rest with the mill owners and administrators, all wield-ing their considerable power from the enviable comfort of their bountiful mill operations, and not from public offices located in the capital.

However, there were certain very real forces that would present a threat to this comfort. Within the total island society itself there were two existing enclaves competing for space and unbounded freedom from restrictions, harsh or otherwise. The primary element, the larger of the two, consisted of the ambitious settlers and struggling small farmers, influential and prosperous planters, underpaid colonial admin-istrators and officials, merchants, slaves, and ambivalent freedmen and -women of color. This first group comprised the formal colonial struc-ture—the structured, orderly colony as a whole. The second group, by contrast, was not regarded as the true colonists on the grounds that this element did not accept or respect the edicts, rules, restrictions, and general regulatory impositions of the Crown, located in far off Madrid. This group elected to operate their affairs, their lives outside the re-strictive margin of colonial order and management. It was character-ized by a wide range of types: from the highly sophisticated and secret community of *cimarrones* to the boisterous, often violent and maraud-ing, assemblage of *bucaneros* and *piratas* described earlier.

Notes

1. Frank Moya Pons, *Manual de Historia Dominicana*, p. 32.
2. Roberto Cassá, *Historia Social y Económica de la República Dominicana*, p. 67.
3. Ibid., p. 69.
4. Ibid., p. 91.
5. Juan Bosch, *Composición Social Dominicana*, p. 40.

10

Hispaniola's Slave-Labor Plantation Economy

The key elements that helped explain the makeup of Hispaniola's highly intensive slave-labor plantation economy included a series of closely connected, mutually interdependent factors. The administrative and political efficiency, along with the strategic position of Hispaniola's chief port city of Santo Domingo as the most important commercial center of the Americas, largely accounted for the island's overall high productivity. This productivity was naturally tied quite strongly to a specific kind of international commerce, totally different and new to world trade: the transatlantic slave trade. The arriving Africans, therefore, not only offset the demographic decline of the early settlement periods, but also contributed to greater social variation in the island. By the mid-1500s, the number of African arrivals was considerable. About two thousand African captives were entering Hispaniola annually. Records housed in Santo Domingo for the year 1542 calculated that some twelve hundred Spaniards—for the most part ranchers and mine owners—had legal possession of between twenty-five thousand and thirty thousand African slaves.[1] Further estimates showed that by the year 1571 some thirteen thousand slaves were working on *hatos* (cattle farms), *estancias* (ranches), and of course numerous *ingenios;* the remaining numbers of Africans were counted among domestic servants.

A Changing Ethnic Picture

Hispaniola easily became the territory in the Americas with the greatest concentration of Africans, whether *ladinos* or *bozales*. Demographically the colony was early characterized by a clearly dominant presence of Africans in a condition of forced slave labor. There was an estimated, soon-to-be-alarming five-to-one ratio of Africans to Caucasians. The constantly increasing numbers of slaves, together with the departure of Europeans, provoked the Spanish Crown to offer various kinds of special incentives to *campesinos* scattered throughout Iberia in order that they might resettle in Hispaniola. The Europeans' departure had been a result of displacement, depopulation campaigns, and emigration. Some of the compensatory measures offered to the *campesinos* included a variety of tax exemptions, franchises, even limited land grants and livestock. However, such enticing benefits did not do much to alter the island's steadily changing ethnic composition.

African captives often entered the island by other than legal means. Smuggling was without doubt the avenue by which the greatest numbers of Africans arrived, well outranking documented entry. It was this form of human contraband trade, openly accepted by many colonists, that accounted for the accelerated rise in the African population. For one observer, there were so many Blacks in Santo Domingo that it seemed as though the city were *una efigie o imagen de la misma etiopía*[2] (an effigy or image of Ethiopia itself). When Spain executed measures to depopulate the island's most northern coastal zones as a strategy for combating the growing menace of smuggling (during 1605–1606), the area had earlier witnessed increasing numbers of Africans. Areas under official orders to depopulate included the towns of Monti Cristi, Puerto Plata, and Yaguana. Many of these Africans were *cimarrones* who were fleeing to the safety of the already established *manieles* and *palenques*. The issue of smuggling was central to the government's plan to depopulate these particular areas.

The colonists petitioned Madrid relentlessly for the abolition of the exclusive trade monopoly that Spain had enjoyed for so long. As with all newly claimed Spanish territories, Hispaniola was prohibited from engaging in free and unhampered trade with other European nations. As the Crown continued denying these concessions, illicit trade grew, spearheaded by the Portuguese, who were at the time trafficking most of the African captives into the entire Caribbean region. Another infamous agent in slave trafficking was the English pirate John Hawkins. This notorious individual, as we have already learned, was directly financed by various groups of English capitalists as well as by the English Royal Crown itself. After having negotiated with the Portuguese and having conducted a series of successful slave raids along the coast of Sierra Leone in West Africa, in 1563 Hawkins arrived with his cargo of some three hundred Africans to be sold in Puerto Plata. Soon after the devastating siege and plunder of the island's capital city—an assault led by the English pirate Francis Drake in 1585—Hispaniola's European population dropped sharply. This was especially the case when many settlers decided to try their luck in the far western portion of the island (today Haiti) or else to relocate altogether to newer territories throughout the Caribbean.

A Declining Trade

The sixteenth century began witnessing the gradual decline of the slave trade in Hispaniola and, as an intimately parallel consequence, the decline also of the sugar industry. This latter industry was rapidly being eroded by the ascendancy of cattle raising as a replacement for the island's principal economic base. Because of the growing demand in Europe for items made from leather, Hispaniola's cattle industry became considerably important. As with other commodities throughout the island's economic development, cattle became the target of a booming contraband trade as well. The industry, therefore, was forced to move its operation closer to the central zones of the country. African slaves, quite naturally, followed this move with the *hatero* (cattle rancher).

Just as cacao (the fruit of the chocolate plant) was being cultivated for major export, and there was hope that cacao would thus be the salvation of the colony's economy, a deadly smallpox epidemic swept the island (beginning in 1651), killing thousands of Africans. The colonists again petitioned Madrid to allow for the immediate entry of more captives from the African continent. Now the number had risen to thirty-five hundred Africans annually entering the Spanish Antilles. Most ironically, in the remote mountain range of the *maniel,* fierce military campaigns were under way against mutinous *cimarrones.* Perversely, there were also official plans to promote massive and immediate migration from the Canary Islands and other poverty-stricken regions of Spain. Without doubt, the island's demographic landscape was changing even more dramatically.

A World of Symbiosis

Santo Domingo's slave-based plantation society was far removed from the society envisioned by the island's earliest-arriving Spanish settlers. That original intent was to duplicate the established pattern of the overseas metropolis. For the most part, the attempts failed. The slave-labor plantation presented a rapidly transitional world that was metamorphosing from an artificially constructed, though quite rigid, society into one that was far more complicated, less contrived. It was symbiotic in that slaves and masters alike combined their individual strengths and talents in order that this unique, new living experiment would prove effective and efficient in the overall operation and survival of the total society. In the distinct ambience and circumstance of the Caribbean, it was actually impossible for these two diametrically opposing forces to develop two separate, alien communities. The uniqueness lay in the very peculiar sociopolitical, interlocking relationship forged from the region's trifold ethnic components; the character, the experiences, and the traditions of the indigenous, European, and African populations. Accommodation and adjustment were the key ingredients operating here. Each segment of the population, the enslaved and the liberated, the master and the marginal—all adjusted to their circumstance as best they had learned how to do. Each group virtually needed the other in this effort to adjust. No group could succeed in living without the other.

There was definitely something beyond the ordinary here in the Caribbean with respect to the process of *mestizaje* (miscegenation or creolization). Caribbean slave society reached its most dynamic phase of evolution by the late eighteenth century, presenting finally its most characteristic face, one of many ambiguities, contradictions, and subtleties all functioning at the same time. All the various segments together made for an intricately patterned, interdependent complex of unquestioned caste and class distinctions. Perhaps more than any other aspect of the plantation culture, these caste divisions were the most apparent. Throughout the plantation society of Hispaniola, there were three distinctly recognized caste divisions that were largely maintained by tradition, legality, and subtle enforcement. The hierarchal ladder was clear enough: on the bottom rung were the African slaves; next in ascendancy were the free individuals of color; on the top rung were the Europeans. Each caste was well aware of its specific parameters of definition and role within the socioeconomic and political context of the island's humanscape. Nevertheless, there were innumerable contradictions and ambiguities that served to cloud the picture.

Very frequently, the system became dysfunctional because of vagueness, relaxed adherence to the rules, and the ever-increasing numbers of mixed-blood individuals among Hispaniola's growing population. This latter element especially, the mixed-bloods, was constantly passing in and out of the social mainstream. Slaves were designated slaves purely on the basis of their having been purchased as chattel—an article of personal, movable property, a piece of merchandise, condemned legally to enslavement status. It was only toward the period of the late seventeenth century that the designation *slave* was very specifically associated with color or race, and more decidedly with persons of African origins and with menial labor. In essence, to be black was to be a slave.

Then there were further subdivisions involving free Africans and free mulattos. On the whole—in fact, throughout the Caribbean region entirely—free mulattos were accorded a status superior to that of free Blacks. From quite early on, Hispaniola's community of free persons of color consistently employed the criteria of complexion and hue, hair texture and thickness of lips, plus any other visible characteristics of distinctive Africanness, to determine an individual's social status and rank.[3] What seemed unquestionably to distinguish the free groups, then, was race and color. Within the Caucasian group, which was naturally free, the circumstances of economics and occupation were the primary determinants of the individual's social position and status on the hierarchal ladder. The more land a European settler possessed, or the larger the plantation with its required number of slaves to work it, the more prestige and status were accorded the island's Caucasian residents.

Within the slave quarters, it immediately became a question of assigned task or occupation that contributed to that slave's designated social rank and prestige. Again, the matter of specific color and hue played a prominent role in the master's assigning particular tasks to his plantation slaves. The more skilled or specialized and the more domesticated slaves—who not surprisingly were overwhelmingly of lighter complexion than the field and sugarmill workers—traditionally enjoyed a far higher social esteem than did the nonskilled common field slaves. This vicious scheme of color-coding was much in evidence as a formidable operative in contemporary Dominican society. The consequences of this system would be especially brutal in neighboring Haiti. The notion of ambiguity appeared constantly as this scheme provided a decisive impetus for social mobility internally. However, it was also true that while this fluid movement served to unify the plantation society in terms of the slaves themselves, this same mobility was likewise very instrumental in provoking a contagious resentment and grievance that would later have tragic consequences.

Notes

1. Roberto Cassá, *Historia Social y Económica,* pp. 88–89.
2. Gonzalo Fernández de Oviedo, "Historia General y Natural de las Indias," in Herrera Miniño, p. 125.
3. R. N. Murray, *West Indian History,* p. 103.

11

Hispaniola's Century of Misery

One highly respected interpretation of the social history of Hispaniola aptly refers to the period of the seventeenth century in the island as El Siglo de la Miseria[1] (The Century of Misery). Throughout the society during that period there was a pervading atmosphere of spiritual despair on practically every level of daily existence. Most disappointingly, for example, cacao never quite reached the point of being the significant export crop it had been expected to become. The severity of the era's unfavorable climatic changes, among other factors, accounted for this failure. Moreover, the period was witness to perhaps one of the worst epidemics of illness and disease in the island's history, nearly completely destroying the bulk of the labor force in the colony. Africans were by far the majority population that fell victim to the smallpox epidemic: *no dejaron manos que cultivasen la tierra*[2] (not leaving any hands to work the land). In a letter written at that time to a friend back in Spain, one settler described the local conditions: *las arboledas de cacao, que de quince a diez años a esta parte se sembraron, están perdidas por no haber esclavos que lo beneficien*[3] (the cacao groves, which were seeded ten or fifteen years ago in this part, are lost as a result of there not being slaves to work them).

Total Paralysis

The *siglo de la miseria* was characterized by economic ruin, by spiritual despair, by shame, and a general loss of local pride. The entire country found itself in a state of paralysis—in the capital as well as in the most distant little towns and villages throughout the island. A total immobility gripped the country in every regard. Hispaniola's treasury was bankrupt. There was no money circulating quite simply because there was no money to be had. Even government administrators and functionaries were paid their salaries with money brought into the island from abroad each year during this crisis. One especially note-worthy aspect of this period appeared in the realm of social interaction between master and slave. Dynamic social changes were emerging that would affect the island's later social character. For example, the Afri-can slave certainly continued being a slave, as well as his offspring. The plantation master was still the undisputed *amo* (master). However, the island's economic crisis now suddenly dictated that the traditional interrelationships be altered drastically. Situations were so perverse that *los amos tenían que andar descalzos como andaba el esclavo y ambos tenían que comer el mismo tipo de comida*[4] (the masters had to go barefoot like the slave and both master and slave now had to eat the same kind of food).

It is quite possible that during this painful era in the social evolution of Hispaniola the first notions of a kind of racial democracy in terms of actual treatment were witnessed. This feature becomes especially im-portant as an observable trait in the contemporary Dominican personal-ity. Perhaps, too, it was during this century of misery that certain national habits were formed, ultimately reaching the level of a national conscience. One such tradition observed throughout the entirety of today's cultural landscape on the island is the basic meal, which con-sists of *plátanos, arroz, habichuelas, y un poco de carne* (bananas, rice, beans, and a little piece of meat). All these items, of course, are locally produced, and were readily accessible to both plantation slave and plantation master alike. So had this terribly demoralizing eco-nomic blow to the plantation master now forced him into a position to treat his slaves as though they were free beings? At any rate, it ap-peared that the century of misery was having the effect of almost equalizing everybody.

Escape from the French Zone

The seventeenth century also saw increasing numbers of African slaves fleeing the western portion of Hispaniola, territory held by the

French, and heading into the Spanish zone. By about 1677 large numbers of Africans managed to escape from the French colony, obtaining
refuge in Santo Domingo. The prevailing attitude of the colonial authorities in Santo Domingo at the time was to grant immediate asylum
to these fugitives. This action was, in all probability, motivated more
by purely political rather than genuine humanitarian objectives.
Sparked by a longstanding political rivalry between the French and the
Spanish, the notion of offering liberty to the escapees was thought to
be a potential stimulus for other French-held slaves elsewhere throughout the Caribbean to flee their oppressors. Thus, a severely felt economic blow would be delivered to Spain's chief competitor. The plan
seemed to work, for within a very short time the numbers of escapees
increased significantly.

In 1678 an official Spanish policy was set in place that carefully
outlined procedures for receiving all those runaways from the western
zone of Hispaniola. A special runaway patrol was created with the
express intention of being constantly vigilant for runaways, then personally escorting them to safe haven within the borders of Santo Domingo. The runaways were literally rounded up and brought to resettle
in a specially designated community given the name San Lorenzo de
los Mina. Situated on the eastern bank of the Ozama River, this historic settlement was named after those very first escapees who themselves were members of the Mina ethnic group from Angola in
southern Africa. Today, in the precise spot of that original community
for African escapees from the French-held western zone of the island,
there exists a bustling district of the capital called Los Minas. The
district is populated overwhelmingly by Dominicans quite visibly of
African descent.

A studied glance at the arrival of Africans to the island during the
seventeenth century reveals appreciable insight into the changing circumstances of these individuals. Between the years 1600 and 1675, the
arriving captives came directly from the African continent. The points
of origin ranged along Africa's Atlantic coast as far north as the Gulf
of Guinea and as far south as Angola. From about 1677, in relatively
diminishing numbers, Africans began arriving from the French-
dominated western zone of Hispaniola. By the mid-1680s, there was a
resumption of considerable traffic leaving Africa's Atlantic coast.
Then by the early 1690s the colony received arrivals from other Caribbean islands, primarily from Jamaica and from faraway Barbados.

Caribbean Battle Front

It was by no means surprising that the pristine tropical waters of the Caribbean soon were transformed into a crimson-colored aquatic battlefield for European imperialists who were in fierce competition for absolute domination of the entire region. Arch rivals France and England first fought three separate wars to drive the Dutch out of the Caribbean, intending to reserve for themselves the lucrative, but heinous trafficking in black flesh. Then these two victors began devouring each other as a result of their wickedly insatiable greed. It became quite common that whatever territorial dispute or commercial rivalry erupted on the European continent quickly played out the decisive rounds in the Antilles. The region became the no-holds-barred field of minor skirmishes and major battles, ending with the colonies' being mere pawns. The tiny island of Tortuga was initially one of the coveted prizes before lustful eyes were cast upon the bigger trophy of Hispaniola. The central protagonists now were Spain and France.

Both these European imperial giants remained steadfast in their aim to expel the other from these lush waters. The Spanish were not totally successful in safeguarding the island from mounting foreign intrusions. Eventually the western end of Hispaniola, especially vulnerable to such encroachment, saw the establishment of full-fledged French settlements. By 1697 France found itself in a particularly lucrative position of strength. France was able to force Spain to cede this western portion of Hispaniola by means of the Treaty of Ryswick—dividing the island so profoundly that this separation, even to this present day, would affect the affairs of both countries. The Treaty of Ryswick formally recognized the existence of two distinct cultures, two different languages, two divergent traditions and demographics. The Spanish-speaking eastern portion would be called Santo Domingo, while the French-speaking western zone would become Saint-Domingue. Most of the 375-kilometer border still remains rather haphazardly guarded to this day.

Competition for dominance continued. With the British joining as an equally determined ally, Spanish forces attacked the French settlements. The French territory's prosperous capital city of Le Cap Français, more popularly referred to as Le Cap, was completely sacked and burned. The capture of Le Cap was of particular significance not only because this city served as the capital both of the northern province as well as of the entire French colony, but important also because the vast majority of the colony's slaves lived in this exceptionally fertile region. Within a few short years, the French had constructed the Caribbean's most productive colony—built, of course, on the exploitation of African slave labor. The victorious Spanish garrisons carried off as many of these slaves as the soldiers could possibly round up, then resettled the rescued souls in Santo Domingo. The Black population in the island's eastern zone thus surged to new records.

Now with official recognition of each other's territorial sovereignty and the mutual acceptance of a permanent presence on the island, war ceased. Both colonies, although divided by a border that was not consistently clear, nor adequately patrolled, engaged in a constructive campaign of coexistence. This period, however, was largely characterized by extremes of impoverishment for Santo Domingo, which proved to be not as aggressive in its production means as Saint-Domingue. Lethargy and servility might readily and accurately describe the eastern neighbor at this juncture. Santo Domingo was constantly plagued by raids, abused by harsh, restrictive economic policies set by Madres, short-changed by a colonial administrative system that censored any attempt at liberalism of religious and educational thought. The period was also revisited by the earlier enacted, ruinous measures of what were called *las devastaciones,* or often referred to as *las despoblaciones* (abandonment), of coastal settlements to curtail smuggling activities.

Ironically, revised and enlightened official policies of the Spanish Crown made possible a new wave of immigration of major and far-reaching proportions. The new immigration, together with the overall slave system, now ineffectual, played a vital role in lessening the harshness of racial antagonisms to a degree that was totally absent in Hispaniola's French-held Saint-Domingue. *Los canarios,* as the Canary Islanders were called, kept up their arrivals, reaching large numbers throughout the major part of the century. These new arrivals to Hispaniola, exceeding perhaps four thousand individuals, established fresh settlements in places like Baní, Neiba, San Juan de la Maguana, Bánica, Las Cahobas, Dajabón, Monti Cristi, Puerto Plata, Samaná, and Sabana de la Mar. In terms of an expanded demographic panorama, *los canarios* began constituting the rather solid base of a vitally important sector of Caucasian settlers. These newer residents in the island would form a growing middle class as well as a newer slave-owning class. They would also be craftsmen, merchants, and ranch-owners of varying degrees of sociopolitical and economic influence.

Notes

1. Juan Bosch, *Composición Social Dominicana,* p. 109.
2. Ibid., p. 118.
3. Ibid., p. 119.
4. Ibid., p. 123.

12

Hispaniola's Demographic Expansion
Interior Colonization

What largely characterized eighteenth-century Hispaniola was a note-worthy demographic expansion as well as an intensive campaign to colonize the interior regions of the island. This accelerated effort to establish settlements deep inside Hispaniola's heartland subsequently began to weaken considerably the dominant role of the island's capital city. This Ciudad Primicia (City of First Fruits) had long been regarded as the undisputed hub and focal point of all manner of activity in the colony. In the eighteenth century, numerous smaller settlements, later evolving into sizable towns, were founded in areas that had previously been abandoned, mainly in the westernmost zones. Two primary fac-tors accounted for this shift in population settlements: These were the precise areas affected by the dislocation/depopulation policies of an earlier period known as Las Devastaciones of 1605–1606, and which were in real danger of being absorbed by the rapidly encroaching French. Also, these were the areas of growing importance for cattle raising, upon which a border commerce was based. Once there were established communities in these frontier zones, these new populations could readily take advantage of the lucrative commerce.

Eighteenth-century Hispaniola also saw a resurgence of the slave-labor plantation system. Restructuring the economy of the colony again made it possible for members of the Spanish colonial aristocracy to accumulate capital. During the latter part of the eighteenth century, many cattle ranchers *(hateros)* and other large landowners in Santo Domingo were purchasing great numbers of African slaves in the neighboring French colony. It was during this period also that the island experienced the growth of another extremely important economic sector—tobacco cultivation. The rich Cibao region was the center of the tobacco estates. Tobacco cultivation had a secure market, as much in the neighboring French colony to the west as in Sevilla, where the export crop provided a major source of raw materials. Special allocations from the Spanish Crown served as an incentive to increase production in the Cibao Valley. Over a period of time, this particular incentive would lay the key foundation for tobacco's gradual takeover as the primary economic base in the entire Cibao. Cattle raising, however, was still supreme throughout most of the eighteenth century, until its economic importance diminished at the beginning of the nineteenth century.

The New Economic Force: Tobacco

Interesting to note is the occurrence in this northern region of an initially small, propertied, agricultural-mercantile class. The birth of this new economic sector gave simultaneous rise to a strikingly new social model in terms of interethnic relations in Hispaniola. Perhaps for the first time on an appreciably large scale, the utilization of free labor would constitute the model for social relations. Thus, in the Cibao, the number of African slaves was undoubtedly the very lowest anywhere in the country.[1] Seemingly, the Cibao region presented a set of favorable social conditions and a rather distinctive milieu that combined to render the area quite unlike the Ciudad Primicia, Santo Domingo, farther south. After all, the colony's economic pulse center, as well as the colonial aristocracy, was concentrated in the southern zone. The island's history and major traditions had created this geopolitical and economic dominance. The country's southern zone was where the large landowners, with their vast utilization of plantation slave labor, predominated. It was here in the island's southern zone that the great sugarmills, the *ingenios,* and expansive sugarcane fields reigned supreme, engulfing most of the surrounding landscape—and humanscape as well. To say that sugar was cultivated on a massive scale would be an understatement. By stark contrast, tobacco cultivation in the Cibao

Valley required neither an extensive labor force nor extensive planting tracts.

Moreover, both the fertility of the very lush soil and the special climatic conditions favored a varied agriculture, not like the unique topographical restraint of sugarcane cultivation. Consequently, more individuals unhampered by the bonds of slave status were literally free to devote themselves to a kind of rudimentary agribusiness. These individuals were now able to engage energetically in profit-motivated agricultural production, however minor the initial scale. By about 1763 the tobacco growers of the Cibao had become so numerous and their crop so abundant—actually having won the status of a major colonial export—that the Spanish Crown established export quotas and fluctuated prices for this highly coveted regional tobacco. By now, the renowned *tabaco cibaeño* (Cibao-grown tobacco) constituted the valley's prime economic base, simultaneously becoming one of Hispaniola's chief export commodities.

New Social Patterns

Also tied very closely to tobacco cultivation were unexpectedly new social patterns, which were unfolding over time. Unlike on the region's *hatos,* where the transplanted Africans—whether enslaved or free— and the Caucasian peons really did not need to be highly skilled in order to execute their tasks, the tobacco farm required a particular degree of technical expertise and specialization. Tobacco growing demanded a thorough knowledge of the entire production process, from initial seeding to curing to determining exactly which leaves should be selected for cigar rolling. Taken together, then, the acquisition of precise skills and social mobility served to distinguish considerably the agricultural workers of Cibao and the bulk of slave-labor plantation workers of Hispaniola's southern zone. This, of course, is not to suggest that plantation slaves were completely lacking in skills. Quite the contrary, so-called specialist slaves—carefully trained and seasoned slave drivers,[2] carpenters, mechanics, masons, millwrights, coppersmiths, sugar boilers, rum distillers, seamstresses, tailors, weavers, potters, shoemakers, and an almost endless list of other occupations essential for the viability and survival of a community within a community—could be found throughout Hispaniola's mammoth and intricate slave system. This labor system was further divided according to either domestic or field categories. The point here, therefore, is that the Cibao Valley presented specific socioeconomic circumstances that quite truly gave rise to a set of very important regional differences that characterized the Cibao and the South. Such differentiation is today heavily evidenced in the cultural patterns of the island—witnessed classically in differences between the Cibao and the South.

With an incessant flow of European immigrants to the Cibao throughout the eighteenth century, the number of Caucasians easily surpassed and remained consistently greater than the number of Africans there. The evolving social structure and patterns peculiar to the region were to have an indelible impact not merely upon this northern zone, but upon the island as a whole. Plantation life in the south was marked by a clear rigidity of social barriers among masters, slaves, free Blacks, and European peons. In the Cibao, by dramatic contrast, there existed a sizable population of free Blacks and mulattos. Much will be discussed later about the forceful impact of *mestizaje* (miscegenation). Both the African slave and the European peasant together found themselves on the same cultural level in this new labor arrangement on the northern *hato,* unlike what was commonly encountered on the southern plantation. Both slave and peon experienced the same narrow relationship of total dependency on the unquestioned *amo* (master).

A New Sophistication

The socialization process relative to the tobacco farm, though, was quite different. Here there was a much broader range of social intercourse, given the nature of the tobacco industry. There were greater numbers of small independent growers, allowing for social and business contacts in the area's urban centers. As a result, the tobacco grower reached a level of sophistication never achieved by large numbers of the island's *hateros.* The tobacco growers of the Cibao thus began to form the base of a kind of *pequeño burgués campesino* (small country bourgeoisie), as one local social historian calls them.[3] Several conveniently interlaced threads helped knit together a social fabric that would be unique among European-held territories throughout the entire Caribbean during this era. Life on the Cibao *hato* featured an intensive, largely harmonious coexistence among Blacks—both slave and free—Caucasians, and property-holding mulattos. There was a great deal more fluidity in terms of interethnicity here than in the south. There was a rapid effort toward the emancipation of slaves. In turn, these former slaves transformed themselves into small producers of agricultural commodities, thereby expanding the ranks of the area's middle-class farmers. These particular social patterns inspired the movement toward national integration that had begun during an earlier period on the island. These new farmers were solidly independent in spirit, resourceful and self-sufficient with their own traditional *conucos.*

Economic Importance of the *Hato*

It was during the eighteenth century that the cattle ranch resurfaced as the island's prime economic and social base. Cattle raising generated a healthy proportion of the colony's total revenue. Moreover, the social dynamic of the *hato* was a major force shaping the mold that would ultimately determine how the entire colonial society would operate, especially in terms of social interaction among the diverse groups. The uniqueness of the eighteenth-century cattle ranch *(hato ganadero)* lay in the peculiar combination of labor forces: a strikingly unconventional blend of labor performed by free property owners alongside slaves. What evolved was a kind of socioeconomic unit that was both patriarchal and feudal. Indeed, one rather fascinating aspect about the milieu of the *hato* was the fact that slaves who formed part of the labor force in this circumstance were actually allowed free time to engage in a variety of nonthreatening activities that would personally benefit them. Quite commonly, for example, a slave would rent out his or her services to neighboring *hateros,* or to family members of the master. With the accumulated earnings from such rental services, slaves would frequently purchase their freedom or that of a family member. Clearly, then, a genuine social mobility was an achievable goal envisioned by many a slave connected with Hispaniola's *hato* system.

If there was a so-called typical *hato,* it might be described as one that had anywhere from two hundred to three hundred head of cattle. The most typical *hato* of the period was basically a self-sufficient, self-contained unit with practically every item it produced being consumed on the premises. It is not certain exactly how many *hatos* were operating in Hispaniola during the eighteenth century, but we do have data to suggest that by the latter half of the century, the number of these productive ranches shifted between eight hundred and one thousand.[4]

From Azua and Bánica, to Cotuí and Santiago and Bayaguana, what determined the dynamism and magnitude of the *hato* was not necessarily the land extension or available grazing area, but more the number of head of cattle. There is evidence that the total number of cattle for export from these areas alone reached about 115,000 in 1780. That export was destined for the neighboring French colony to the west. That same year recorded some 250,000 head of cattle in the whole of Hispaniola. Approximately ten thousand to fifteen thousand individuals—a considerable portion of the colony's total residents at that time—were living permanently on *hatos*. Thus, with the exception of the slave-labor plantations, these cattle ranches housed the island's most productive labor force and resulted in establishing an impressive and very fundamental economic base.

Notes

1. Roberto Cassá, *Historia Social y Económica,* p. 121.
2. Drivers were normally the highest ranking slaves in privilege and importance on the plantation. They were work-force leaders, or gang leaders, the pivotal managerial agent of work routines assigned to slaves. Drivers could also, and usually did, administer corporal punishment to resistant or rebellious slave-crew members.
3. Juan Bosch, *Composición Social Dominicana,* p. 213.
4. Roberto Cassá, *Historia,* p. 131.

13

The Neighbor to the West

Saint-Domingue

Not at all surprisingly, the French colony at the western end of Hispaniola played a key role in forming the fundamental commercial and trade policies of eighteenth-century Western Europe. The development and growth of Santo Domingo's western neighbor, called Saint-Domingue, naturally found itself very closely linked to such policies, especially in terms of territorial expansion and the frantic search for untapped markets. The whole of the Caribbean was already well in the throes of being transformed into a multitude of quite profitable single-crop export factories. This transformation was made possible by the rigid institution of slavery by the time that France jumped into the open-competition fray in the late seventeenth century. However late France entered the scramble for high-yield Caribbean profits—and indeed it was rather late—she nevertheless managed to equal, then ultimately surpass, her envious rivals in sugar and coffee production.

With fierce tenacity and an obstinate commitment to become the supreme power in the region, France by 1716 was regarded as a serious contender for the reigning sugar producer in the Caribbean. The overall sugarmill productivity of the French-held territories of Martinique, Guadeloupe, and later Saint-Domingue itself soon positioned France at the top of the heap in export productivity. Meanwhile, at least by the late 1700s, Spanish-speaking Santo Domingo in the east had established rather firm economic ties with her western French-speaking neighbor, with an impressive trade in hides and meats in exchange for desired manufactured goods.

The World's Richest Colony

Saint-Domingue in the period of the 1780s was producing nearly one-half of all the sugar and coffee being consumed in Western Europe and the Americas.[1] To meet the spectacular consumer demand for these items, the colony facilitated the parallel rise in expanding the number of new coffee estates and sugar plantations. Most significantly, especially for future generations in Haiti, the abundant mountain forests were randomly cut down to accommodate this expansion. By about 1789 the French territory could count easily eight thousand plantations that were producing crops for export alone.

One element had to be firmly in place, however, if Saint-Domingue was to be the undisputed regional leader in sugar production. That indispensable key ingredient was labor—and lots of it. Slave labor was absolutely essential for an ever-expanding, extremely profitable, yet abominably grueling sugar industry. Over a relatively short period, millions upon millions of African captives were forced into perhaps the cruelest and most inhumane labor system ever conceived, with maximum profitable production the single objective. As a result, the Caribbean became an active participant in a massive, unprecedented, incoming wave of human souls on its shores—via the transatlantic slave trade. Quite easily also, the trafficking in African slaves and the institution of slavery were powerful co-conspirators in the rapid evolution of sugar production as the economic base of the French colony in the West.

As sugar and its chief byproducts of rum and molasses became the mainstay of the expanding economic prosperity, as well as a solid indicator of success for the colony of Saint-Domingue, so too did the slave population there. The French colony rather quickly, but with measured caution, experienced the largest slave population in the Antilles. Even with the campaigns by the authorities to bring more Caucasians into the colony and the rising numbers of free coloreds and mulattos, Saint-Domingue clearly was turning overwhelming Black. At the same time, sugar was enjoying its unrivaled position as king, generating more than two-fifths of France's foreign trade and overall wealth. By the end of the eighteenth century, the Caribbean colony of Saint-Domingue had reached its long-desired aim of being crowned not just the richest colony in the region, but the world's richest colony.

A Very Different Neighbor

The neighbor to the West was quite different from the eastern Spanish-speaking colony in many more aspects than merely language and customs. Beginning very early in the territory's evolution, there were outstanding differences in such areas as economics, society, demographics, and culture. Even though there were indeed certain basic, immediately recognizable patterns following the traditional three-tiered structural framework that describes all the sugar colonies throughout the Antilles, some uniquely important patterns emerged in Saint-Domingue. The considerably small number of Caucasians there, while tightly linked in formation by a purely racial solidarity, were nevertheless disjointed bitterly by class or caste. Despite the growing abundance in material wealth of the colony, there were equally growing racial caste and class antagonisms that would ignite with a devouring vengeance this explosive socioeconomic and psychological circumstance. The division, with the accompanying hostilities, proved to be noticeably unusual for the region. The colony was producing, along with increased material richness, a social elite, an economically successful caste, that began perceiving itself as a new nobility, however alarmingly insignificant their numbers.

Privileged Caste: Divided Loyalties

The class antagonisms soon produced a situation that placed not only the colony's sugar and coffee barons at opposite, hostile poles, but also these rich estate owners against traders, doctors, and businessmen. The tensions further alienated all of these individuals, who were actually part of the landed proprietary class or *grands blancs* (great whites), from the larger masses of poor Whites, or *petits blancs* (little whites). This latter group of vocally disgruntled Whites was comprised of street venders, store and office clerks, shopkeepers, seamen, and plantation managers and overseers. This group was certainly not a part of the colony's social elite of the colony.[2] The so-called *grands blancs* were separate from the other groups of Caucasians by considerable degrees of privilege, wealth, and plantation productivity. As the colony's wealthiest grew richer, they began viewing themselves more and more as the single legitimate spokespersons for the entire colony. With the colony priding itself in having become the pivotal center—not just in economic terms, but in strategic terms as well—questions were being asked regarding who would be the authentic voice for this divided territory and exactly how the colony would be administered as a solid whole.

Then there was the colony's impressively large, influential, and economically prosperous community of free coloreds, mulattos, or as they were called locally, the *gens de couleur* (people of color). So here was another unique aspect about Saint-Domingue, making it quite apart in character from the traditional sugar colonies of the Caribbean. Across most of the region, the free persons of color usually were a relatively small segment of the general populace and seldom evolved in influence and privilege beyond being independently comfortable, even prosperous craftsmen. This circumstance, however, was dramatically altered in the French-speaking Saint-Domingue. Here this category of *gens de couleur* greatly surpassed the Whites in numbers, also often in formal education, and, frequently, even in wealth. This situation is easily explained by the prevailing nature of the colony's metropolis during the period of territorial expansion. France was a much more populous nation than England, Spain, or the Netherlands, and certainly had fewer overseas territories. It was therefore conceivable that Saint-Domingue lured many more unskilled, unemployed, illiterate, and destitute young adventurers than did Western Europe's rival states to their respective Caribbean colonies.

The world of the tropical plantation society was a complete, comprehensive society unto itself, quite remote from anything the metropolis had known back in Europe. An overwhelming ethnic homogeneity in Europe largely accounted for notions of ready or automatic acceptance and conformity and established tradition. On the other hand, the precise cultural and ethnic diversity in the Caribbean made for razor-sharp divisions and most definitely color differences. In Saint-Domingue, an individual with an African ancestor, regardless how distant, suffered unimagined and often humiliating indignities and harassment, particularly from the increasingly envious and usually uneducated *petits blancs*. The *gens de couleur* formed the colony's most ambiguous sector among the general population. Many such individuals could naturally point to both Africans and Europeans for close relatives. These persons moved rather freely, but were still restricted and subjected to certain prohibitions—which will be discussed in detail in a later chapter. This group was neither slave nor White. Their members' status within the local society ranged conspicuously wide: concubines of wealthy White planters, talented and skilled artisans, even some slave owners themselves and members of the dreaded slave patrols; others were recently emancipated slaves and estates owners—yet still never regarded as White.

Manacled Africans

The slaves unquestionably formed the bulk of the population, generally categorized in Saint-Domingue as being either creoles (locally born) or *bozales* (imported into the colony). Most estimates indicate that during the period between 1785 and 1790 alone, well over forty thousand African captives in shackles and chains were hustled annually into the French colony in order to assure uninterrupted economic prosperity for the metropolis. It can be said that as dangerously fragmented as the tiny Caucasian population was, Saint-Domingue's Black slave population was far more splintered, and definitely not homogeneous.[3] Blacks represented diverse ethnic and linguistic groups from the African homeland, bringing vastly different traditions and religious beliefs, and commonly at different phases of the acculturation process. Blacks as a unified whole nevertheless constituted the essential core of colonial Caribbean exploitation, classically displayed in the model of Saint-Domingue. This exploitation, by its very nature, from the outset was a growing threat to the privileged position of the colony's small number of Caucasians, whether *grands blancs* or *petits blancs,* or the remaining numbers of *gens de couleur.*

Natural Barriers

The geography and demographics of Saint-Domingue combined quite conveniently to divide still more sharply, and ultimately in most ruinous dimensions, the fundamental unit of the society during this period. For instance, the fertile northern plains of the colony, Plaine du Nord, comprised one administrative unit. The large and very prosperous sugar plantations of the colony were located in this zone. Here was the colony's economic and strategic pulse. The administrative capital for the North

Province and at the same time the chief administrative center for the whole colony, Le Cap Français, more commonly called simply Le Cap, was thus the nucleus of power and policymaking for the *grands blancs*. As would be expected, the majority of the colony's slaves lived here as well—indispensable to the sugarmills. The colony's principal mountain chain, the Massif, separated this huge, enslaved population from the rest of the colony. The West Province was the second zone, located in the center of the colony, just south of North Province. Port-au-Prince is today the southernmost town in this province. Here the estates were smaller and the crop production featured a wider variety than in the north. This West Province had fewer slaves than elsewhere, and the *petits blancs* dominated this zone, a combined sociohistorical factor that would have major consequences later upon the widening stage of events in the French colony. The overall population here tended to be scattered throughout numerous small villages and hamlets.

The colony's third administrative unit, South Province, is today the long strip of peninsula jutting westward out into the Caribbean Sea. At the time, sparsely populated and featuring the colony's highest concentration of mixed-race mulattos, South Province quite early on established a firmly unified, closely knit community of traditionally energetic, often rich, free *gens de couleur*. A reluctantly acknowledged irony with the *gens de couleur* was the fact that an impressive number of this sector was Whites from either category. More and more the propertied persons of color were a force not to be ignored readily. For too long, this group had been systematically denied access to any meaningful or active role in the affairs of the colony. Present-day Haiti's former General Raoul Cedras and his very aggressive wife are from this zone and are most representative of the predominant socioeconomic class. Interesting also from a historical perspective, this group of *gens de couleur* by the 1780s had begun dominating the rural police force and quickly formed the nucleus of the colonial militia. Later in more modern times, members of this particular social group would evolve into the highest-ranking military officers.

Separate Agendas

Cohesiveness, therefore, certainly was not among the more dynamic and essential ingredients in the social mix of Saint-Domingue during the period of the late 1700s. The various splinters within the French colony at the island's western end began forming painful blisters as legitimate grievances of divergent groups affirmed a stance in accordance with their particular colonial interests and circumstances. At the outbreak of the French Revolution in 1789, for example, all the colonial *grands blancs* hurriedly and pompously announced that they were now Frenchmen. Their expressed agenda called for total autonomy within the Caribbean colony, with specific concern for unrestricted trade. Notions of liberty for this sector translated easily into purely economic terms. Like the more haughty *grands blancs,* the colony's *petits blancs* without hesitation embraced the ideals of the revolution in order to garner support for their collective agenda in the metropolis. This sector drafted an agenda that called for liberty and equality, yes, but for only the colony's White population. The *petits blancs* expressed the idea that the landed proprietors were not the single recipients of Saint-Domingue's benevolence and thereby should certainly not be guaranteed any manner of special class privileges.

Overall, the White population responded with an open display of utter resentment and rage in the face of the mounting socioeconomic prominence of the mulatto community. Eventually this bitterness took the form of the almost overnight enactment of a series of humiliating and discriminatory laws clearly aimed at obstructing any further upward mobility of this mixed-race class. The officially restrictive measures were extremely successful in assigning all mulattos to a rigid, inferior status only slightly above that of the colony's Blacks. Overt disdain and unharnessed hostilities against the mulatto community spread throughout every segment of Saint-Domingue's White population. The social tensions and divisiveness were undoubtedly a logical consequence of the very nature of the plantation slave society itself. Such a society presented the spectacle of colonial Whites dominating a very tiny handful of an uncomfortably large, exploited and angry mass of Black and mulatto residents.

The mulattos of Saint-Domingue were now made unequal by law and subsequently rendered totally defenseless against daily insults and gross personal affronts—not unlike the customary dehumanizing process inflicted upon the colony's Black majority. For example, it was now unlawful for free coloreds to wear European-style clothing, to play traditional European games, to ride in carriages, to attend church with Whites, or to enter certain professions such as law or medicine. With seemingly inexplicable irony, however, mulattos could indeed continue to accumulate wealth and property, but could expect no justice when wronged by a White person. Mulattos could send their children abroad to be educated in Paris, but were banned altogether from holding public office in the colony. Before the Haitian Revolution, this sector enjoyed the active support of the leading abolitionist group in France at the time, the Societé des Amis des Noirs (the Society of Friends of the Blacks).[4]

In terms of outside advocacy, the *grands blancs* could count on the conservative planter-based Club Massiac in Paris. This activist support organization had been formed by elitist absentee planters in order to protect their financial interests in the Caribbean, and naturally were very pro-slavery. It soon became clear—perhaps it was always an unspoken acknowledgment—that the colony's Whites lived in constant fear of the legitimate aspirations of the free mixed and enslaved masses. The striking numerical ratio did not do much to allay the nervous feeling among Whites that one day they would be besieged. On the eve of the monumentally historical Haitian Revolution, the White population reached a dismal 6 percent of the total colonial population—even given that colonial records are not always reliable. On the part of the nonsettler class of Whites, the racial fear, or more precisely, the fear of all non-Whites, was more immediate. This sector was numerically outranked by discontented slaves and resentful free persons of color. Thus, the Whites together feared that any measure of political and social equality of any non-White group would not only undermine the entrenched institution of slavery, but would also jeopardize the heretofore unquestioned mechanism of social control that was reserved for Whites only. Finally, any disruption of the slave plantation system would automatically result in severe economic and social losses for the colony. The impact would be felt on property, wealth, commerce, social status, and the psyche of all the players. Before the inevitable Haitian Revolution, the elite caste had tried relentlessly to gain full, unchallenged control in Saint-Domingue. They wanted to be the single, authentic vocal representative in the French parliament, for example, or the constituent body of a locally elected assembly. Their efforts would prove very much in vain. Their days were truly numbered. The coming tropical storm was near.

Notes

1. Robert and Nancy Heinl, *Written in Blood: The Story of the Haitian People, 1492–1971*, p. 36.

2. The term "elite" is used today by Haitians themselves to refer to members of the upper socioeconomic class. This segment of Haitian society comprised the colonial freedmen. Once the French colonial aristocracy was destroyed (by massacre or exile), the mulattos took control of much of the wealth, and claimed the political and social dominance once held by Whites. After about 1843, the mulattos lost control to the Blacks, thereby becoming a kind of silent, less obtrusive aristocracy.

3. Robert and Nancy Heinl, *Written in Blood,* pp. 39–40

4. The Societé des Amis des Noirs was an important French antislavery society in Paris that became more prominent in the colony. Initially, the society protested solely against trafficking in slaves and for equal rights for the *gens de couleur,* but not against the institution itself. Total abolition of slavery, considered by most individuals except the Black masses as only a remote possibility at some future point, was not part of the organization's agenda. Most certainly, however, the *gens de couleur* conducted themselves like the slave owners and took every precaution not to have their campaigns confused with the Black agenda.

14

The Haitian Revolution and the Neighbor to the East

The storm finally came in the unmasked fury of the triumphant Haitian Revolution. Not to be overlooked, however, is the fact that almost as soon as slavery began in the French colony of Saint-Domingue, turbulent slave revolts and other acts of rebellion served consistently as distant antecedents of the ultimate explosion in the colony. With the powerful Haitian Revolution, the most massive and most successful of slave uprisings history had seen, came an interlinking of the realization of racial equality, the unconditional abolition of slavery, decolonization, and the birth of a nation—the very first in not only the Caribbean, but in all of Latin America. The rallying call not just in Paris, but in faraway Saint-Domingue as well, was Fraternité, Egalité, Liberté. The rapid outbreak and then prolonged succession of bloody warfare in the French colony between 1791 and 1803 was both praised and condemned at the same time by slaves and slave owners respectively throughout the hemisphere. Former slaves had brought about the destruction of the world's richest colony, had destroyed an otherwise thriving economic system, and eliminated totally the class of individuals who had ruled over this system. Indeed, from the perspective of world history, the Haitian Revolution was certainly unique. This war involved Blacks, mulattos, French, Spanish, and English participants—with the fearless ex-slave Toussaint L'Ouverture emerging as Haiti's most charismatic hero.

The Fall of the Divine Monarchy

There is very little doubt in terms of the historical implications, together with closely interwoven sociopolitical factors, that the French Revolution of 1789 served as the spark that most immediately ignited the conflagration in the distant French colony in the Caribbean. For years and years, a steady buildup of tensions, antagonisms, discontent, and the rising aspirations of all segments of the colonial society precipitated that society's ultimate fall. There is little question that events in Paris had a powerful ideological impact in France's most prosperous colony. Everyone had a platform in Saint-Domingue, echoing the thunderous proclamations of the French Revolution: the *grands blancs* clamored for autonomy, the *gens de couleur* championed equality, the masses of Black slaves called for immediate emancipation. The French Revolution signaled the definitive end of the feudal system in France, the destruction of the privileged castes and the divine monarchy, as well as the authentic recognition of the rights of the common man. Such lofty ideals proclaimed by the fiery revolutionaries in the streets of Paris were especially unsavory for Caribbean colonial societies, all of which served as the classic feudal models the revolutionaries were determined to destroy. The traditional plantation world of tropical Saint-Domingue, however removed geographically from the social structure of the metropolis, nevertheless was a blatant contradiction to the rallying ideals of the French Revolution.

France would be transformed forever. The Great Revolution of 1789–1792 decapitated the king and his queen, tearing down permanently the legendary myth of a divine monarchy. Sweeping changes in practically every aspect of French society sent devastating shock waves to even the remotest corner of the Caribbean French-speaking colony to the west of Santo Domingo. In the metropolis the republicans embarked on a path to destroy the old order in which circumstances of birth and wealth alone ceded power and privilege, and to erect in its stead an anxiously awaited, more equitable society wherein talent, merit, and industry would be the determinant factors for a niche in society. In the new order everyone would be a citizen. The French Revolution meant the economic modernization of France, paving the way for the committed development and influence of political power of a rising bourgeois capitalism. Clearly, then, the implications for the entire Caribbean were not hard to fathom.

Armed Revolt in the West

Despite laborious attempts by many observers to portray the situation differently, the plain truth of the matter is that Haitian history and nationalism have been inextricably linked to the domestic affairs of its eastern neighbor, La República Dominicana. Comparisons between them are quickly accompanied by contrasts—some subtle, others blatant, but always entwined throughout their duel histories of development. True, the armed slave revolt in Hispaniola's western end had tremendous repercussions among all the slaveholding societies in the Caribbean, but the reverberations were ear-splitting on the other side of the Artibonito. Next door, the Spanish-speaking colony would eventually become the second Caribbean society to win its political independence (1844). The Haitian Revolution began as a slave uprising; it was in every sense of the term a social revolution. This was no convenient reshuffling of the ruling elite, exchanging one obnoxious, dominant caste for another one later.

Quite the contrary, in this revolution the African slaves became the absolute masters in a now free state. What ignited as a spark of insurrection unexpectedly erupted into an uncontrollable wildfire of civil war proportions, before eventually turning into a war along undeniable color lines. When news of the revolution in France reached the Caribbean colony, the settler class was confronted with the dilemma of deciding which faction would prove most beneficial to its interests. The settlers had to ally themselves with either the republicans or the royalists. But so too did the people of mixed blood have to decide which side of the racial struggle, the Black or the White, it would be in their best interest to join.

Mulatto Activism

The opposing factions of Caucasians armed their slaves and readied themselves for war.[1] Initially the republicans, the *petits blancs,* wanted to exterminate once and for all the mulattos and simply expropriate their property. The *grands blancs* made early gestures indicating their intention to join forces with the wealthy mulattos. One very prominent activist from the mulatto community, Vincent Ogé, went directly before the French Assembly in Paris to present the case for his class. Ogé then traveled to the United States where he was successful in collecting arms and ammunitions for the armed struggle back in Saint-Domingue.

His return to the colony in 1790 served to announce the so-called mulatto uprising. The revolt, led by Ogé and another mulatto companion named Chavannes, was immediately crushed by the authorities. Ogé and the other leaders were executed. Then the truly unexpected happened. The French National Assembly in 1791 decided to admit into all colonial assemblies all those mulattos who were landowners, as well as all other *gens de couleur* who had been born free. Slavery, however, was to continue in the colony for as long as the local assemblies there desired it. This decree did not go unnoticed by the slaves themselves in Saint-Domingue, steadily gaining a more sophisticated political consciousness of their plight. Careful strategies were planned and fighting units were organized and trained. The Blacks had waited more than patiently, painfully, watching, even aiding their masters as they slaughtered one another without mercy. They too had shouted Fraternité, Egalité, Liberté as they fought alongside their masters to defend the narrow interests of one faction or another. No one, of course, was paying any attention to the mounting anger, bitterness, and restlessness of the enslaved masses. No one, neither the Whites nor the mulattos (many of whom themselves owned slaves and did not want them freed), were concerned with the remotest possibility that these exploited, oppressed masses had legitimate grievances to be heard and acted upon.

The Vengeance of Boukman

The impact of an official decree in 1791 to enfranchise the property-owning mulattos of Saint-Domingue resulted in two very important consequences there. First, all the Whites were forced to put aside their traditional caste distinctions and hostilities long enough to enter into hastily formed coalitions. This common front now consisting of Whites and mulattos saw the frightening specter of a society dominated by Blacks. Secondly, in late summer of 1791 the slaves of the Plaine du Nord, responding to the call to arms from the dynamic slave leader named Boukman, launched a violent, indiscriminate assault against all plantation owners of the northwest region. The destruction was quick and far-reaching. The slaves torched the canefields and the town of Cap Français. They robbed, tortured, and massacred any Whites caught in sight. The single objective of the rebels was to destroy once and for all the slave system in every regard, an action seen as the only way by which to guarantee unconditional emancipation. It was executed with unrelenting vengeance.

Toussaint L'Ouverture

As the ravages of war grew in intensity, and chaos prevailed throughout Saint-Domingue, power was gradually shifting toward the side of the Blacks. Soon the rebels were joined and later commanded by an extraordinarily talented former slave named Toussaint L'Ouverture, who earlier had become a high-ranking officer in the Spanish colonial army. L'Ouverture was regarded as an extremely shrewd military genius. He introduced rigid discipline and professional fighting tactics into the ragtag slave army. He was widely perceived as a military strategist of keen ability and a man of superior integrity and personal dignity. It was Toussaint who managed to convert naked vengeance into a sophisticated ideology associated with the ideals of the French Revolution. Repressed anger and hatred were unleashed and transformed into the calculated campaign to destroy the colony's slave system. So astounding was Toussaint's reported shrewdness and talent for manipulation that he was able to augment his army by winning over disenchanted free coloreds and even some French soldiers to his cause.[2]

As Toussaint's heralded victories struck increasing terror into the opposition, the struggle itself began to acquire an international character. English and Spanish troops from around the Caribbean were dispatched from their respective outposts in order to bolster the slave system and the plantation economy in Saint-Domingue. Toussaint, however, capitalized on the occasion of the invading forces by actually strengthening the resolve of the ex-slaves to enhance their military skills and tactics with which to crush the onslaught against the slaves' freedom. The National Convention in France issued a decree (1794) abolishing slavery in Saint-Domingue, a move designed to enlist the support of the Blacks in a counterassault against the invading British. Then the important Treaty of Basel (1795) resulted in Spain's ceding its colony of Santo Domingo to France. By 1797, Toussaint completed the difficult task of consolidating the various ex-slave fighting units. His now superior armies, numbering twenty to forty thousand men, were victorious against the Whites, having driven back both the French troops and the invading British expeditionary forces. He held back the free colored opposition in the southern zone of the colony. By 1800 Toussaint had carried the war directly into neighboring Santo Domingo. He proceeded to unify both parts of the island under a new constitution. A new society and a new reality were being forged—all to the expressed horror of White settlers everywhere. There was a mass exodus of Europeans from Hispaniola to places regarded as safe havens such as Louisiana, Cuba, Puerto Rico, Venezuela, and elsewhere, seen as more comfortable and accommodating for slaveowners.

Enter Napoleon's Armies

Toussaint's bold march into the island's eastern territory, seizing the Spanish-speaking colony without regard to the provisions of the earlier treaty between France and Spain (Santo Domingo was now a French territory), enraged Napoleon. This was an act seen as clear and daring aggression. However, there was no doubt in anyone's mind that the French were intent upon reinstituting slavery in the island. Napoleon's planned invasion was viewed as the definitive campaign to have the plantation-slave system remain under French control. The prospect of a new society of free and equal citizens was diametrically opposed to the traditional notions of France's overseas territories. The chilling image of a free Black population in total charge of France's prized Caribbean jewel must have produced nightmares for the White settlers.

Although Toussaint succeeded in ending the ruthless massacres of Whites and mulattos, encouraged the resumption of operating the vital sugar and coffee estates, and reopened limited trade channels with England and the United States, the French nevertheless found the case of Haiti distasteful and unacceptable. It was at this point during the winter of 1802 that Napoleon sent the first of an elite force of about twenty thousand French troops to retake Haiti. Under the command of Napoleon's twenty-nine-year-old brother-in-law, General Charles LeClerc, the French combat soldiers represented the Western world's most skilled fighting army at the time. LeClerc, but more so the diabolical General Rochambeau, was determined to launch a war of genocide against the Black population. By spring, the French in Saint-Domingue were waging open war against the whole non-White population there. LeClerc failed, however; his troops were either defeated by superior combat strategies or decimated by yellow fever. Toussaint L'Ouverture was finally betrayed by some of his own generals, kidnapped by the

French, and died (1803) in exile, in a dungeon in France. In that same year, though, Napoleon was forced to admit defeat of his scheme to acquire a fiefdom on this side of the Atlantic. The French were forced to abandon their once-profitable Caribbean colony.[3]

Anti-Haitian Phobia

Toussaint's exile and subsequent death fueled the destructive passions of Saint-Domingue's Black masses even more for an uncompromising freedom. That freedom would be had at whatever cost, even if it meant the total annihilation of Saint-Domingue itself. The campaign against the French armies became more ruthless and relentless than before. The rebel forces were now under the skillful command of ex-slave leaders Jean Jacques Dessalines (1758–1806) and Henri Christophe (1767–1820). These formidable and legendary leaders, unlike Toussaint, realized all too well that the French could not be trusted to recognize the emancipation of the enslaved populations. Determined resistance lasted until the enemy capitulated. Dessalines proclaimed Saint-Domingue independent on New Year's Day, 1804, and renamed the free nation by its indigenous name Haiti, an unmistakable symbol of an independent identity altogether from Europe. Haiti thus became the modern world's first free Black republic and second independent nation in the Western Hemisphere. Dessalines, imitating the arrogance and egomania he despised in Napoleon, crowned himself emperor. In order to ensure that his empire would be a solidly Black one, he ordered a monstrous slaughter of all remaining Whites. He was obsessed with the notion that Haiti could be salvaged only by truly hard work. Thus, every able-bodied man was assigned tasks and responsibilities in an effort to rebuild the nation.

Henri Christophe was likewise one of the most intrepid warriors in the struggle for Haitian independence. Christophe had earlier volunteered to fight under Lafayette in the American Revolution. Like Dessalines, he too instituted harsh military discipline in assigning men to work the long-neglected cane fields and coffee estates, returning the nation's agriculture to productive status. Both Dessalines and Christophe were ultimately targets of assassination.

To this very day, socioethnic relations between Haiti and La República Dominicana are sometimes strained and tense, resulting in what more than a few Dominican observers have referred to as *la fobia antihaitiana* (anti-Haitian phobia). The roots of this so-called fear are often traced back to this particularly ugly and disquieting aspect of the Haitian Revolution. Did the vindictive, uncontrollable obsession for personal freedom from enslavement weigh more heavily than any measure of collective concern for a newfound nationalism and restoration of the state economy? It must be remembered that former slaves had destroyed the wealthiest plantation system in this hemisphere and, in the process, had defeated the experienced armies of France, Spain, and Britain. Now these ex-slaves and free coloreds were actually daring to structure laws for the new society in attempts to build a cohesive nation. Haiti was definitely a threat. To what degree, one might further wonder, did genocidal practices and naked hatred against Whites during the violent Revolution exact a lasting toll on the psyche of the *dominicanos* next door?

Finally, in the years following this sometimes heady, sometimes chaotic period, there would be the equally serious issue of vengeance. Numerous Dominicans had been directly affected by, as well as terrified by, the degree of horrendous violence that took place during and after the period of Haitian liberation. As a result of this history, contemporary relations have engulfed both Haiti and its eastern neighbor in oftentimes acrimonious diplomatic exchanges. Dr. Anthony Barbier, sociology professor at the Université D'Haiti, has in modern times (as recently as 1994) made this assessment of Haitian society:

> We have a very violent society today because Haitian society was created and developed in an atmosphere of violence. Our first regime was violent; it was the regime of slavery, followed by a violent slave rebellion, which continued the system of inequity and used violence to maintain that system. From the nineteenth century into the twentieth century, that inequality grew more intense.[4]

Notes

1. In early eighteenth-century Santo Domingo, the Spanish authorities reversed previous traditions and practices regarding Blacks in the colonial militia and now offered free Blacks various posts in the army.
2. CEDEE, *Escarbando las Raíces de la Explotación,* p. 22.
3. It was not until about 1825 that France decided to abandon all claim of possession of Saint-Domingue, but only after the Haitian government had agreed to pay an enormous indemnity for expropriated settler holdings. The French colonists had been expelled altogether and all Caucasians, under the new Haitian

constitution of 1804, were prohibited from owning land anywhere in Haiti. Most historians seem to concur that the huge debt resulting from indemnity agreements was one of the prime factors that actually stunted Haiti's economic development throughout the nineteenth century. Moreover, trade concessions given to French business interests also placed Haiti's export economy under foreign control quite early.

4. Professor Anthony Barbier, on the occasion of a seminar presented in Santo Domingo, summer 1994.

15

The After-Shock
Consequences of the Haitian Revolution

When Toussaint's successor Dessalines proclaimed the independence of Saint-Domingue from France, the after-shock of this traumatic social upheaval produced both local and distant consequences of gigantic proportions, as suspected. The repercussions of the Haitian Revolution were felt across a wide spectrum of economic, political, social, and cultural arenas throughout the whole island, as well as throughout the Caribbean region and beyond. Some Dominican history scholars have made the observation that the slave revolt in Saint-Domingue can be more properly described as the classic model of an all-encompassing social revolution.[1]

The revolt was at the same time a decisive class struggle between slaves and masters and a bitter, bloody civil war between the races in the colony: Blacks, mulattos, Caucasians. The international aspect surfaced once the struggle engaged France, England, and Spain. Finally, the aspect of national liberation became evident once the war battles ended with the actual proclamation of freedom and the establishment of the first free republic in all of Latin America. Haiti's example, without question, contributed immeasurably to the cause of emancipation and decolonization everywhere in the hemisphere. Fraternité, Egalité, Liberté echoed loudly throughout the colonized territories of the Nuevo Mundo (New World). It was a leading Haitian general, Alexandre Pétion, for example, who provided the desperately needed support to the great Simón Bolívar (1815) in order for the hero from

Caracas to remount his weakening military campaigns for the determined liberation of the South American continent. Pétion's single condition of payment was that Bolívar abolish slavery in his own homeland, Venezuela, a solemn promise that was indeed honored once the Spanish yoke of colonialism had been lifted from South America. Haiti truly represented a major psychological threat to the existing order of things, and the new republic's example said much about the future of the Caribbean region. Beginning from about 1792 or 1793, all kinds of laws were hurriedly enacted throughout the slaveholding Caribbean and in the North American South to deal even more harshly (if such could be possible) with slavery, suspected conspiracies, and actual slave rebellions. Everywhere slave owners trembled at the thought of another Haiti.

In the Wake of Success

On both sides of the dividing frontier of the island, both during the prolonged, brutal course of the fighting and in the wake of the revolution's success, prevailing circumstances affected the manner in which the two societies evolved concerning the delicate question of color. From the very beginning, Haiti had been different: the prideful centerpiece of colonized territories with the French Empire, structured upon a slave-labor plantation economy, populated glaringly by a Black majority, seized violently by means of a vengeful slave revolt that literally decimated the White population. The eastern neighbor, on the other hand, was not nearly so central in the scheme of a declining European imperial giant. Nor was Santo Domingo as homogeneous demographically as its neighbor to the west. Here on the Spanish-speaking side of the island was a much smaller total population, featuring perhaps equal proportions of Europeans and Creoles (i.e., Europeans born in the colony), mulattos, and Blacks. Of particular note also was the fact that Santo Domingo could well be described as exhibiting or even harboring a far lesser degree of racial hostility and very much diminished interethnic tensions than evidenced on the French-speaking side. Here too the dominant political entity was the mulatto community, which ardently defended and fostered Hispanic or Creole, not necessarily Spanish or Peninsula, ideals. These mulattos actually behaved as though they were White. The rise of *la fobia antihaitiana* occurred early, but was quite exaggerated beyond the point of reason during the Haitian slave uprising. Therefore, the fledgling Dominican society perceived itself as being menaced by a voracious Black neighbor.

Abolition of Slavery

During the campaign of Toussaint L'Ouverture to liberate the French-held territory, the first significant action he executed when he took the war into Santo Domingo was to abolish slavery in the eastern zone (1801). Landowners in Santo Domingo, who had never been partisans of social reforms of any kind, supported the French during the invasion that began the following year. The mulattos allied themselves with the French rather than with the Blacks precisely because of self-perceptions of race. Although this mulatto group was constituted of *gens de couleur* who were of African heritage on one side, they nevertheless identified themselves solidly with—and considered themselves—*españoles,* and hence White.

In Santo Domingo, what was of maximum social importance to the economically poorer stratum of the colony at the time was not to be completely Black or *too* Black in color. So then, such thinking on the part of this group prompted the creation of an altogether new socioethnic category, *blancos de la tierra*[2] (Whites of the land). This imaginative color designation, referring to a Dominican or Spanish Creole, while in all accuracy describing an exploited, landless peasant, placed this individual yet above the perceived inferior status of the people of color. How tragic that a community of a majority colored population would actually risk their lives in efforts to assist LeClerc in his mission to extinguish the slave revolt, with the ultimate objective of re-establishing slavery next door! There had never been any widespread support for abolition voiced by the eastern neighbor. Both Haiti and Santo Domingo in the aftermath of the Haitian Revolution would experience a deep internal agony of multilayered complexity. The revolution had aggravated a growing identity question rooted in color, ethnicity, and race. On the rise also was the sense of overt apprehension about all Blacks felt by non-Blacks. This fear in turn sharpened the antagonisms toward the Black segment—often in the majority—of populations everywhere throughout the Caribbean.

Social Transformation

The disintegration of Saint-Domingue's slave society ushered in a lengthy era of social collapse, followed by a rebirth. Not just in Hispaniola, but in the whole of the region would there be an intense transformation. For a long time to come, the changes would profoundly affect practically every aspect of the various societies. Perhaps the changes were viewed by some as completely unwarranted, painfully difficult, and unfair. Of course, those harboring this view were a very tiny, yet shamefully privileged segment of the population. Those changes represented the total demise of their privileged world. The number-one accomplishment was the destruction of the long-standing, weighty, undeniably inhumane and unjust slave-labor plantation system.

Another significant liberating element in the former French colony's transformation process had to do with the mixed-race populations. Among them were free laborers of color who had long experienced a kind of passing-in-and-out status within the colony. These free coloreds were for a long time without a clearly defined identity. In the after-shock of the revolution, these individuals began a self-assessment of their traditional role and their uncertain future in terms of the thorny legacy of feeling not totally belonging anywhere.

This was the group that had traditionally been marginalized in Saint-Domingue, forming a separate world from mainstream society, but easily making up a majority throughout the neighboring Spanish-speaking portion of the island. In Santo Domingo the mulatto majority, especially following the Haitian Revolution, became the formidable segment of the population that capitalized significantly upon the cultural uniqueness of being mulatto and used this characteristic to the socioeconomic advantage of the group. In terms of economics, the Haitian Revolution produced far-ranging implications. The physical destruction of Haiti alone was staggering in dimension, due largely to a scorched-earth policy that was designed to demoralize the French forces. The destruction of the colony's economy, however, served to stimulate coffee and sugar production throughout the rest of the Caribbean region, especially Cuba. A stepped-up agricultural expansion in Cuba, for instance, resulted immediately from the transfer of labor, technology, and methods of cultivation to that island. Cuba very quickly replaced Saint Domingue as the world's leading sugar producer.

Although the Haitian Revolution did bring an end to the institution of slavery, the former slaves soon found themselves embroiled in a senseless civil war between Blacks in the north, commanded by Christophe until his suicide in 1802, and mulattos in the south led by Alexander Pétion. This hideous and violent race war would divide the already fragile new society, as the national plantation economy was fast deteriorating under the growing appearance of small, independent peasant farm plots. This new peasant economy, severely limiting, was inadequate to sustain a viable national agricultural production and thus played a major role in leading Haiti to its ultimate decline. Tragically, too, the deep-rooted ethnic and color divisions would plague Haitian society throughout its history, and be manifested in contemporary internal matters.

Notes

1. Valentina Peguero and Danilo de los Santos, *Visión General de la Historia Dominicana.*
2. Frank Moya Pons, *Manual de Historia Dominicana,* p. 197.

16

French, then Haitian, Domination of Santo Domingo

Chaos and resentment seemed to define not merely the newly independent Haitian nation, but the entire island as well. Almost immediately
following independence, the island found itself embroiled in a state of
utter turmoil, both internally and externally. Tranquility and stability
were still a considerable distance away. On both sides of the Río
Artibonito, separating the two sister republics, absolutely chaotic conditions prevailed. Chaotic readily described government operations,
national economic policies, and efforts to ward off external threats.
What seemed to mark the independent western zone as well as the still
colonized eastern portion of Hispaniola was an even greater threat: a
sociopolitical ideology pointing toward a new militarism in the region.
Such militarism made possible the inevitable surfacing of brutally
strong, dominant, and often oppressive *caudillos*[1] (rural chieftains),
who were determined to gain total control of a particular zone. Also,
after the war of liberation, a contingent of embittered, stubborn French
troops disobeyed the orders of their commanders to leave the island
and return to Paris. Instead, the roguish band marched arrogantly into
the Spanish-held territory in the East and established a government
there. Authorities back in Paris openly supported the action and even
officially appointed General Louis Ferrand to serve as territorial governor (1804) there. Ferrand occupied the colony until 1808, when the
unrelenting efforts of an outraged Dominican citizenry dislodged the

French invaders. During the occupation, however, Ferrand systematically transformed Dominican society, forcibly restoring law and order, reactivating the national economy, resisting another invasion attempt from neighboring Haiti, and—most dramatically of all—reinstituting the slave system.

Reconquest by the *Hateros*

Professor Juan Bosch reminds us that in any human aggregation, social authority in the final analysis is much stronger than authority derived from politics.[2] This was certainly the case with the *hateros* throughout La República Dominicana. In a little less than forty years, they had strengthened their position both economically and socially to such a degree that they were ultimately the key figures in negotiating the nation's future. Along the course of the island's developing socioeconomic sectors—the sugar barons, the merchants, the lumber cutters— none had risen to the impressive heights of forming the influential nucleus of social power as had the rancher class of the *hateros*. This pioneering community of Dominican ranchers presented a strong, cohesive group of high-minded individuals who increasingly saw their role as self-appointed defenders of an evolving national consciousness.

From the start of the Haitian Revolution, Santo Domingo began the first of a series of traumatic but very important societal transformations. By 1795 the country was ceded to France; by 1801 the country was being invaded by Toussaint L'Ouverture; by 1804, there was French domination and occupation by Ferrand; more invasions followed, this time by Haiti, in 1805; the campaign of Reconquest *(la Reconquista)* began in 1808; then finally the eastern colony was back under domination by their old masters, the Spanish Crown, in 1809. Throughout the succession of these rapidly paced events, the *hateros dominicanos* remained a consistently unified, impenetrable community. Perhaps this fossil-like solidarity was nowhere more prominently displayed than during the Campaign of the Reconquest, which was almost exclusively the task of the *hateros*.

The Supreme *Hatero,* Juan Sánchez Ramírez

Bitter resistance against French occupation sparked the awakening of an embryonic national consciousness of indignation and the resolve of the Dominican people to retake the territory.[3] Anti-French sentiment boiled to the dangerous point of inspiring efforts to mount a War of Liberation. A wealthy Creole *hatero* from La Vega, named Juan Sánchez Ramírez, became the leader of the rancher group. He distinguished himself and his organized band of resistance fighters with victory against the French at the famous Battle of Palo Hinchado (1808). Spanish troops stationed in Puerto Rico, together with English squadrons from Jamaica, aided Sánchez Ramírez.

With victory won, the *hateros* from the Cibao began to realize the enormous potential—politically and socially—of their group. In about twenty years' time, all the other previously influential sectors involved in managing or dominating the country's affairs had literally fled the island. It was now the turn of the newly assertive rancher class to be in control. This relatively small, yet socially and economically prominent rancher class, ironically strongly favored the continued Spanish domination and control over the island. At the same time, it must quickly be pointed out that there existed a rival group of petite bourgeoisie who were decidedly opposed to the social hegemony of slaveholding *hateros* like Sánchez Ramírez. Unfortunately, however, because of the victory over the French, it was Sánchez Ramírez who was forced into negotiations with the English. During the Reconquista battles, the English had provided a most effective maritime blockade of both the capital city and Samaná, thus aiding tremendously the *hatero* leader in his objectives for victory. The strategic negotiations at war's end led calculatingly to a set of special trade concessions with the English as compensation for their military support. Sánchez Ramírez therefore granted lucrative commercial privileges to his English allies.

Unquestionably, stewardship of Santo Domingo now rested, however uncomfortably and most incompetently, with this new rancher class, which was actually quite naive and unfamiliar with the intricacies and nuances of governance. Santo Domingo, in ironic contradiction of its western neighbor that had just recently waged and won an agonizing and brutally exhausting struggle for national liberation and sovereignty, was plunged as deeply as before into an abyss of political and economic dependency. This period is what Dominican historians refer to as *La España Boba* (Idiotic Spain).[4] The revolution of national reconquest that had been launched by the *hatero* leader Sánchez Ramírez saw its end with Ferrand's suicide in 1809 and the beginning of a twelve-year neocolonialism by a disinterested, preoccupied Spain.

La España Boba

This revisited colonial circumstance began with Sánchez Ramírez at the helm (1809) and lasted until a successful coup (1821) led by José Núñez de Cáceres. Although it was Núñez de Cáceres who boldly proclaimed the independence of Santo Domingo, it was also he who renamed the country Haití Española (Spanish Haiti), and placed the Spanish-speaking territory under the protectorate of Colombia!

This twelve-year period witnessed nothing but shameful ineptness and ridiculous official government policy. ¡España Boba! All of the territory's maladies—illiteracy, massive poverty, cultural and economic isolation and stagnation, feudalism, colonial oppression—all persisted during this horrible period.[5] Moreover, this period in Dominican socioeconomic and cultural development featured the gradual decline of the formerly powerful slaveholder class and the transition toward the rise of a new petite bourgeoisie consisting of tobacco growers and merchants. This same slowly bulging middle class of merchants and entrepreneurs would be responsible for the formation of a national consciousness that had been born under the stewardship of earlier *hatero* rule and the ideals of Sánchez Ramírez. Thus the opposition to the government's general ineptness was rooted primarily in the colony's very social sector that simultaneously was creating the new relations in production. A succession of social battles was being waged against colonial domination and against the socioeconomic and political hegemony of the island's plantation slave owners, aristocrats, and traditional *hateros*. What we witness, then, throughout this era—actually for the first time in the island's cultural formation—is a class struggle that found vocal political expression and began structuring a true political agenda.

The era of España Boba saw a kind of retrenchment of attitudes and practices on the part of the Spanish colonists. This class, by its very nature, was obstinate about undertaking even the slightest measures that would favor a natural evolution of the traditional colonial economic base. This group, in like fashion, was unyielding in its opposition to altering the existing social relations. For example, slavery as an institution was on the decline, despite Ferrand's previous enactment to restore it. Among several other important factors, this decline was a result of the more advantageous and popular practice of granting land to slaves. In addition, slaveholders on many occasions would actually hire out their slaves to neighboring ranches and plantations. A kind of feudal relationship emerged as a consequence. This new relationship involving labor, management, and production impacted quite heavily upon the older, more traditional forms of plantation-labor slavery.

The Rise of El Cibao

Emerging also during this period was a more aggressive mercantile activity, along with the creation of a vital commercial network encompassing several of the important port cities of the Dominican Republic. Puerto Plata, Monte Cristi, Samaná, and Azua took on greater significance by acquiring a revitalized economic as well as social prominence. Most ironically, in fact, the period of La España Boba saw the region of El Cibao being converted into the most dominant region of the country in terms of economic, social, and political vitality. It was Santiago de los Caballeros, the premier city of El Cibao, that had served so gloriously as the spiritual center and seat of strategic operations during the War of Reconquest. Both the economic and social prosperity of the region now marked it almost as if it were a totally distinct country, separated and isolated from the rest of the country, so progressive and dynamic was El Cibao by comparison.

Finally, the era of La España Boba also witnessed perhaps more than its share of unwelcome antigovernment conspiracies and insurrections. While most of these conspiracies were of a clear political nature and were conducted mainly by a very small, urban bourgeoisie, the slave insurrections were unmistakably different in this regard. One major slave uprising in particular, called La Rebelión de Mendoza y Mojarra (1812), was led by the slave Pedro de Seda. The uprising occurred on the outskirts of the capital city, in the parishes of Mendoza and Mojarra, and was described rather aptly as an eminently serious movement executed by skillfully organized and astute slaves and freedmen whose objectives were primarily social and were apparently quite alien to the notion of national independence.[6] Rather, the immediate goal of Pedro de Seda and his comrades was the abolition of slavery and the subsequent granting of certain rights and privileges in accordance with their anticipated, newly acclaimed social status within Dominican society.

La Rebelión failed. The colonial authorities were so fanatically determined that another Haitian-style revolution was not to be repeated

that they meted out horrendous and brutal punishment to the condemned slave insurrectionists as a lasting example to other individuals
secretly harboring similar notions of rebellion. Pedro de Seda and his
co-conspirators were hanged, and their corpses later quartered and dis-
membered, before finally being fried in sizzling hot fat. What must be
remembered is that while slavery overall was indeed moving into ob-
solescence as the primary means of production throughout most of the
island, remnants of this odious forced-labor system persisted stub-
bornly on those plantations still in the hands of the old-line colonial
aristocracy. By the year 1812 also, the country's dominant social sector, the *hateros,* who were still in the seat of the territory's government, began a slow decline themselves. Replacing this sector in both
economic and political influence was the small group of tobacco growers and merchants of El Cibao.

Notes

1. *Caudillos* were strong-arm military leaders who had gained a position of
absolute regional supremacy and commanded loyalty by defeating all other adver-
saries and rivals in fierce battle.
2. Juan Bosch, *Composición Social Dominicana,* p. 14.
3. Frank Moya Pons, *Manual de Historia Dominicana,* p. 207.
4. Roberto Cassá, *Historia Social y Económica,* p. 167.
5. Ibid., p. 169.
6. Ibid., p. 170.

17

A Haitian President in Santo Domingo

The era of La España Boba did manage to produce a spirited national consciousness and was able to lend impetus to the development of an aggressively active mercantile class. This dynamic sector held new and rather progressive economic theories. Even so, Dominican society as a whole still lacked a single-purpose social class capable or strong enough to serve as the nation's spearhead of resistance against the ever-present threat of outside invasion. The earlier heroic actions of Sánchez Ramírez and his *hatero* resistance fighters notwithstanding, there was still a void of societal cohesiveness as well as a vacuum of sociopolitical leadership. The result was a profound weakness of Dominican society at the precise moment of the new Haitian invasion of 1822. This circumstance was a consistently debilitating flaw that would have indelible sociopsychological consequences for *el pueblo dominicano* for many years beyond that historical date.[1] The Haitian invasion and occupation of 1822 under Haitian President Boyer is one of the most controversial and bitterly argued incidents (second or maybe third in importance to the Era of Trujillo or, as some individuals would continue to argue, to the United States military invasion of 1965) in the history of La República Dominicana. A tremendous amount of emotionalism invariably accompanies any sincere attempts to analyze the events in question. More than an isolated cadre of the country's historical analysts and commentators, as well as ordinary citizens today, have concluded that much of the contemporary Haitian

147

phobia has its genesis in Boyer's invasion. As has been noted elsewhere in this work, an observer of today's Dominican society frequently hears a Dominican or a Haitian quickly exclaim, "Oh, but we're so entirely different; we're not the same; everything about us is so different." However, the more significant reality is that one cannot possibly view or begin to understand Dominican history and culture without fully realizing or recognizing the intricately interwoven textures and threads flowing between the two neighboring cultures, Dominican and Haitian. Their evolving societies on the jointly shared island of Hispaniola have been quite intimately interconnected since the earliest periods in the island's history. Therefore, any analysis of the twenty-two-year Haitian occupation of Santo Domingo, beginning in 1822, will tend to depend largely upon the particular social orientation (biased, perhaps?) and personal agenda of the observer. Some observations will casually comment upon Boyer's nobler enactments such as abolishing slavery or the questions of church-state separation or attempts at agrarian reform, while other depictions of Boyer will attempt to vilify the occupying Haitians by describing them as savages, rapists, and murderers. Without any dispute, however, is the one fact of lasting visibility: the population of the eastern end of Hispaniola was made considerably *más oscura* (darker) as a result of both increased Haitian-Dominican intermarriages and the White flight of greater numbers of Spanish colonists from the invaded territory.

Jean-Pierre Boyer, Foreign Invader

Undoubtedly, one of the initial ironies of the first proclamation of independence of Santo Domingo by Núñez de Cáceres (1821) was that there was ample support at the time for the incorporation of the Spanish-speaking colony with the Republic of Haiti. While clamoring for independence from Spain, a sizable number of individuals, mainly the territory's political and military elite, voiced their desire for union with their French-speaking neighbor in the west. In the years of chaos and madness that came in the wake of Haitian independence, Haiti was a unified republic by 1819, much to the credit of Jean-Pierre Boyer. The new republic's capital was at Port-au-Prince, with Boyer himself as president. His skillful leadership and persuasive style had assisted him in successfully bringing together under one central command the two formerly bitter rivals within the Haitian nation. There had actually existed two Haitian nations, one with Christophe in the north, and the other under Pétion in the south.

Some Dominicans today argue vociferously that Boyer invaded and occupied the eastern portion of the island precisely at the moment he did as a crafty strategic measure. It is suggested that Boyer's design was to thwart efforts by zealous slaveholders who were determined to launch an invasion of Santo Domingo in order to return the society to its former slave-plantation status, on both sides of Hispaniola. There is also speculation on the part of a number of Dominicans that Boyer's invasion was a consequence of the Haitian president's scheme to fulfill his obligation to loyal military officers and army soldiers: that of parceling out land to them as payment for military service. Haiti had no more available land; Santo Domingo, on the other hand, had more than enough. Boyer's solution to the land distribution question, therefore, lay to the east.[2] However persistently one might argue, though, what is certainly clear is that Boyer was adamant about bringing into realization as quickly as possible the unification of the entire island. All the island's inhabitants would thus be converted into *verdaderos haitianos, fueron estos blancos o libertos, negros o mulatos*[3] (true Haitians, whether they be White or freedmen, Blacks or mulattos).

Haitian Domination

In true revolutionary fashion, Boyer proceeded to enact specific measures that were clearly designed to place the Spanish-speaking eastern zone in balance with the tone of political and economic realities being played out in the western part of the island. His first significant proclamation, therefore, was the abolition of slavery. He next moved on agrarian reform by distributing land parcels to newly freed slaves. Boyer then shifted attention toward the church, confiscating land and other properties traditionally held by this hallowed institution, as well as expropriating real estate of absentee landowners. A final example of Boyer's revolutionary and indeed controversial intentions was his measure to institutionalize the judicial and political machinery in such a manner that there would be a genuinely representative government. Boyer's overall design was to redirect completely the daily life throughout the island.

It would be a serious understatement to suggest that more than a few individuals within Dominican society at the time were both unhappy and outraged by Boyer's measures—perceived by some sectors of the population as perhaps draconian or radical. While Boyer's occupation brought about important sociopolitical changes, the Haitian domination was not without grave problems and cause for deliberate opposition. Mostly, Boyer's land reform measures, however controversial and subject to varying historical and social interpretations, nevertheless had the resounding effect of destroying the traditional, exploitative land monopoly held by the society's dominant groups. Soon there was widespread, general discontent on both sides of Hispaniola. There had been little economic development under Haitian rule. In fact, the economy was failing, again, on both sides of the Artibonito. Boyer was apparently interested more in encouraging and stimulating the agricultural sector than in any other economic activity, especially urban mercantilism. Church real estate was being arbitrarily transferred to the state, a first in the tradition of Hispaniola. There were even rumors of a Spanish invasion (which never materialized). There was also a resurgence of the decades-old rivalries between the governing Haitian elite (mulattos) and the masses of the Black population, most notably throughout the western end. Embers of a struggle for absolute national independence were ignited at a series of historical, secret meetings that were taking place throughout midsummer of 1833 in Santo Domingo.

The Trinitaria Movement

Opposition to Haitian domination and President Boyer grew more intensive than ever expected. What many individuals considered increasingly abusive and intolerable in Boyer's reform measures, the Boyer government regarded as progressive and necessary for meaningful societal redirection and restructuring. At about this time, Juan Pablo Duarte, a young, energetic Dominican intellectual, son of a Creole merchant, had been studying in Europe. Upon completing his studies, he returned to his native Santo Domingo filled with impressionable theories of the new liberalism and ideals of nationhood then sweeping the continent during this intoxicating opening period of European Romanticism. Young Duarte, upon his return to the milieu of the Caribbean, was especially incensed by what he thought to be the excesses of Haitian rule. By July of 1838, a clandestine group of mainly young liberal-leaning professionals met in the capital city of Santo Domingo to form a secret society that carefully outlined a single-purpose agenda: to organize local resistance to dreaded Haitian domination and separate their territory once and for all from Haiti. This spirited and intrepid group of individuals was called *La Trinitaria* (the Trinity) and was founded by the young idealist Duarte.

When Boyer finally relinquished office (1843), his successor, General Charles Herard, prolonged the struggle for Dominican independence by his staunch determination to annihilate the countergovernment forces. After a series of both temporary setbacks and decisive victories, the revolutionaries were able at last to crush the Haitian onslaught. Herard was forced to abandon all designs of conquest, retreating back across the Río Dajabón. The date of February 27, 1844, thus opened an altogether new political and social era in the ongoing evolution of Dominican culture. That date marks the official birth of a new nation, an independent República Dominicana. Perhaps this is the only nation that can boast proudly of honoring not one, but *Tres Padres de la Patria* (Three Fathers of the Nation): Juan Pablo Duarte, Francisco del Rosario Sánchez, and Matias Ramón Mella, each playing equally prominent roles in the struggle for the ultimate creation of an independent, liberated nation.

Notes

1. Immediately following Haiti's proclamation of independence (1804), Haitian leaders were very cautious about executing any designs to intervene in neighboring or regional slaveholding colonies. Following the earlier example of L'Ouverture, these leaders did not wish to provoke a maritime embargo or an invasion by the slaveholding powers in the region. Dessalines proved to be the exception when he attempted annexation of his eastern neighbor in 1805. The mission was nevertheless completed by 1822.
   2. Roberto Cassá, *Historia Social y Económica,* p. 175.
   3. Frank Moya Pons, *Manual de Historia Dominicana,* p. 226.

18

After Independence, More War

Quisqueyanos everywhere, whether on the island or in New York City's Washington Heights district, or in Miami, Philadelphia, or Barcelona, jubilantly celebrate February 27 as their Día de Independencia. On that triumphant date in 1844, the *trinitarios* and their loyal followers, although minus their founder Duarte because he lay seriously ill in Curaçao, were successful in overtaking the fortress of the Puerta del Conde in the city of Santo Domingo, forcing the Haitian commander to surrender. In a very short time, the other major towns around the island held by the occupying Haitian army capitulated. La República Dominicana was officially born and subsequently separated from Haiti. But even after independence was proclaimed, there were still some lingering and more than merely vexing internal problems and issues facing the now liberated Dominican citizenry. The new nation was still haunted by several of its earlier, weightier liabilities: a lack of firm national cohesiveness and unity of purpose, a deficit in national loyalty, an unusual dispersion of population over much broader areas of the country, a totally uncomfortable and unacceptable level of educational, political, and religious turmoil.

These were problems that, taken as a whole, might well point toward a deeply rooted weakness in the intrinsic nature of Dominican culture since its earliest beginnings. Did there truly exist some inexplicable inability of the Dominicans to maintain a sense of real stability? Whether derived from the more liberal or more conservative faction, this apparently elusive stability was simply not present in a community that was not socially organized. That is to say, here was a community that did not as yet have at its helm a social group or class holding uncompromisingly to clearly defined, articulated ideals and purposes agreed upon by a consensus of the population. After independence, the only undisputed common accord was *no volver al dominio haitiano* (not to return to Haitian domination). So narrowly focused upon was this single notion that both the *hateros* and the petite bourgeoisie alike were making overtures and later actually initiating concrete steps toward some form of protectorate status by a foreign power at the very moment of the nation's birth!

Quite significantly, the newly independent República Dominicana had a seriously divided leadership. Ultraliberals like Duarte and his faithful *trinitarios* were bitterly opposed by ultraconservatives like Pedro Santana and Buenaventura Báez, who were even suggesting the strong possibility of annexation by an influential and powerful foreign country as a realistic means of safeguarding their new nation against any external threats. The specter of Haiti just wouldn't go away. In the mind of many conservative *dominicanos,* Haiti still presented itself as a menace that lurked in the shadowy psyche of all Dominicans, especially the ruling elite.

Although the country had won its lengthy struggle for independence with the loyal support of fervent liberals of both France and Haiti, there were Dominicans who nevertheless regarded Haiti as a vengeful neighbor, an ever-present and potential invader intent upon recapturing its lost territory. This more powerful group, representing the very limited, egotistical class interests of the *hateros* and the *pequeña burguesía* (petite bourgeoisie), was able to continue dominating the nation's political and economic scene in the aftermath of independence. Men like Santana, Báez, and Tomás de Bobadilla (each of whom would serve later as the nation's president) had considerable prestige among the elite and were engineering forces behind the creation of the country's new Central Governing Board (*la Junta Central Gubernativa),* which now had complete control of the affairs of state for La República Dominicana. It was this very powerful body that conveniently found Duarte, Rosario Sánchez, and Ramón Mella traitors to the independence cause, then exiled them! Again, traditional class interests prevailed over any broader ideals of national cohesiveness.

Annexation and Restoration

After the country experienced a senseless, exasperating—although short-lived—Revolución de Julio de 1857, there were reawakened gestures toward annexation, looking this time across the seas in the direction of Madrid. By 1860 North American adventurers and calculating mercenaries concocted schemes of their own for annexation of República Dominicana to the United States. One has only to point to the dastardly case of the notorious William Walker and his exploits in Nicaragua as the classic example of such schemes.[1] Finally, against much general indignation by the Dominican people, a formal Proclamation of Annexation came in 1861. La República Dominicana was to be regarded as an additional overseas province of Spain. Annexation was to guarantee military and financial protection to the new *provincia.*

As soon as annexation was proclaimed, massive demonstrations of protest flared, despite efforts by the annexationist-led government to convey the impression that the entire populace had overwhelmingly registered a consensus of support for the measure. Conflict between the masses of outraged and humiliated Dominicans and the overconfident Spaniards was inevitable from the start. After twenty years of an embittered coexistence with the occupying Haitians and then another seventeen years of an independent lifestyle (and yet nervous psyche), the Dominicans could not help feeling serious contradictions and agonizing conflicts in terms of both culture and politics under renewed foreign domination. The Spaniards, upon arriving at the island, discovered that the population they had come to govern this time was not as Hispanic (i.e., Spanish) as expected. It was the color question again. Especially serious were those cultural conflicts that dealt with color and race, since the majority of the population was constituted by people of color, and their customs had differed enormously from those of the Spaniards.

As the convolutions of classic irony would have it, the very same Dominicans, *los anexionistas* (annexationists) who had been in the vanguard of the annexation campaigns, became victims themselves of Spain's very racist ideology. The entire Dominican society, comprised of *criollos, mulatos, negros,* all suffered the extremes of humiliation brought by the Spanish bureaucracy during this period. The nagging question of slavery was equally paradoxical in light of the prevailing circumstance that slavery was still operating shamelessly in the nearby

Spanish-held islands of Puerto Rico and Cuba. There were frequently reported incidents in the city of Santiago in El Cibao, for example, that began being duplicated throughout Dominican society. The more Caucasian-appearing *dominicanos* began modeling their behavior after that of the governing *españoles* vis-à-vis their fellow *dominicanos* who were darker in skin color or more African in physical appearance. This former group perceived themselves as superior to their darker sisters and brothers in order not to run the unwelcome risk of being assimilated to them, or being regarded as inferior by the occupying Spaniards. The aim was to be accepted as social equals by the Spaniards.

The War of Restoration: 1863–1865

Neighboring Haiti, despite horrific internal woes and its ongoing struggle to maintain an appreciable level of normalcy, was continuously in fear of reenslavement, a fear perceived as based on reality. Haiti's sense of uneasiness was readily provoked by any manner of foreign presence anywhere on the island of Hispaniola. That discomfort quickly intensified once it was felt that such presence even remotely gestured toward reinstituting the practice of slavery. Spain, once again the colonial master (this time with an annexed province next door in República Dominicana), was clearly a slaveholding foreign power in the Caribbean region, and her other Antillean possessions created a hostile environment for a newly independent, yet weak and uneasy, Haiti. So Haiti did not need any cajoling to be convinced that she must join those *dominicanos* who were anti-annexationists.

On August 16, 1863, a small but tenaciously intrepid band of just fourteen anti-annexationists headed by Santiago Rodríguez—and bolstered by the offered commitment of Haitian fighters—crossed the border into Dominican territory and atop the Cerro de Capotillo hillside unfolded the Dominican flag. Thus the signal was ignited. The *Guerra por la Independencia y la Restauración de la República* (War for the Independence and the Restoration of the Republic) had begun in earnest. All the communities in the surrounding area took up the call without hesitation. One after another, the towns and villages dotting El Cibao announced their unflinching allegiance to and support for the Restoration Movement. The cibaeño towns of La Vega, Moca, Puerto Plata, San Francisco de Macorís, Cotuí—each with its own contingent of prepared and willing sons and daughters of liberty—marched on the Spanish military stronghold at Santiago.

Opposition to Annexation

Perhaps one of the most significant actions of the War of Restoration was ordered instantly: the burning of the entire city of Santiago as a strategy to rout the Spaniards holed up there. Before war's end (1865), the whole country from one end to the other—with very few exceptions—had risen up against annexation to Spain. La Guerra Restauradora had begun as a rebellion of insurgent campesinos, but promptly turned into a war of very major social and psychological implications. Of special note was the fact that Dominicans of color, indisputably now the majority of the population, feared that they would be automatically reenslaved by their former plantation masters.[2]

It soon became evident that what started as a populist uprising set in motion all the nation's talents, resources, and energies in order to preserve its hard-earned independence—to restore its sovereignty and integrity. This period has been viewed as one of the most important of the nineteenth century in terms of the country's social struggles. La Guerra de la Restauración had become another milestone in the reaffirmation of a declaration of independence for the Dominican people.

Principally by employing the tactics of guerrilla warfare, the revolutionaries waged a fierce war that became a nightmare for the Spaniards. But in terms of devastation and human suffering, the war brought havoc to the entire country. One immediate casualty that would linger and fester for decades was political fragmentation. This factionalism left La República Dominicana hounded by scores of selfishly ambitious military leaders, resulting in frequently violent power struggles among themselves for absolute dominance in a given region of the country. This rivalry was the beginning of modern caudillismo. Another of the war's unfortunate casualties was renewed geographical divisions in socioeconomic terms. Resurfacing were those animosities dormant since the late eighteenth century that sharply divided the country into two separate, competitive economic and social zones: El Cibao and the south.

Beyond any degree of doubt, the one gigantic personality that emerged during the period of the Restoration was that of Gregorio Luperón. This avowed progressive thinker, a genuine champion of

Dominican nationalism, a man of exceptional military prowess, battled relentlessly against all forms of enemies to Dominican sovereignty. Luperón embodied in his daily conduct and spirit the very best ideals of the era. It was Luperón alone who was able to consolidate the various rival factions and regional caudillos into a single-purpose national leadership. It became evident then that the *trinitarios*, those earliest members under the charismatic influence and inspiration of the movement's founder Duarte, had successfully planted the seeds of liberalism for later patriotic defenders of national sovereignty. The earlier *trinitarios* had proved to be ardent proponents of *ideas más avanzadas* (the most advanced ideas) of the period. Their legacy had been passed on to the leaders of the Restoration campaign. La República Dominicana under the presidency of Gregorio Luperón (1879–1880) was characterized by a new, liberalist vision that began the task of reordering society. His was a bourgeois reasoning, according to historian Cassá, that centered upon the delicate process of transforming the national economy into a modern, export-based economy.[3]

Notes

1. William Walker, a fanatical ex-slaveholder from Tennessee, arrived in Nicaragua (1855) and seized the city of Granada. He made himself commander-in-chief of the Nicaraguan army, then later proclaimed himself president of the country. All of Central America waged a personal war against Walker and his followers. By 1860 he had been captured and executed by the allied regional forces.

2. James Holly and J. Dennis Harris, *Black Separatism and the Caribbean, 1860,* p. 66.

3. Roberto Cassá, *Historia Social y Económica,* pp. 86–90.

19

After Restoration, More Chaos

The fifty-year period that immediately followed La Restauración was plagued by still more chaos. The Dominican Republic fell into serious ruin. There were crippling political fragmentation, revived socioeconomic competition between El Cibao and the south, paralleled by regionalized economic production, plus the nagging question of the Samaná territory. From the period of 1865 until 1916 there were thirty-six presidents, some serving multiple terms in office. The era was marked by heavy foreign loans, the difficulty of debt payments, power struggles among regional caudillos, and a series of bloody civil wars, all compounded by a stagnant national economy. The fragile Dominican government with its ruinous indebtedness eventually prompted United States military intervention. First, though, came the humiliating Fiscal Convention of 1907 that placed the nation's customs operations completely in the hands of the United States. Later, in 1916, the United States Marines landed. One might say that the truly modern era for Quisqueya began with the unceremonious introduction of United States imperialism.

Two Opposing Societies

Attempts to restructure Dominican society were both the primary focus of, and the overriding provocation for, much of the political unrest in the years after the Restoration. The sociopolitical struggles engaged two dominant rival sectors—the petite bourgeoisie and the *hateros,* and these battles can be readily described as bitter skirmishes between two ideologically opposing societies. On the battlefields were two dissimilar economies, two diametrically opposed modes of thinking, and two antagonistic political objectives. Thus, essentially what prevailed in the island between 1865 and 1879 was continued political instability and social tension. Despite the unsettling political conditions throughout the country, the triumph of El Cibao over the south, seemingly a perpetual rivalry between the two opposing geoeconomic zones, strengthened economic activity in the north. Tobacco became king, forming a most solid economic basic there.

However, as perhaps an indirect consequence of the War of Restoration, the modern sugar industry was born in the southern zone at about the same time. The origins of this now modern industry were tightly linked with the enormous wave of Cuban immigration to Hispaniola at the outbreak of Cuba's first war of independence against Spain (1868). Of major significance in this sudden and new wave of immigration was that astute Cuban capital investment bought up huge land tracts for the sole purpose of cultivating sugarcane. But this time the sugar plantations could boast of modern, industrialized methods: the employment of the newly developed steam machinery, the construction of railroad tracks, the use of engines to transport the cane directly from the fields to the nearby processing plant. The proprietors of the new industry were all foreigners; following the Cubans in dominance of the industry were North Americans and Italians. This particular circumstance, as did so many exterior factors in the process of the island's evolving culture, would have grave ramifications later for the Dominican people.

Some Dominican social historians have noted with some acerbity that throughout the whole of Dominican society there has been a serious flaw: a kind of lingering social void that seems to have evolved and then festered as a consequence of the dismal failure of the sugar oligarchy of the earlier sixteenth century.[1] More specifically, some historical analysts on the island feel that had the slave-holding elite sector developed normally—in other words, run its natural course as it did, say, in Cuba—then that sector probably would have given way ultimately to the formation of a rather powerful bourgeois society.[2] If not a totally bourgeois society, then at least there might have emerged a society with a strong bourgeois core. Instead, what developed in La

República Dominicana was a weighty patriarchal slave-holding oligarchy that dragged the entire society down into a deep preindustrial
stagnancy.

Rival Ideals

After the Restoration, stagnancy reached dangerous levels of sociopolitical polarization in the island. Political activity centered largely
around just two dominant, bitterly antagonistic factions, *los azúles* (the
blues) and *los rojos* (the reds), symbolizing two rival ideals. Simply
viewed, *azul* represented liberalism, while the color red meant reac-
tionary and dictatorial. Upon closer inspection, however, the actual
party ideology oftentimes represented a fusion of diverse alliances.
The liberalism of the *azúles,* for instance, was frequently limited by the
narrow scope of a specific personality and the individual interests of
the party's military leaders. The hero of the Restoration, Gregorio
Luperón, was unquestionably the supreme party chieftain of the blues
and exemplified the best traditions and practices of a liberal platform
for the country. By stark contrast, his very faithful protégé and skillful
minister of war, who later would himself become a five-time president
of the Republic, Ulises Lilís Heureaux, had pronounced in a letter of
1887 that *mi política y mis propósitos de conciliación tienen por limite
la necesidad del orden y la garantía de los intereses sociales*[3] (my
politics and my purposes of conciliation have, because of limitation,
the necessity of order and the guarantee of social interests).

The *azul* party, with its striking platform of progressiveness, consisted overwhelmingly of bourgeois liberals. But by the time Heureaux
gained the presidency (1882), the party ideology was undergoing a
dramatic transformation. Many of the old-line liberals who had been
nourished on the hallowed ideals of Duarte and his early *trinitarios*
began registering deep suspicions about General Heureaux's increasing militarism and his lustful appetite for personal power. The irony in
all this, of course, was that both mentor and protégé, Luperón and
Heureaux, had each personally experienced the best possible example
of spiraling social mobility as a result of the practiced ideals of
society's liberalism. Heureaux had come from a background of Black,
lower socioeconomic origins; the orphaned Luperón also had grown up
in circumstances of economic deprivation. Therefore the surprise must
have been rather jolting to some individuals when Heureaux wrote that

he subscribed to the need for order and the guarantee of social interests,[4] referring undisguisedly to those narrow, very selfish interests of
the bourgeoisie sector. This was the group that Heureaux intended
establishing as the socioeconomic and political core of the new
República Dominicana. This sector would be the basis for reordering
Dominican society. It was intended, or so Heureaux envisioned, that
the void be filled, at long last and at whatever cost.

Peacemaker of the Nation

By the third time that Heureaux had occupied the presidency, his title had
become—in a rather sadistic sense—*Pacificador de la Patria* (Peace-
maker of the Nation). Never mind that the electoral campaign itself had
witnessed blatant instances of persecution, imprisonment, and even assassination of the opposition. Heureaux ultimately succeeded in converting
the constitutionality of the presidency into an authorization for tyranny.
One particularly crucial step he took was to eliminate all nationalistic
tendencies in the country's economic sphere. The economic pattern that
had been established by previous administrations was replaced altogether
by policies that put the nation at the disposition and mercy of foreign
investment interests. Economic interests, taking on more and more a
North American face, were served by profitable franchises and other
investment incentives designed to generate capital. When La República
Dominicana perceived exterior threats, again from Haiti, El Pacificador
himself sought the aid and protection of a foreign power. By 1889, negotiations were under way between Santo Domingo and Washington for
Samaná Bay and the peninsula to be purchased by the North Americans.
Heureaux offered the long-term leasing of Samaná to the North Americans in exchange for economic aid and substantial military protection
against any external threat, most especially the proverbial invasive enemy
to the west. These negotiations failed. This was certainly not the first of
such designs on Samaná. Dominican sovereignty regarding this strategic
bay had been threatened earlier (during the 1850s) when scheming Dominican annexationists were eager to sell the Samaná territory to the
United States. That plan also had failed.

A Nation Mortgaged

When a group of adventurous North American financial speculators
(among them the United States secretary of state and other high-ranking

government officials) formed an investment company called San Domingo Improvement Company, the Dominican government under El Pacificador Heureaux responded in predictable fashion. He began soliciting gigantic, often questionable loans from these creditors. In a few short years (1896–1898) the entire country was mortgaged to this company. Thus began a swift plunge into a pattern of heavy, ruinous indebtedness to foreign investors. The financial failures that resulted were unparalleled in the long history of Quisqueya. Once the San Domingo Improvement Company stepped into the financial and economic life of the country, the United States subsequently gained a sizable foothold in the island's internal affairs—an influence that penetrated to truly unimagined depths.

The worsening debt crisis eventually provoked the so-called dollar diplomacy objective of United States foreign policy in Latin America.[5] When European creditors finally threatened an armed invasion of the island in order to seize customs revenues, United States President Theodore Roosevelt sought justification in his personally tailored corollary to the historic Monroe Doctrine. Roosevelt snatched up Dominican customs operations, accordingly, to prevent European intervention and influence in the hemisphere.[6]

It was readily apparent almost everywhere that La República Dominicana was experiencing a serious economic transformation. The major source of income was now being generated from the production of sugar for export. Cacao and coffee were the other important export crops. San Pedro de Macorís, which during earlier periods in the country's social and economic development had been a nondescript fishing village, was now a pivotal, new export hub, having quickly become a major center for enlivened commerce and culture. Large numbers of bourgeois merchants and sugar producers were becoming extremely rich, powerful, and influential.

Foreign capital was in evidence throughout the entire island. Specially tailored laws were hastily enacted to give foreign investors almost absolute power; it was almost as if they were *un gobierno sin restricciones* (a government without restrictions). The sugar industry appeared to benefit most spectacularly. It is probable that all the *ingenios* were owned by foreigners. The national bank, which had been established in 1885 by the French, eventually fell under solid North American ownership. Accompanying the expansion of export sugar production, the Royal Bank of Canada was set up in 1908, becoming the island's first stable credit institution. Finally came the decisive blow that would usher in a radically new era in the evolution of Dominican society.

In 1907 a very unusual document, La Convención Dominico-Americana (the Dominican-American Convention) was drafted and approved by the National Congress in Santo Domingo. This unprecedented document impacted most profoundly upon both the economic and political life of Dominican society, and produced grave consequences for many other vital aspects of the community as well. This document literally prepared the way for United States intervention. Very importantly, such pending foreign intervention now had the official sanction of the Dominican government. Essentially, by naming the president of the United States as general collector of revenue, this proviso placed the United States in absolute control of the financial life of the Republic. The Convention of 1907 actually transformed the island into a modern-day protectorate of the United States. Of course, for this to occur, there had to be a decided measure of duplicity and collaboration on the part of more than just a few *dominicanos.* One Dominican president in particular, Ramón Cáceres, believed firmly that La República Dominicana could best achieve impressive economic development and political stability under the direct protection of the United States government. So, with perhaps blind admiration for the colossus to the north, Cáceres became one of the most ambitious architects behind the design to deliver the nation's fate into the eagerly outstretched hands of North American capitalist interests and imperialist policies.

Notes

1. Roberto Cassá, *Historia Social y Económica,* p. 168.
2. Ibid., p. 172.
3. Emilio Rodríguez Demorizi, *Cancionero de Lilís,* p. 256.
4. Ibid., p. 258.
5. Dollar diplomacy was the often controversial interventionist foreign policy of United States Presidents William Taft and Woodrow Wilson, calling for the hastened expansion of North American economic interests in Latin America and the Caribbean. Taft was especially intent upon converting the economy of the Central American region into a veritable monopoly of a handful of United States business ventures.
6. The administration of customs, mainly at the vital ports of Puerto Plata and Santo Domingo, by the Improvement Company, lasted until after the death of President Heureaux (1899). Then customs operations were taken over by the United States government in 1905, and thereafter United States officials held complete control of the operation until 1940!

20

Invasion from the Northern Colossus

One of the most hotly debated issues concerning La República Dominicana, especially in contemporary times, is the controversial and onerous United States military intervention and occupation of 1916–1924. In fact, as we mentioned earlier, most of the reference material in English about the island nation deals almost exclusively with rather isolated aspects of the country such as the instances of North American military intervention. Dominicans themselves, whether serious commentators and analysts of history or ordinary citizens engaged in a fast-paced game of dominoes, still argue passionately about exactly why the United States invaded their small island. The Dominican Republic without its western neighbor Haiti is truly a tiny country. A mere 18,800 square miles, Quisqueya could easily fit twice inside the borders of either Nebraska or Kansas, with room to spare. There are more people living in metropolitan Philadelphia— some nine and a half million—than the total population of the island. What possible threat did this minuscule Caribbean nation pose to the colossal United States that military intervention was deemed necessary? What circumstances, real or imagined, warranted the total seizure of the country's customs operations, as well as the takeover of other internal financial institutions? And then for the United States Marines to remain for a period of eight years there—why?

Expanding United States Hegemony

Even the most cursory overview of North American entanglement in the domestic affairs of various Latin American countries after the

Spanish-American War (1898) reveals the evolving of a steadily aggressive interventionist policy. So the case of the Dominican Republic in 1916 was certainly not an altogether unrelated incident in the total scheme of things. The United States' presence in the Caribbean Basin became immediately prominent upon official North American acquisition of the tropical island paradises of Cuba and Puerto Rico. The very brief but bitter Spanish-American War ended with the vanquished Spanish Crown having to surrender Cuba, Puerto Rico, and the Pacific islands of the Philippines to United States jurisdiction.

These territories subsequently were transformed into colonial dependencies of Washington, D.C. As the Northern Colossus penetrated ever more deeply into the internal affairs of the individual islands of the Caribbean, the more it was perceived—at least by Washington— that the route of military intervention in the region was essential for maintaining order and stability there. The United States military invasion and accompanying occupation of 1916–1924 in Quisqueya, therefore, was merely a key component of the rapidly emerging pattern of expanding North American political and economic hegemony in the Caribbean and Latin America generally. According to leading proponents of the widening role of North American capitalism during the era following the Spanish-American War, economic stability was regarded as the single basic tenet upon which any thoroughly modern, sophisticated nation could successfully be erected. All across the region, the United States had been fast positioning itself as mentor and master in terms of the ideal example for political and economic maturity. Direct United States intervention was thus inevitable once policymakers in Washington convinced themselves that solely by means of responsibly managing the finances of these countries could it then be feasible to restructure the existing political conduct—considered immature by North Americans—in the Caribbean.

Inter-American Relations: An Era of Shame

Upon examining inter-American relations from a historical perspective, one will readily find, without exaggeration, that such relations have been tarnished by gross misunderstanding and much misinformation, constantly resurfacing hostilities and antagonisms, dangerous suspicions, and mistrust over a rather lengthy period. In large measure and in a very shameful fashion, the United States in its dealing with the nations of the Caribbean and Latin American, historically, has been propelled by a two-pronged objective: (1) to prevent the entry into the hemisphere of any competing economic rivals, and (2) to guarantee and secure the politico-economic hegemony of the United State alone in the region. Therefore, it has been perceived as absolutely vital that governments in the region be maintained as stable and dependable allies that could safeguard North American economic interests. Initially it was a matter of simply developing trade and financial investments; but these efforts were hampered by severe limitations imposed by belligerent European nations with similar motives.

Earlier, in 1823, after recognizing the sovereignty of the newly independent Hispanic nations,[1] and in part after preventing designs by either Spain or its European cohorts to attempt acquisition anew of American territories, United States President James Monroe issued a kind of restraining order. The Monroe Doctrine (1822), admit some commentators, has profoundly influenced United States foreign policy in Latin America by proclaiming its serious opposition to European intervention in the hemisphere. This doctrine established the very foundation of United States continental hegemony, clearly expressing the idea of political spheres of influence. Not unnoticed, however, were the frequently repeated instances of shameless hypocrisy on the part of the doctrine's creators. The United States itself appears to have been left unchecked regarding similar condemned acts of intervention.[2] North American commercial and political interests completely ignored the restraints. Never referred to as an act of intervention were such subsequent actions as the series of events leading to the United States–Mexico War (1846), Puerto Rican annexation of 1898, or the takeover of Cuba between 1901 and 1934.

The Big Stick and Dollar Diplomacy

It is generally conceded that the American public figure most closely associated with United States expansion into the Caribbean and Latin America, at the cost of regional sovereignty, is Theodore Roosevelt, the Rough Rider. Under President Roosevelt, the United States government began fostering the view that it alone had an absolutely legitimate right to control the region of the Caribbean and Central America. Aggressive economic investment or political and military pressures would achieve this hegemony. This same Rough Rider in 1904 redefined the

Monroe Doctrine by justifying those so-called pressures when he declared that it was "the duty of the United States to intervene in those wretched banana republics in order to protect and assure the economic investments and interests of the civilized nations."[3] This novel interpretation of the original doctrine, the Roosevelt Corollary, thus introduced the period that became known as the Era of the Big Stick. Typical of the period was the frequency and degree of violent military interventions executed by the United States government. After Roosevelt, United States Presidents William Howard Taft and Woodrow Wilson both continued this interventionist policy in the region. The Caribbean Sea was fast being converted into the North American Sea. Taft's program focused on substituting dollars for bullets and was a program designed to insure regional stability by means of rather hard-to-ignore economic incentives. Taft's particular reading of the Roosevelt Corollary became the cornerstone of what was called "dollar diplomacy." La República Dominicana, among several other countries, was a classic example of just how initial North American private investment capital in the region almost overnight positioned the United States into easily monopolizing the national economies of these indebted nations.

President Wilson, for instance, promoted his own personal philosophy regarding how and what should be the specific nature of government in the countries of Latin America and the Caribbean. True liberty and democracy for all the countries in the region were not the lofty ideals allowed for determining the direction of United States foreign policy there. Under a variety of pretexts, United States military forces intervened most violently in Latin America: Panamá (1903–1914 and again in 1918–1920), Cuba (1898–1908 and 1917–1922), Nicaragua (1912–1925 and 1926–1933), Mexico (1914 and 1918), Haiti (1915–1934), and finally the Dominican Republic (1916–1924). So for the first three decades of this century, the United States had acquired supreme domination of a major portion—actually the lion's share—of the national economies of several strategic countries in the region.

This domination, perhaps most especially in the Caribbean, established a debilitating and certainly humiliating state of political dependency and subservience of these nations to the will and might of the northern colossus. Finally by 1933, another Roosevelt, a cousin to the former Rough Rider, Franklin D. Roosevelt, tried improving relations between the United States and Latin America. His Good Neighbor

Policy was designed to reject direct intervention into the domestic affairs of neighbor states. Repealing several notoriously offensive measures and withdrawing the Marines from occupied areas, Roosevelt sought to build a positive new spirit of cooperation and unity among the hemisphere's family of sovereign nations. Nevertheless, the utter shallowness and continued hypocrisy of this new focus became apparent with Roosevelt's approval and support of strong economic investment in the region. Roosevelt declared gone forever the earlier days of dollar diplomacy. Now more aggressively than previously, however, economic expansion was the clear and single objective. Of course, before such expansion could occur, totally assured social and political stability had to be solidly in place. Before any meaningful progress and modernization could be realized, the sociopolitical climate had to be most favorable.

The United States Marines in La República Dominicana

The assassination of the Dominican President Ulises Lilís Heureaux (1899), in addition to creating a leadership vacuum that pushed the nation to the brink of yet another revolution, seriously aggravated an already uneasy financial dilemma. The country was plagued by heavy financial indebtedness to various European creditor-nations, all demanding immediate repayment of outstanding loans. The creditors were threatening armed invasion of the island in order to collect their debts. At this precise moment, the United States stepped in with calculated strategies to prevent a foreign government (i.e., any of the European creditor-nations) from invading the hemisphere. Washington would act as a kind of collection agent for the foreign creditors. The United States was successful in exerting pressure on the Dominican government to permit American financial experts to assume total responsibility for the customs revenue of La República Dominicana. According to American officials, such a measure would satisfy the assertions of foreign bondholders that the *dominicanos* were "financially inept and irresponsible."

By the time Juan Isidro Jimenes was inaugurated as the new Dominican president (1914), a now irritated United States had imposed additional reforms on the Dominican government.[4] This was without question a government that the North Americans had assisted very intensively in creating. Among the amended list of proposals tailored to restructure the island's government was one in particular that prompted naked outrage in the Dominican Congress. This measure stipulated that a North American official be named director of public works in the island. Another bitterly contentious measure called for a special financial adviser, again another so-called American expert, to assist the Dominican president. This adviser would actually be responsible for shaping and drafting the national budget, which would then be enforced by requiring the adviser's personal authorization for each listed expenditure! Still another humiliating stipulation in the new set of structured reforms concerned the all-important customs receivership. This receivership was broadened by means of an entirely new and essential function: collecting and controlling all the internal revenue of the country.

Finally, the United States demanded that the Dominican government disband its armed forces and replace them with a national police force—commanded by North American officers. When the Dominican Congress vociferously refused to accept these drastic proposals, and after repeated threats by the United States to dispatch armed troops to force compliance and implementation of the reforms, the United States Marines finally landed in Santo Domingo in April and May of 1916. Occupation of Quisqueya was under way, with ominous warships sailing to Puerto Plata, Sánchez, and San Pedro de Macorís. The United States military government was set up under Marine Captain Harry Knapp. A parade of successive North American military governors was appointed to La República Dominicana with names like Anderson, Pendleton, Fuller, Snowden, and Robinson—none of whom, by the way, spoke a word of Spanish!

Remaking Dominican Society

The United States military government under the newly appointed military governor Knapp attempted to remake Dominican society from top to bottom, redefining and redesigning various programs to be executed on the island. These measures were meant to transform the country's political, economic, and social life. Any discernible degree of social discontent had to be quelled; any flames of insurrection had to be immediately extinguished. From the very moment that the occupation forces landed at Santo Domingo, the country had lost its autonomy. The United States was quite secure in its perceived mission of something called Manifest Destiny—a vague, self-professed notion of destined grandeur coupled with the obsession for territorial expansion. The northern colossus remained steadfast in its conviction—as it saw it—of manifesting the moral obligation to police and dominate the hemisphere, and also presumably to instruct the Latin Americans in self-governance and fiscal responsibility following a prescribed North American formula, until which time the North Americans regarded the Latins as having *advanced to maturity.*

One of the first measures enacted by the occupying government to ensure total control of La República Dominicana was to disarm the general population, prohibiting the citizenry from carrying armed weapons. If nothing else, some commentators have remarked, this action was effective in bringing about an end to the violent local wars among rival caudillos. Another enactment was local press censorship, thus putting an end to public hostile expression against the United States' military presence in the island.

In addition to the general resistance mounted by *dominicanos* who populated the major urban centers around the nation, a most spectacular resistance movement grew out of the popular antagonisms that had been long smoldering among the masses of inhabitants in the rural eastern region of the country.

In the province of El Seibo, in particular, the *campesinos* waged a tactical guerrilla war against the new foreign invaders. What was noteworthy about the character of this resistance campaign here (as opposed to the other, urban middle-class sector) was that this rural sector was made up of a heterogeneous sociopolitical cadre, unified by the common repudiation of the unwelcome presence of foreign military troops, the common enemy. The study of Dominican resistance during this period is a very pivotal component in the complete story of the occupation because the resistance itself is so closely tied to the military government. The opposition campaign became so strong that it seriously impeded the overall operation of the military regime, subsequently forcing the invaders to act upon definite plans to withdraw. Sugarcane workers, along with other agricultural laborers in the eastern region, were most defiant against the sophisticated weaponry and professional military training of the invasion forces. However, for all the technological superiority possessed by the United States forces, to their disadvantage they understood neither their Dominican target nor the nature of the war being fought.

The resistance effort of the rural eastern region was aided by certain outstanding notions about the region itself. The greatest number of *ingenios* was located here. This region had been the hardest hit by the effects of the earlier expansion of sugarcane estate owners, most of whom were foreigners. Even most of the export-import trade was in the hands of foreign ownership. North American and other foreign sugarmills were being converted into elitist capitalist enclaves, wholly insensitive to and disconnected from the lives of the masses of field laborers living in the area. Smaller sugarcane cultivators were rapidly being absorbed by the larger, better financed sugar producers. The smaller regional farmers became little more than *peones* (common day laborers), cane cutters, or even idle vagrants in many instances. Of special note in the new socioeconomic circumstances at this juncture throughout the eastern zone was the increasing degree of foreign domination of the region's industries—again, sugarcane and its byproducts. Outright disdain and resentment greeted this foreign domination. The anger grew out of the widely held opinion that monopoly of the local economy by foreigners was clearly an overt attempt to create a kind of neocolonial dependency. Most foreign investment, often eagerly encouraged by the Dominican governments over the years, in setting up sugarmills to supply the market of the investor-nation (or for export only) did nothing to stimulate development of local entrepreneurship. Consequently, there was no demonstrated concern or sensitivity on the part of these foreign investors for local economic growth or even employment.

Guerrilla Warfare in the East

Two crucial elements predating the North American invasion were present in the eastern zone that help further explain the growing hostility and resentment of most of that region's inhabitants. The zone was first of all in the midst of the economic transformation described above. The entire area changed quite rapidly from one that had long been dominated by traditional subsistence agriculture and grazing into a modern, capitalist-oriented sugar-producing center. Secondly, the unusual political system traditionally prevalent in the region was a key factor in trying to understand the nature of the resistance movement there. The archaic political model of the traditional caudillo system, a relic of nineteenth-century Latin America, might describe political power in the East. Long remaining out of the mainstream focus of progress and modernization that factored into the development of the

Republic's more sophisticated urban centers like Santo Domingo, Santiago, or Puerto Plata, that portion of the rural eastern zone only minutes outside the important urban hub of San Pedro de Macorís was ruled by very powerful, influential caudillos. These militaristic strongmen operated with unopposed authority and frequently by violent intimidation. They enjoyed a significantly wide popular allegiance among the inhabitants of very carefully delineated territorial boundaries.

Los Gavilleros

So with clear reasons, for five and a half blood-soaked years, the United States Marines were totally unsuccessful in controlling most of the eastern half of the occupied República Dominicana. The *campesinos* engaged in a formidable guerrilla insurrection in the east that nearly wrecked the reform campaign being implemented across the entire country. This impressive rural guerrilla movement was called *los gavilleros,* a word in the Dominican cultural context meaning rural bandit. But were these patriotic resistance fighters really bandits? Above all else, according to the island's most respected historians, *los gavilleros* were fiercely nationalistic, authentic Dominicans who were determined to reclaim the sovereignty of their beloved Quisqueya. Their goal was simple and direct: to end the United States occupation of the island. This was not unlike the goal of the original sandinista movement in Nicaragua some years later, in the 1920s.[5]

Many of the men and women who fought with the caudillo-led bands of *gavilleros* were laborers from the *bateys*[6] (sugarcane workers' quarters) of the area. The battle contingents were made up of the rural dispossessed, the unemployed, the exploited sugar plantation workers, and even the threatened small landowners—all engaged collectively in an intensive campaign of resistance to the presence of armed and dominating foreigners. All too often, as has been recorded, the animosity among these easterners was fanned by the attitudes and practices of racial superiority on the part of the occupying military personnel. Such abusive, belligerent anti-Black sentiment openly exhibited by more than a few members of the invasion forces often heightened existing tensions and provoked physical altercations, even random murder of innocent Dominican citizens. The *gavilleros,* of course, were not unmindful of such arrogant and unacceptable abuses. The overwhelming rural population in the eastern zone was then, as it is currently, dark-skinned. By contrast, the inhabitants of the island's northern zone are usually much lighter in skin color and were not met with nearly the degree of blatant racial bigotry from the North Americans.

One of the most well-known groups of *gavilleros* operating in San Pedro de Macorís and the eastern provinces was that commanded by Eustacio Bullito Reyes. The movement's most prominent leader overall, however, was a *campesino* named Ramón Natera. On many occasions group leaders had previously been popular regional caudillos who had participated actively in any number of uprisings against various Dominican governments during the period before the United States intervention. Martín Peguero, Vicentico, Chacha, and Tolete were leaders whose legendary names and heroic resistance are still remembered throughout parts of the eastern region. This nationalist peasant resistance was probably the very first instance in Latin American/Caribbean history wherein North American interventionist forces employed aerial bombing and machine gun artillery against local insurgents.

Consequences of United States Military Occupation

The occupation lasted a total of eight grueling years, with the occupying forces learning very little about the Dominicans, their history and culture, or their psyche. Exactly what, then, was ultimately accomplished by the designs of such a lengthy and costly military expedition on foreign shores? What may be questionable in the view of some contemporary analysts and interpreters of that particular episode in Dominican history is the actual extent of economic growth and modernization. On the other hand, what is certainly not debatable is the brutal enforcement of an obsessive policy of political stability favorable to North American investment interests in the island. This stability was guaranteed by the implementation of major programs and reforms such as the creation of the Dominican Republic's first adequate road network, expansion and improvement of the country's public education system, and the beginning of national public health and sanitation programs. There was also significant overhaul of the Dominican treasury, the tax system, the tariff structure, and the courts and the judiciary. It was precisely during this controversial and bitter period of military occupation that the notion of a public works program became a keystone in the strategic arsenal of future local administrations. Good and efficient government came to be synonymous with massive construction projects.

A very important economic consequence of the United States military occupation centered around major protectionist measures shrewdly tailored to favor the tax-exempt entry of North American manufactured consumer goods into La República Dominicana. Without question, such measures stifled the development and growth of local industry much in the same way that today's system of *zona franca* (free trade zone) operates in the country. The military government encouraged and was largely responsible for the almost miraculous expansion of the sugar industry. In fact, through a series of carefully crafted albeit questionable legislative maneuvers, North American sugar firms were permitted legally to expropriate land for the expansion of sugar plantations. The traditional Dominican land titles system had been completely altered and twisted in order to accommodate United States capitalist investments. As a result, the island's economy was converted into a plantation economy, dependent upon world sugar prices.

On the sociopsychological front, the military occupation must be viewed as having left indelible scars on the Dominican psyche. It may indeed be difficult to measure the exact severity of the North Americanization process that most assuredly took place in the island. A definite cultural incursion became obvious, however. Even in terms of seemingly innocuous social recreation, for example, this incursion was felt in considerable depth. North American–style baseball replaced forever the more widely played soccer (called *fútbol* in Latin America), which is easily the most common sport played throughout all Latin America. Simultaneously, though, the United States military presence engendered a stronger Dominican nationalism than would perhaps have been expected. What became evident was a more forceful and deliberate self-conscious celebration of things Dominican. The country's social elite, for instance, attached themselves more fervently with what was to become the national dance, the merengue. This dance and its rhythms had traditionally been closely identified with the proletariat class.

Finally, on the issue of sociopsychological consequences, some commentators have pointed out that the racism ingrained in the attitude and behavior of members of the occupying forces noticeably intensified the more subtle forms of this disease that existed in the island's society well prior to the 1916 invasion. Every conceivable facet of Dominican life was touched by the superimposed military presence of the United States Marines. For eight years, the notion of Dominicans exercising the right of governing themselves was abrogated completely. One especially macabre aspect of the military governance was that it taught by painfully direct example the advantages of repressive methods of controlling human beings. The lesson was undeniably vigorously received by members of the Guardia Nacional, now solely responsible for maintaining order throughout the island.

Final Withdrawal

The cruel irony of the massive effort of the United States military government to bring order, stability, progress, and modernization to La República Dominicana was that the biggest winners were not the Dominicans but the North Americans. In fact, *los dominicanos,* according to many contemporary commentators, ultimately paid very heavily. The occupying military government had implemented a series of major reforms with the intention of remaking the very core and character of the Dominican system, sociopolitical and economic. While the eight-year ordeal of occupation did produce some rather tangible changes, nevertheless to this day the question remains controversial and debatable whether such changes were essential to the overall vitality of Dominican traditions. For all the pragmatic and immediate solutions to several lingering, pressing domestic issues and concerns, the ultimate consequences of the invasion were harmful in the view of many *dominicanos* today.

One of the most damaging results was the infectious anti–United States sentiment and antagonism that lasted for a long time afterward. Another harmful aspect of the military occupation to the *dominicanos* was their humiliating loss of hard-won gains to determine the course of their own national destiny and to charter creative, self-tailored blueprints and schemes for maximally developing their nation. The relentless struggle waged by fearless Dominican nationalists, both men and women alike, to regain and protect their sovereignty, ridding the island of foreign invaders and occupiers, was the primary cause of the inevitable United States military withdrawal. The intensely fought wars of resistance were extremely successful in making more difficult the already arduous task of operating a military government on foreign soil. For all its internal divisiveness and petty squabbling, the newly formed National Party (Unión Nacional) gained broad support across the island and mobilized divergent segments of the Dominican populace in committed response to the intolerable repressiveness of military rule.

Upon its final departure from Quisqueya, the North American military machine did not dismantle altogether its repressive operation. Rather, probably the single most undisputed legacy of United States intervention was the very important introduction of a new stabilizing force in the country, the Guardia Nacional. Working hand-in-glove with the implemented reforms (especially the new, improved system of roads and communications facilities), the elite corps of Dominican military personnel was super-efficient and zealous in maintaining order. It quickly became the supreme instrument of control throughout the land. The Dominican masses, having been thoroughly disarmed, now lay naked and defenseless against the excesses of power executed by whichever military officer—now Dominican instead of foreign— was willful and bold enough to attempt grabbing absolute control of the Guardia.

Such an individual could ultimately reign with impunity over the entire country. With the exit of United States troops, the job of keeping the peace would be left to the new North American–created and trained Dominican military machine. The new commander-in-chief, El Jefe, of the sophisticated Policía Nacional Dominicana (National Dominican Police), whose name would change in 1928 to Ejército Nacional (National Army), was an obscure but obsessively ambitious young career soldier named Rafael Leonidas Trujillo. On September 18, 1924, after eight years of frustrating occupation, the United States Marines withdrew from La República Dominicana.

Notes

1. The proclamation of a slave-free, independent Republic of Haiti in 1804 did not receive official diplomatic recognition from the United States government until 1861.

2. The Platt Amendment of 1902 (named for United States Senator O. H. Platt of Connecticut) was designed to place restrictions upon Cuba's activities in order to make the island safe for foreign capital investment. Among other provisions, the Cuban government was limited in its power to make treaties with foreign nations. The Cubans also promised to provide fueling or naval stations to the United States. However, the most horrendous feature of the measure was the provision that unmistakably defined Cuba as a protectorate of the United States, virtually sanctioning the United States military takeover of the island. Abrogation of the amendment would not come until 1934.

3. CEDEE, *Escarbando las Raíces de la Explotación,* p. 34.

4. The United States was particularly vexed since it had covertly manipulated Jimenes's successful bid for the presidency. The new president, in addition to being grateful and indebted, was quite amenable to almost all the United States proposals for reform in the Dominican Republic.

5. During the period of United States intervention in Nicaragua, guerrilla leader General Augusto César Sandino refused to accept the imposition of North American military rule and thus led a protracted resistance struggle throughout the country. Sandino is regarded by Nicaraguans today as their most genuine patriot and national hero. The name Sandino symbolizes courage and resistance to oppression throughout Latin America generally.

6. *Bateys* are company-owned worker camps or villages adjacent to the sugar-cane fields.

21

The Era of Trujillo
1930–1961

In describing the Era of Trujillo, which refers to the period in Dominican history when the country was under the tightly clenched iron fist of General Rafael Leonidas Trujillo, one noted present-day social commentator puts it this way:

> Para ser dominicano auténtico e integral es necesario conservar una memoria permanente e inmodificable de las vicisitudes y las declinaciones sufridas por la personalidad nacional en todos los sentidos, durante la Era de Trujillo.[1]

> (In order to be an authentic and complete Dominican, it is necessary to preserve a lasting and unalterable memory of the vicissitudes and deterioration suffered on the part of the national personality, in every sense, during the Era of Trujillo.)

These are the words of Dr. José Francisco Peña Gómez, leader of the Partido Revolucionario Dominicano.

Peña Gómez, quite the eloquent polemicist, over the years has argued vehemently the case for remembrance. It is now a generally accepted truth that the Trujillo Era converted the Dominican nation into a kind of chamber of psychological tortures, as well as physical and spiritual horror. Peña Gómez has presented the case for the neces-

178

sity of creating a national consciousness in the island's newer generations. Today's generations in La República Dominicana are being reminded constantly that the Trujillo Era, which saw the country turn into a tightly run prison camp, operated under the absolute control of a single man, governing with the roughness and oftentimes insanity of a sadistic plantation overseer of the earlier centuries in the island's history.

The power of Trujillo's reprisals was so great that it stretched even to the interpretation of intentions of practically every Dominican. Many people today say that, during this nightmarish period of fear and intimidation, some citizens were actually punished for not mentioning El Jefe (The Chief) at solemn public functions, or for listening to inflammatory anti-Trujillo radio programs that were, of course, broadcast from outside La República Dominicana.[2] One of the clearest consequences of the United States occupation by the marines from 1916 to 1924 was the very powerful military machine erected by the North Americans, and eventually the particular Dominican personality selected to head up its operation, Rafael Leonidas Trujillo. This ambitious military officer rose to prominence in the midst of a national economic crisis stemming from foreign debt obligations. He ruled in the most brutal and ruthless manner imaginable, eliminating his opposition by direct means of forced exile, torture, extortion, imprisonment, and even murder. Trujillo had organized a band of professional terrorists called La Cuarentidos (the Forty-Second), that spread fear throughout the island.

Trujillo's shameless acts of rape and pillage of the nation's economy began by his obtaining an exclusive contract with the Dominican army to provide laundry service to soldiers, whose monthly salary was taxed for this expenditure. From prostitution to house paint, from exporting fruit to acquiring monopoly rights to the production and sale of such staples as salt, meat, rice, and milk, Trujillo used cunning political power and the military to enrich himself and his family. *El banquito* (the little bank) was a loan-shark service managed by his wife, María Martínez. The operation, which was housed in an actual bank building, allowed public employees to cash their salary checks ahead of time—and they were encouraged to do so—for a stipulated fee. Moreover, all public employees, whether Supreme Court justice, senator, or humble office filing clerk, were required to pay 10 percent of their salary to the Partido Dominicano. It was said that during Trujillo's rule *los dominicanos* couldn't eat, sleep, wear shoes, or put on any article of clothing without Trujillo or a member of his family benefiting in some form or another. From the very start, the Dominican government was a vehicle for Trujillo's personal aggrandizement. The reconstruction of state apparatus was a convenient pretext for the exaltation and promotion of his self-perceived glory. Trujillo was made to appear as the restorer of financial independence, for example, when he enacted measures to liquidate the enormous foreign debt. The administration of customs was placed back in the hands of Dominican functionaries, but all the collected revenue was deposited directly—and immediately—in the National City Bank of New York.

Economically, the thirty-two-year dictatorial reign of Trujillo uncannily duplicated the Somoza model in Nicaragua and the Duvalier pattern somewhat later in neighboring Haiti. Trujillo meticulously and very shrewdly brought huge portions of the Dominican national economy under his personal control. He turned the island into his personal fief. When it became expedient for him to occupy the presidency, he presented himself as a candidate amid the spectacle of farce. When it better suited his purposes on occasion for the country to offer an "acceptable image" for the international community, Trujillo duly appointed carefully selected individuals to occupy the presidential chair. Four such personally appointed individuals for this purpose included Jacinto Peynado, Dr. Manuel Troncoso, Hector Trujillo (one of El Jefe's brothers), and Dr. Joaquín Balaguer. By the end of his life, Trujillo and his family controlled nearly 80 percent of the nation's industrial production; they possessed well over half of the island's economic assets. More than 45 percent of Trujillo-owned enterprises employed more than 40 percent of the total work force in La República Dominicana. Again, like the Somoza dynasty in Nicaragua, Trujillo industries were employing about 15 percent of the country's population. An estimated 60 percent of Dominican families depended upon Trujillo's economic octopus. It came as no surprise to anyone that all the newly constructed roads easily led directly to Trujillo's plantations and factories; most certainly the new harbors benefited Trujillo's shipping and lucrative export enterprises.

Father of the New Nation

Trujillo had hoped that the Catholic Church would bestow upon him the supreme title, Benefactor de la Iglesia (Benefactor of the Church).

However, the Church refused to do so. In just two or three years in power, all the institutions in the Dominican Republic were surrendered as pawns to the ruthless will of El Benefactor and his despotic reign. In an act of self-paid homage, he daringly changed the nation's capital city—which for centuries had been called Santo Domingo—to Ciudad Trujillo (Trujillo City). From the very outset, Trujillo the tyrant and Trujillo the capitalist were two distinct characters that were forged together in monolithic and calculating fashion, ultimately presenting an overpowering persona. As he grew richer and richer, gaining spectacular economic power and unquestioned supreme domination over the entire country, Trujillo simultaneously constructed a jealously guarded autonomy in terms of the nation. By the time of the outbreak of World War II, La República Dominicana found itself governed by the Trujillo Machine, not by Rafael Leonidas Trujillo the man. Throughout the long, agonizing thirty-two years of dictatorial rule, the Trujillo government executed the most grandiose plan of public works ever undertaken in the island until that time.[3] These massive construction projects created an economic infrastructure that catered shamelessly to and benefited the exclusive interests of the bourgeois capitalist elite. This privileged sector was headed by none other than El Padre de la Patria Nueva (The Father of the New Nation).

In terms of agricultural development, La República Dominicana under the Trujillo Machine encouraged an effective campaign to stimulate crop production across the island. It might correctly be noted that a rudimentary kind of agrarian reform program was initiated when large numbers of *campesinos* were resettled on abandoned farmland, introduced to innovative methods of production, and then given the seeds to plant. The hope was to lift the country into the position of self-sufficiency in those designated areas of basic crop needs: corn, beans, rice. Another control of this traditional industry by Trujillo complemented the modernization process that was under way in the nation's economic and industrial sectors. Trujillo's economic power was still considerably less than that of the North American sugar corporations, which were growing steadily more intrusive in the economic, political, and social life of the country. El Benefactor utilized both state funds and his own private resources to buy up most of the other foreign *ingenios* that were operating around the island, thus easily becoming the principal noncorporation sugar producer. The only profitable sugarmills that Trujillo was not successful in acquiring were those belonging to the highly influential and shrewd Casa Vincinci, and the powerful South Porto Rico Sugar Company, under ownership of the super-wealthy Central Romana.

The Parsley Test

Question: How do you distinguish on sight a Haitian from a Dominican? Answer: You can't. So, you give him or her the parsley test! This is exactly what happened during the infamous *Masacre de los haitianos* (Massacre of the Haitians) in early October of 1937, when Trujillo's death squads were given direct orders to kill Haitians! The macabre and sinister *operación perijil* (the parsley test) was considered the one foolproof method of uncovering who actually was or was not Haitian among the Black population within the Dominican society, especially those individuals of African descent living along the Dominican-Haitian border zone. Here, the term *castiza*[4] is used to describe persons born to a cross-cultural Dominican/Haitian couple. Even today, many such unions in the border zone are quite commonplace. Trujillo had devised a strategy whereby the Dominican soldier would simply hold up in front of the suspected Black person a leaf of parsley and ask him, "What is this?" Haitians living among Dominicans, although possessing a thoroughly convincing knowledge of Spanish, often have serious difficulty pronouncing the language correctly. For instance, the Spanish *r* and *j* are especially troublesome for French speakers. Thus, for French- and Kryol-speaking Haitians, it is practically impossible to pronounce with any degree of authenticity and rapidly the Spanish word for parsley, *perejil*.

During the 1937 massacre that began in the border town of Dajabón, roving bands of Trujillo militia administered the parsley test to unsuspecting Haitians who tried to pass themselves off as Dominicans. But not just Haitians became victims of the persecution. Throughout the border zone, anyone of African descent found incapable of pronouncing correctly, that is, to the complete satisfaction of the sadistic examiners, became a condemned individual. This holocaust is recorded as having a death toll reaching thirty thousand innocent souls, Haitians as well as Dominicans, and spread across perhaps seventy-five localities of La República Dominicana. Some observers today ask whether General Trujillo was afterwards satisfied that he had succeeded in diminishing the African presence in Dominican national life and on

Dominican soil. Throughout contemporary Dominican society, Haitians number perhaps one million among the nation's population.

Trujillo's Haitian Phobia

It was often said that Trujillo was relentless in his attempts to gain acceptance into the select inner circles of the country's bourgeois elite. He had never been regarded as one of them. Rather, he was always the outsider, or the interloper. Although Trujillo was admittedly one of the nation's wealthiest individuals, he nevertheless possessed neither the prerequisite family geneology nor the racial stock nor the moral character that traditionally typified the composition of this exclusive sector of Dominican society. He therefore paid his way into favor by means of classic Machiavellian tactics, which he had mastered superbly. Trujillo quite early in his lengthy career had learned to manipulate to his best advantage a given situation or event that had potentially explosive properties if ignited. Haiti again proved one such instance.

Driven primarily by chronic economic depression and abject misery in their own homeland, Haitians seeking a better life for themselves and their families had been quietly trekking across the border into territory of their eastern neighbor since the period of the First Republic (1844–1861). They would settle as squatters on abandoned farmland, and work in the sugarcane fields as cutters or in Dominican households as servants. These Haitian immigrants also engaged heavily in commerce as traders and merchants. These various Haitian workers were always marginal people, staying safely just inside the limits of the law and avoiding all manner of conflict or antagonism with local Dominicans. Intermingling, intermarriage, and commercial interchange had long been commonplace. Haitian currency, for example, had been welcome as the medium of exchange in Mao and Santiago, and as far south as Azua. It is still not entirely known to what extent this occupation by large concentrations of Haitians seriously antagonized the masses of Dominicans in these areas. When Trujillo traveled to the border town of Dajabón in 1937, he is reported to have used the occasion to launch a venomous tirade against the growing presence and influence of Haitians throughout *la frontera:*

> ¡Los haitianos! Su presencia en nuestro territorio no puede más que deteriorar las condiciones de vida de nuestros nacionales. Esa

ocupación de los haitianos de las tierras fronterizas no debía continuar. Está ordenado que todos los haitianos que hubiera en el país fuesen exterminados.[5]

(Haitians! Their presence in our territory can't do anything else but worsen the living conditions of our own people. The Haitian occupation of the border zones must not continue. It is ordered that all Haitians that are in the country be exterminated.)

The Massacre

A few days later, Trujillo gave the order literally to kill Haitians wherever they might be found throughout La República Dominicana. So quite insanely began the indiscriminate pogrom of thousands of Black Haitians and Dominicans alike. The River Dajabón after the horrendous butchering became known as the Río Masacre (Massacre River). Even as the international community expressed a numbed disbelief and outrage at this barbarous act of genocide, within the Dominican Republic itself there were staunch supporters of the regime who orchestrated an effective propaganda campaign to portray El Benefactor as having acted to defend Dominican sovereignty and nationhood. What had provoked this Caribbean holocaust? Was he uneasy about the widening sociopolitical influence of the Haitians residing in these border zones? Was he motivated by the already evident racism that was a traditionally persistent element in the psyche of the dominant social stratum into which the dictator himself fought so obsessively to penetrate?

The Process of Dominicanization

While we will perhaps never know the exact reasons, psychological or otherwise, that explain Trujillo's nefarious actions, we do know that just a few years following that gruesome event in 1937, Trujillo was fostering an aggressive immigration scheme to entice Jewish, Spanish, Lebanese, and other European refugees to resettle in Dominican territory. About 1939–1940, for example, the Trujillo government arranged for Jewish refugees, particularly German and Austrian Ashkenazim, to be settled at Sosúa on the north coast, on land donated by El Benefactor himself. The influx of Caucasians into the island was therefore not unintentional. Had this been El Jefe's way of *blanqueando* (whitening up) a nation that he personally felt was just a bit too dark? Even by early 1937, the tone of the island's immigration policy had been set by a rather clear statement by Trujillo himself:

> Se precisa una gran cantidad de inmigrantes de la raza blanca. Los emigrantes deberán de ser españoles, italianos y también de orígen francés. Los de orígen caucásico deberán pagar seis pesos por el permiso de residencia; los que no sean de ese orígen deberán pagar quinientos pesos.[6]

> (A great quantity of immigrants of the White race is needed. The immigrants shall be Spanish, Italian, and also of French origin. Immigrants of Caucasian stock shall pay a fee of six pesos for the residency permit and those not of such origin shall pay 500 pesos.)

What followed next in El Jefe's design to offset the disgrace of the so-called border conflicts, as the regime chose to refer to the holocaust, was a calculated government process that came to be known as Dominicanization. This scheme was to be implemented throughout the border zone. The plan included actually constructing entirely new towns and full communities, together with the required military installations, all along the freshly drawn borderline between the two countries. The underlying idea of this Dominicanization process was to regain Dominican territory that had been lost to Haiti during the period dating back to Toussaint L'Ouverture and to the Haitian invasions of the First Republic.[7] With these successful efforts, the border issue was perhaps finally settled once these traditionally disputed zones were at last integrated into the central Dominican administrative unit.

The Fall of Trujillo

Generalissimo Trujillo succeeded in winning, although not surprisingly, the approval and support of the United States government by means of various channels of appeasement and compromise on the part of the Dominicans. Despite whatever manner and intensity of human rights atrocities were perpetrated against the Dominican (and Haitian) people, as long as Trujillo stabilized the country and made it safe and profitable for United States investment, Washington had totally deaf ears and blinded eyes on Trujillo's corrupt fiefdom. "Trujillo is a true son of a bitch!" President Franklin Roosevelt is often quoted as having said, "but he's *our* son of a bitch!" By the late 1940s, Trujillo was proclaiming himself champion of anticommunism in the Americas. Of course, Duvalier and Somoza would do likewise. This particular stance of El Jefe garnered him considerable favoritism from United States government and business sectors.

The era of the 1950s really ignited the smoldering undercurrent of discontent and disillusion throughout La República Dominicana. Anti-Trujillo conspiracies became almost commonplace. A threatening economic crisis of major proportions in the country consumed the attention of the regime. Trujillo reacted with anticipated irrationality. His exclusion of foreign capital from lucrative domestic ventures and his unforgivable, despicable assassination attempts against the lives of strongly vocal opposition, both inside and outside the island, all became openly negative factors in the arsenal against El Benefactor. Trujillo's inevitable fall must also be placed within the broader context of the Caribbean regional crisis at this precise juncture, politically, economically, and socially. Instead of taking positive, rational steps to confront this regional turmoil, the Trujillo Machine, fast disintegrating as it was, greatly aggravated matters with counterproductive measures.

With the unexpected success of the Cuban Revolution (1959) when the young Fidel Castro trampled the United States–backed Fulgencio Batista government, tremendous fears surfaced that Trujillo himself was fomenting conditions for another Cuba. The names Enrique Jiménez Moya, Juan Isidro Jiménez Grullón, and Manuel Tavárez became names associated with an armed anti-Trujillo movement, Movimiento Clandestino 14 de Junio (Clandestine Movement of June 14). A bold, heavily armed expedition force made up of exiled *dominicanos* and *revolucionarios* from several other Latin American nations attempted an invasion of the island (1959). Although the invasion failed to achieve its determined mission of bringing down the Trujillo machine, its overall impact upon the political consciousness of *el pueblo dominicano* was incalculable.

Another sensational incident took place in 1960 when Trujillo made a truly bold assassination attempt upon the life of the president of Venezuela, Rómulo Betancourt. In immediate response and repudiation, the Organization of American States (OAS) imposed comprehensive economic sanctions, supported by the international community, against the Trujillo government. Again, however, as was true in the earlier case of Trujillo's Haitian Massacre of 1937, there was a sizable and loyal contingent of waiting apologists for the regime. Even so, anti-Trujillo activity accelerated around the island. The government's reaction was again predictable: increased repression in the form of brutal reprisals, terrorism, torture, more assassinations. The jails throughout the Dominican Republic were nearly overflowing with arrested political prisoners and suspected conspirators. Still talked about today in the island is the almost storybook incident of *las hermanas Mirabal* (the Mirabal sisters). The Mirabal sisters came to symbolize most dramatically the dangerous yet strong resistance to Trujillo. Coming from one of the most socially prominent families in the town of Salcedo, the three sisters were murdered in brutal fashion because of their political activism against the Trujillo machine. The tragic tale of Patria, Minerva, and María Teresa, who refused to succumb to El Jefe's rule of terror, is presented with poignancy by the extremely talented contemporary Dominican-American author Julia Alvarez in her 1995 novel, *In The Time of the Butterflies.* It was becoming increasingly more apparent in all quarters that with each new incident, Trujillo was becoming more of a real problem for Washington and United States business investment interests. Trujillo had long outlived his usefulness to the United States. In May of 1961, Trujillo was assassinated by a trusted cadre of his personal staff officers, who are said to have used weapons that had been supplied by the CIA. The Era of Trujillo was brought to a close, but still today many *dominicanos* will openly admit that La República Dominicana continues living in the shadow of Trujillo.

Notes

1. José Francisco Peña Gómez, as quoted to the author by Helson Cruz Pineda in a series of taped interview sessions during the summer of 1993 in the town of Barahona. Cruz Pineda is in the process of compiling an anthology of the political and social commentary of Dr. Peña Gómez.

2. During the Trujillo Era it was extremely dangerous to be caught listening to radio programs like "Trinchera Antitrujillista" (Anti-Trujillo Ditch) or the very popular "La Voz de Quisqueya Libre" (The Voice of Free Quisqueya), both of which were broadcast from Venezuela. Most anti-Trujillo propaganda campaigns were naturally conducted from outside the country because of tightly monitored government censorship.

3. The public works ideal had begun at the opening of the century by Ramón Cáceres and was accelerated during the period of United States military occupation.

4. Although in standard Spanish expression, the word *castiza* usually means pure-blooded or of noble descent, throughout the border zone the word takes on—even today—a somewhat ironic twist. Here *castiza* more commonly refers to the offspring of a Haitian-Dominican union.

5. Quoted to the author in a personal interview with local historian Don Julio Félix of Barahona, summer 1993.

6. Francisco R. Herrera Miniño, *Raices, Motivaciones y Fundamentos de la Raza Dominicana,* pp. 67–68.

7. The First Republic was the period between 1844 and 1861, following the success of the Trinitaria Movement leading to the separation of the Dominican Republic and Haiti, and the proclamation of Dominican independence. Turmoil and chaos followed immediately.

22

Living in the Shadow of Trujillo

The period from 1961 to 1966 in Dominican society was undoubtedly one of the most difficult periods in the entire history of La República Dominicana. It was a time for serious reflection and regrouping by every segment of the society. Reflection was in terms of considering the future direction of a community that had been rendered nearly comatose and paralyzed by thirty years of personal excesses of one unquestionably powerful individual, along with members of his family. Regrouping was mainly from the perspective of a drastic sociopolitical conversion and a reawakening of a national consciousness that had been formerly repressed. Democratization and organization, followed by a gripping civil war and yet another agonizing foreign military invasion and subsequent occupation, were the key elements characterizing the period that came in the far-reaching shadow of Trujillo's assassination. Reaction to the Trujillo machine took the form of the emergence of various new political voices with a wide range of objectives and agendas.

New Voices from the Shadows

A few of the new organizations were of lasting influence and popularity. The Movimiento Popular Dominicano (MPD), while of extreme leftist orientation, had been cleverly sanctioned earlier (1960) by El Jefe himself. The bold Unión Cívica Nacional (UCN) enjoyed widespread support under the leadership of the highly respected Dr. Viriato Fiallo. Along with several other exiled intellectuals and political activists, Professor Juan Bosch returned to the island and set up the Partido Revolucionario Dominicano (PRD). Manual Taváres Justo headed up a militant organization, the Partido Revolucionario 14 de Junio, which he had hoped would duplicate in the Dominican Republic the success of the Cuban Revolution. Later on, Dr. Joaquín Balaguer, the last president appointed by Trujillo[1] and kept in office with the backing of the country's new military leadership, would establish the Partido Reformista. By 1978 when Dr. Balaguer won the presidential seat for this fifth term, he would overhaul and strengthen *los reformistas* (reformists; members of the Reformist Party) by altering the name of the defunct Partido Revolucionario Social Cristiano (PRSC), or Christian Social Revolutionary Party, in order to present a new political image. The PRSC would now be known as the Partido Reformista Social Cristiano (Christian Social Reform Party). It was wisely suspected by party leaders that being seen as Christian Democrats would easily win supporters and sympathizers from the international community, who, during this period, were strident in the battle against atheistic Communists.

Calls for a New Constitution

In December of 1962, La República Dominicana held its first free elections in forty years. Some observers say these were the first free elections ever in the island. The people elected Juan Bosch, the PRD candidate, who called for the drafting of a completely new constitution. Because Professor Bosch held theories of government and society that were considered extremely progressive, perhaps even radical for many people in the country, his candidacy was seriously questioned by some groups within the society. Bosch's ideas were regarded as especially threatening to the country's traditionally wealthy landowners, industrialists, businessmen, the military, and the church. Bosch, an intellectual giant, an enlightened visionary whose two principal sources of inspiration have been the country's own history and the social reality of the island, was consequently branded a communist. The tactics of the professor's opposition worked quite effectively, producing a tidal wave of anticommunist sentiment directed against the new constitutional presidency. Throughout the country, Trujillo loyalists and North American business interests, together with a determined band of resident Cuban exiles fanatically opposed to Fidel Castro and the new Cuba, led the anti-Bosch movement to topple the freely elected Dominican government. Bosch had won by a very comfortable margin of over 70 percent of the vote. That didn't seem to matter to his opponent, however. Professor Bosch was overthrown by a right-wing military coup in September of 1963, having held the presidency a mere seven months.

The Triumvirate

In only a few days following the coup, Bosch was replaced by a triumvirate comprised of the Dominican corporate elite and their cadre of attorneys. This governing triumvirate was buttressed by the unified support of the United States government, important segments of the island's Catholic church, and the Trujillista generals of the armed forces. The widespread unpopularity of the new government, scandalously corrupt and abusive in terms of power and privilege, prompted equally universal reactions and counteractions. Various political conspiracies, carefully orchestrated and clandestine military opposition, persistent general strikes by workers and students all sought a common objective—to overthrow the triumvirate. Despite government reprisals, which were swift and severe, public opinion was mobilized in favor of a restoration of the constitution and the reinstatement of the legally elected Bosch government. Most observers today agree that Bosch, with his election victory of more than 70 percent of the voters, had provided the Dominican people with a long-awaited, genuine taste of democracy. Hope ran very high for the Bosch government—at least on the part of the impressive numbers of his supporters throughout the island.

Civil War: April 1965–September 1965

When the new self-appointed military government repudiated the constitution and reversed all of Bosch's reforms, a forceful popular uprising exploded. Once the civilian population was armed by pro-Bosch military officers, civil war erupted on April 25, 1965. Intensive and bloody fighting overtook every corner of the capital city. The Constitutionalist forces were about to launch a decisive final strike against the strategic San Isidro Base, but junta leaders, backed by reports from the United States embassy in Santo Domingo, informed the United States president that a Communist takeover of the country was imminent. President Lyndon Johnson, telling the American public that he was responding to the threat to American lives and economic interests, ordered the immediate deployment of some forty-two thousand United States Marines to the shores of Quisqueya. This second North American military invasion was mammoth in scale. The rationale quickly became one based around the need to prevent a second Cuba in Latin America.

So, for a period of two months, the regular Dominican army, under the command of the invasion forces (but now called an inter-American peace force) battled the *constitucionalistas* (the supporters of the constitution) in the streets of the cities and in the countryside. Once the fighting reached a critical point and the rebels seemed to be heading toward victory, the war between the Constitutionalist faction and the conservative military became a bloody contest involving what many segments of the Dominican armed forces described as "atheistic Communists and their sympathizers determined to take control of the government and zealous supporters of the United States eager to restore order and eliminate the threat from the left."[2] From the American embassy in the capital, intelligence reports to Washington grossly exaggerated the numbers and the degree of influence of Communist sympathizers among the ranks of Bosch's *constitucionalistas*. These reports also dangerously misrepresented the genuinely democratic commitment of many key rebel leaders. Labeling Bosch's forces as being heavily infiltrated by international Marxists and Communist sympathizers strongly bolstered Washington's claim that military intervention was an absolute necessity. Public declarations that sending American troops to the Caribbean was required in order to protect American personnel and property quickly gave way to statements that troops were "saving the Dominican Republic from falling into the clutches of the Communists." Moreover, there had been the prevailing thought underlining the whole of United States foreign policy in the region: the so-called No-Second-Cuba ideology that many analysts offered as the primary rationale for the intervention.

An Illegal and Immoral Invasion

What was surprisingly new about the character of this particular invading army was the immediately noticeable array of Latino faces making up the ranks of the soldiers. Heavy pressure exerted by the United States upon the OAS forced a commitment of fighting troops from several Latin American nations. Brazil, Costa Rica, Honduras, and Paraguay sent battle contingents in order to lend the appearance of legitimacy to this otherwise illegal, immoral, unilateral intervention of the United States. There was no question that the United States had clearly violated the fundamental charter of both the OAS and the United Nations. This illegal invasion resulted in the deaths of more than three thousand *dominicanos.* In June 1966, still under the vigilance of the much-resented North American military presence, an election was held to determine who would be president, Juan Bosch or Joaquín Balaguer. It is no secret now—as it certainly was not then—that the Balaguer candidacy was strongly endorsed by the United States, the traditional Dominican oligarchy, and Trujillo loyalists. In fact, *trujillista* (Trujillo loyalists) military officials sponsored a terrorist campaign against Bosch and his PRD followers. More than 350 Bosch supporters and political activists throughout the island were reported murdered between the months from January to May of 1966, months leading up to the critical and controversial presidential elections.

There were literally thousands of political activists who felt genuinely intimidated and thus fled into exile to Miami and New York. It is said that during the campaign Professor Bosch himself was not able to leave his home in Santo Domingo. Some Dominican military officers made public pronouncements that if Bosch ventured outside his house, he would be confronted by them (the officers) and would likely be assassinated. The Balaguer camp won the presidency, also two subsequent elections, remaining in power for the next twelve years. The professor went into exile, residing more than three years in Spain. The United States, once again, succeeded in restructuring Dominican society and especially the Dominican armed forces. When President Balaguer took office in 1966, he found himself at the helm of a Dominican government that was under the bureaucratic control of perhaps four hundred United States federal civil servants and career officials functioning at just about every imaginable level of government administration. United States technical advisers and counselors, not *dominicanos,* made all the vital decisions. Certainly the armed forces, the security forces, as well as the Policía Nacional, all received direct orders from a team of United States advisers, some of whom were unmistakably CIA operatives. A number of other Dominican government agencies and departments were administered by non-Dominican chiefs. However, Dr. Balaguer was ultimately successful in having the control of his government returned to Dominican hands, whereupon, not surprisingly, he proved to be an extremely intelligent and astute administrator.

Twelve Years of Balaguer: 1966–1978

The shadow of Trujillo was cast long and hard. Violence begot more violence. Bitterness lingered and festered. The venomous civil war was really not over. Without the Dominican military, very few soldiers who had been Constitutionalists were forgiven for their perceived betrayal by their comrades. Many of the so-called traitors were executed during the period of transition from the provisional government to the permanent presidency of Balaguer. Throughout the capital city the former civil war combatants were now replaced by a systematic campaign of anticommunist, anticonstitutionalist terrorism conducted by paramilitary groups. Urban guerrilla warfare scarred the face of major cities and towns across the country. For a few very turbulent years La República Dominicana suffered the pain and torment of a climate of hate, fear, and terror imposed upon the citizens by militaristic Balaguer forces. President Balaguer collaborated with the United States government to eradicate what remained of the popular leftist movement. The United States police training program that had been discontinued under former President Bosch was reactivated. Expert military personnel from Washington quickly reorganized the controversial Dominican security forces. Many people still say that what resulted was bloody repression and human rights abuses against student activist groups and trade unionists. The organized Left had been effectively destroyed, and repression against labor, students, and disgruntled slum dwellers kept popular protests subdued. During the 1966 elections, it must be recalled, candidate Balaguer had promised a return to peace and order.

Nevertheless, the intimidation and violence had become so commonplace throughout the country by 1972 that the United States and other Western nations insisted that Balaguer get his house in order. Perhaps one individual more than any other is credited with drawing international attention to the notoriety of human rights violations in the country. Dr. José Francisco Peña Gómez, a party leader of the PRD, waged an intensive, tireless campaign throughout Europe, Latin America, and the United States to have external pressure brought upon the domestic crisis in the Dominican Republic. Peña Gómez would go on to become head of PRD in 1973 when Bosch realized the party would probably not ever move toward fomenting the kind of socialist revolution he envisioned for the country.[3]

A Development Miracle

Large-scale economic development throughout the island was intended as the other factor in the strategy for preventing any resurgence of civil unrest and radicalism. It was at this point that United States officials were directed by the president of the United States himself to begin implementing what was referred to as a development miracle. The central strategy here was based on pumping huge amounts of United States private investment capital, government aid, and specifically tailored loan packages into the Dominican economy. Unprecedented amounts of money in grants—unprecedented at least for the Caribbean region—from the United States Agency for International Development (AID) financed the impressive building of an infrastructure designed to entice foreign investors to La República Dominicana. A true miracle did indeed take place. There was a boom in public construction projects. President Balaguer was aggressive in building new port facilities and upgrading old ones, building highways, aqueducts, streets, bridges, and energy systems. He also invested heavily in the construction of new public housing, schools, and health clinics. It was during this period also that plans were being laid for the future development of a major tourist industry, amazingly long overlooked or neglected as a vital source of revenue for the island, given the truly spectacular natural wonders of this Caribbean Eden.

The miracle also accounted for a serious modernization of the country's cities. Of course, Santo Domingo and Santiago, because of their traditionally shared status as the nation's premier cities, would receive the lion's portion of urban development funding and public investment. However, important population centers such as Puerto Plata, San Cristóbal, Haina, La Romana, San Juan, San Francisco de Macorís, Moca, La Vega, Mao, and Nagua also witnessed an amazing renaissance of impressive economic growth, physical renovation, and modernization. High world sugar prices coincided with the influx of North American aid dollars, and so Balaguer's economic strategies produced rapid growth. Thanks largely to foreign investment, the economic stimulation of the country during the early 1970s was among the highest in all Latin America. Some critical observers, however, have reflected upon what they call the extreme generosity with which the Dominican government offered conditions of investment to foreign companies. For example, one of Balaguer's first acts of such generosity was to entice the United States multinational giant Gulf & Western to construct an expansive Dominican empire of sugar interests, beef export, and luxury tourism. At the same time, though, Gulf & Western deliberately maintained a low wage scale for its cane cutters and other sugar industry workers by swiftly smashing the central union located in the company town of La Romana. According to union activists, many foreign corporations have been given practically free rein to exploit Dominican and Haitian laborers. Firms like Falconbridge Dominicana, Rosario Dominicana, Shell, Nestle, and Philip Morris have received highly lucrative incentives to operate in the island, even if such operations have meant sometimes weakening competitive domestic entrepreneurship. Many of these multinationals have raised the necessary capital on the local financial market and have obtained economic advantages by negotiating their contracts with the help of the Dominican government itself.

Geopolitical Destiny

The question of the extent of foreign investment, especially United States investment, would continue being a central issue in Dominican sociopolitical and economic life. The Balaguer ideology, shared by a very large and influential segment of the populace, seemed to adhere to the notion of the geopolitical destiny of the Caribbean region. This view necessarily implies that La República Dominicana would forever be a regional satellite of the United States, mainly in order to prevent the emergence of another Cuba in the region. In turn, the United States State Department in Washington would determine the national agenda for the island. Everybody well remembers that massive North American military force had twice already been deployed to ensure the uncompromising protection and expansion of American interests in Quisqueya.

Therefore, in view of this acknowledged *destino geopolitico* (geopolitical destiny), it was difficult for Balaguer and his Reformist Party to accept defeat in the election of 1978 against PRD candidate Antonio Guzmán. Charges of election irregularities, even fraud, were leveled against the *reformistas*. Scandalously and shamelessly on the night of the general vote counting, several *balaguerista* military chiefs (supporters of Balaguer) stormed into the headquarters of the Central Election Board, interrupted the official counting, which was showing Guzmán the unexpected but obvious winner, and confiscated, then destroyed the ballot boxes. There were cries of indignation and outrage from all over La República Dominicana when the *balagueristas* tried ignoring the election results. The new Carter administration in Washington, which was widely regarded as far more sensitive to human rights issues than any previous United States administration, took the rather bold step of demanding unequivocally that the PRD victory be acknowledged and immediately accepted.

A Nation Again in Crisis

The election of Antonio Guzmán (1978–1982), former minister of agriculture in the Bosch government and a wealthy landowner-businessman, in all probability reflected the people's urgent call for change. What the Dominican people received instead was a quite harmful dose of unabashed nepotism and new levels of government corruption. Guzmán's initial popularity dissipated quickly as his administration was perceived as fraudulent. His critics accused him of having used the Partido Revolucionario Dominicano (PRD) as a direct avenue toward personal financial gain, as well as economic enrichment for his family and intimate friends. Under steadily escalating corruption and a plunging national economy, the devaluation of the Dominican peso, falling world prices of sugar, increased government borrowing from foreign banks, plus the devastation of Hurricane David (1979), Guzmán was losing his very last measure of credibility. Even the hurricane relief aid that poured into the island from the international community became a target for gross misappropriation and abuse, with Guzmán being blamed. Now the PRD itself, in a rare move indeed, decided to withdraw all official party support from their own sitting president. The country was seated in the threshold of bankruptcy. In a state of extreme despondency, Guzmán committed suicide on the night of July 3, 1982. La República Dominicana was in shock.

Economic Restructuring

Economically, La República Dominicana was in such abysmal chaos prior to his election that Salvador Jorge Blanco (1982–1986) was engaged in critical discussions, and even in making secret agreements, with the International Monetary Fund (IMF) in Washington, well before occupying El Palacio. He had agreed to implement certain austerity measures that were required by the IMF. Jorge Blanco's earlier campaign pledge of *democracia económica* (economic democracy) for the island was totally blown out to sea. Freezing wages, closing state-run hotels, and removing subsidies on food and fuel were just a few examples of the economic restructuring moves that were implemented by Blanco's government in order to meet IMF accords. Moreover, further United States aid to the Dominican Republic was made contingent upon absolute compliance with the stipulations of the fund. The Dominican government denounced the unpopular and harsh demands of the IMF, but to no avail. Growing hardships and dangerous discontent on the part of the general populace did not go unnoticed. During La Semana Santa (Holy Week) of April 1984, violent street demonstrations and rioting erupted in Santo Domingo and in towns around the country. Soldiers, having been ordered to put down the rebellion, killed more than one hundred of their compatriots, wounded hundreds more, and arrested more than four thousand angry protesters. The price of basic food items like bread, cooking oil, milk, and sugar rose by more than 50 percent in dramatic response to the new austerity measures that had been imposed upon the nation.

Balaguer Returns: 1986–1990

The Jorge Blanco government, as well as his official party (PRD), had been thoroughly discredited by now. A sordid record of government corruption and piracy severely weakened the party organization. Internal ideological differences also splintered the ranks of the party membership perhaps forever. The specific choice of a presidential candidate for the upcoming elections caused the most irreparable damage in terms of party cohesiveness. The dilemma centered around the candidacy of either Peña Gómez or Jacobo Majluta. When Jorge Blanco finally lost all support of the military, he had lost every possible hope of recovery and so Balaguer and his faithful *reformistas* won by a very narrow margin.[4] The preferred Reformist candidate was again Joaquín Balaguer. Many ordinary *dominicanos* literally expected miracle cures from Dr. Balaguer. Many people believed that Balaguer would eradicate corruption and graft and would rebuild confidence and efficiency in government operations. Balaguer, it was thought, would simply "put things in order." Upon occupying *El Palacio*[5] this time, Balaguer initiated a high-profile anticorruption crusade. In April of 1987, former president Jorge Blanco was ordered arrested on a series of charges, including sedition, misappropriation of government funds, even conspiring to commit murder. Blanco fled the country with his family, arriving in the United States after having been denied political asylum in Venezuela.

Dr. Balaguer returned to the presidency for the fifth time in twenty-five years. This amazingly multifaceted personality on the Dominican political and cultural scene, now a frail, nearly blind octogenarian, was completely unnerved by what might have been considered a debilitating, handicapping condition by less courageous individuals. He was successful in totally reorganizing and in fact strengthening his Reformista Party. Always the methodical and analytical, consummate politician, Balaguer immediately orchestrated the plan to deliver the conclusive blow to the already discredited ex-president Jorge Blanco and the PRD. When Balaguer reinstated previously ousted military personnel, who would be strategically helpful, he destroyed permanently any future attempts of Blanco to reenter the island's political arena. Besides, Jorge Blanco was now safely in exile in the United States.

The Sugar Crisis

More importantly, *el pueblo dominicano* were by and large quite preoccupied with the real dilemma facing the country now: the national economy and the gradual demise of sugar. Of all the countries in the Caribbean region, La República Dominicana has been the only one traditionally to have depended so heavily and singularly upon sugar exports. When beet sugar and high fructose corn syrup, a very formidable sugar substitute, gradually began conquering the world market, Quisqueya became the region's heaviest casualty. Demands for sugar had fallen; the United States and Europe increased their subsidies to domestic producers. The Dominican economy plummeted. Balaguer's main thrust to try offsetting this national crisis was to enact measures in three specific areas that the government hoped would replace sugar: (1) tourism, (2) agro-industry, and (3) the expansion of foreign-owned manufacturing in so-called *zonas francas* (free trade zones). By 1988, the country's foreign exchange revenue from a rejuvenated and restructured tourist industry almost doubled its combined earnings from cacao, coffee, and sugar. Balaguer also personally undertook an ambitious, carefully planned urban renewal program that entailed massive new construction of roads, bridges, public housing units, and other public buildings in and around the capital city. Economic growth soon took on the dimensions of what offered the appearance of an economic revival.

Then in 1989, the nation was jolted by the menacing realities of a staggering foreign debt, the agonizing question of how to pay it, and a sharper, downward turn in the already frightening energy crisis. Fuel supplies dwindled, causing severe shortages in every part of the country. The entire island suffered from the impact of this pervasive crisis. Dominicans began getting accustomed to receiving no more than three or perhaps four hours daily of electricity usage. These notorious *apagones* (power outages or blackouts), as they were called, became so routine that they even found their way into the lyrics of popular merengues.

More Controversy and Adversity

Some individuals view as cruel irony the country's energy crisis as it focused upon the now completed, truly breathtaking and mammoth construction of El Faro a Colón (the Columbus Lighthouse). Amid a ruinous shortage of electrical energy, a lighthouse stands, believed to be the world's largest and expected to overtax the limits of energy consumption under any normal circumstances. El Faro was built (1992) at a cost in the billions and is surrounded by much controversy. This imposing structure, in the shape of a gigantic cross, projects a powerful beacon of light for miles and miles across the Caribbean night sky. The crowning event of the island's Quinto Centenario (Five Hundredth Anniversary: 1492–1992) was the long-awaited inauguration of El Faro a Colón. The ceremonial transfer of Columbus's remains to the lighthouse and a mass said by Pope John Paul II capped the spectacular celebration.[6]

Still, the immediate reality was economic misery for nearly all Dominicans, disregarding altogether any notion of specific allegiance to this or that party, or their views about the lighthouse. Further devaluations of the *peso dominicano* continued eroding domestic purchasing power and playing havoc with the national psyche as well. By October 1990, the exchange rate reached almost RD15 pesos to the United States dollar, sending inflation soaring well beyond control. Food prices rose to astronomical heights, sparking an angry wave of food riots across the island. Basic public services, already having reached intolerable levels, deteriorated even further into nonexistence. Statistics for 1990 indicated that the majority of Dominican citizens had been forced into the ranks of poverty. La República Dominicana came near the brink of yet another major upheaval. Numerous groups and organizations, political as well as professional, openly demanded Balaguer's resignation. The people's unbridled anger in response to the worsening circumstances of daily economic pressures took the form of organized protests against the government, violent street demonstrations, worker strikes, and demands for salary increases. The violence left scores of protesters dead and many more arrested. There was even a relentless campaign of harassment, originating inside the government, that was directed at the business and financial communities. The government publicly accused several of the country's most prestigious financial institutions of illicit trafficking in dollars, resulting in indiscriminate persecutions against this particular sector. A dreadful period of economic misery and panic provoked widespread pessimism among the masses of Dominicans.

The continuing impoverishment spreading throughout the island was reflected also in stepped-up migration. The targeted areas of choice were the United States, Venezuela, Puerto Rico, and even Spain. A steady exodus of new boat people to Puerto Rico, for instance, gained unwelcome publicity when several of the *yolas* used to transport the fleeing refugees capsized and the passengers drowned or were devoured by sharks.[7] Immigration authorities in nearby Puerto Rico estimated that between 1989 and 1990, a monthly average of three hundred undocumented Dominicans were deported from Puerto Rico. In 1990 there were some 900,000 *dominicanos,* legal permanent residents as well as individuals without official documentation, living in the United States. A very sad commentary indeed: an estimated 12 percent of the Dominican population had fled the grim, nightmarish economic reality assaulting Quisqueya la Bella. Yet, forever undaunted

by economic hardships or political crises, the proud and expertly resourceful Dominican people braced themselves with even firmer resolve and determination for the upcoming elections, first of 1990, then of
1994. Paralyzing general strikes, national financial downfalls, seemingly
endless energy shortages, more crippling IMF stringencies and accords, threatening social unrest, and still more agonizing frustration
among an already impatient citizenry, topped by worsening Dominican-
Haitian relations, together conspired to paint a quite dismal picture of
life in the island. Perhaps not to anyone's astonishment, Dr. Balaguer
was returned to the presidential command post for the sixth time
(1990–1994).

The Electoral Crisis of 1994

¿Valió la pena? (Was it worth the trouble?) Many *dominicanos* were
asking that very question after the hotly contested 1994 elections. Mo-
mentum had been building an entire year in advance. That was the
burning question posed by a genuinely worried observer in just one of
literally hundreds of informal postelection conversations and discussions by ordinary citizens around the island. One elderly voter, for
instance, Don Roberto Sánchez, asserted that "nunca soñé que
treintitres años después de la caída de Trujillo el pueblo dominicano
todavía no tendría una democracia definida" (I never dreamed that
thirty-three years after the fall of Trujillo the Dominican people still
wouldn't have a definite democracy). Don Roberto pondered the validity of the 1994 elections, insisting that democracy be fully respected.
He felt that democracy would surely die and that the efforts of all those
brave men and women, the death of *las hermanas Mirabal* (the
Mirabal sisters), the young people of El Movimiento 14 de Junio, all
the other valiant heroes and heroines over the years who sacrificed
their lives to the cause of Dominican freedom, would be without meaning. Yet, like Sánchez, many *dominicanos* never dreamed that thirty-
three years after Trujillo's execution, his shadow would still engulf the
island. Who could possibly dream that passenger cars would be
stopped along the country's highways and bridges, and the occupants
searched to see if they were concealing weapons beneath their clothing? Such horrors actually were reported during the 1994 electoral
crisis that electrified the entire nation.

The outgoing United States ambassador, the usually jovial, often laid-back Robert Pastorino, appeared at a postelection banquet in Santo Domingo where he reportedly "listened approvingly" as the keynote speaker, the chief losing candidate, firmly denounced the evident voting irregularities in the elections. Ambassador Pastorino's very presence, it was thought, lent an element of credence to the serious allegations of election fraud. But undoubtedly the most vitriolic of postelection denunciations appeared in a boldly worded *New York Times* editorial that addressed the issue of "The Doubtful Victory of Mr. Balaguer." The commentary was reprinted almost the same day in Santo Domingo's leading newspaper *Listín Diario,* in the Spanish version *(La Dudosa Victoria del Señor Balaguer).* Stinging charges of fraud were leveled against Balaguer, charging, among other things, that Balaguer had reclaimed his victory behind a campaign marred by racism and a discredited voting process. The article, meticulously translated into Spanish and circulated throughout La República Dominicana, alleged that during the campaign Balaguer made constant references to the race of his principal rival, Dr. José Francisco Peña Gómez, who is Black, and who, if he won, would be the first Black president elected in the country's history. Not-so-subtle remarks never failed to point to Peña Gómez's Haitian origins, even though he was in fact born in Dominican territory—La Loma del Flaco, near Guayanaces and Mao in the region of El Cibao, Valverde province. Other obviously irrelevant issues found their way into the *New York Times* commentary: the crisis in Haiti, the uncontrollable smuggling of fuel across the Haitian-Dominican border, Balaguer's open antipathy toward deposed Haitian president Jean-Bertrand Aristide, and Peña-Gómez's suspected "practice of Vodún."[8]

The article concluded with the strong recommendation that the international community not recognize the so-called victory of President Balaguer because of substantiated allegations of election fraud and voting irregularities reported by international election observers. A significant number of these monitors and observers said that it was probably true that the Dominican authorities did nullify the votes of some 200,000 sympathizers and supporters of candidate Peña Gómez. Serious pre-election apprehensions and concerns for fair play surfaced a full year prior to the scheduled elections. The author of this book journeyed with extreme intimacy and confidence from one corner to the other of the island, recording all levels of conversations and various kinds of commentary. There was animated engagement in discussions with *dominicanos* from practically every walk of life, from widely differing socioeconomic groups, plus an array of political ideologies. Invariably, commentary about the upcoming elections reached a fever pitch—depending upon, quite naturally, whether the respondents were *perredistas* (PRD), *peledeistas* (PLD), or *reformistas* (PRSC). But almost overwhelmingly noticed was the injection into any level of political discussion the point of Peña Gómez's Haitian origins! The point was totally inescapable.

Of course, this section is certainly not intended even remotely to be another postelection analysis or personal interpretation of *¿Qué pasó?* (What happened?). The many noted Dominican sociologists, historians, and political pundits are far better able, better justified, and no doubt more personally motivated to do that than this author. However, there are certainly a few salient features about the May 1994 elections that do make for spirited discussion and studied reflection. To begin with, this election turnout was undoubtedly the largest in the island's history, following the collapse of *la tirania trujillista* (the Trujillo tyranny). With roughly three million Dominicans participating, out of 3.3 million registered, the numbers were truly extraordinary. The two principal rivals, President Balaguer and Dr. Peña Gómez, received over a million votes each. Another point was that the early pre-election polls and surveys had indicated that the margin of victory would be extremely close. In actuality, there was universal insistence that there be a recount of the ballots. The Junta Central Electoral (JCE), or Central Election Board, complied with the demands of the people on this issue. Another significant surprise was Joaquín Balaguer's victory in nearly the whole of El Cibao, where in 1990 Juan Bosch had won handsomely. It was said that there was such strong sentiment here to defeat *el haitiano* (the Haitian, Peña Gómez) in this region, at whatever cost. Still another feature was that Peña Gómez easily won the capital, El Distrito Nacional. Finally, there is the pressing issue of the huge number—some two hundred thousand—of nullified votes around the country. *¿Y es fácil?*[9]

Going into the election initially were just two major candidates. One was Peña Gómez, the Harvard-trained economist and leader of PRD, who served as Secretario General de la Internacional Socialista for Latin America. People were constantly being reminded that Peña Gómez is a descendent of a family that had been butchered along with scores of others during Trujillo's heinous Massacre of Haitians in

1937. Dr. Peña Gómez has been an ardent opponent of historical human rights abuses—whether in neighboring Haiti, carried out under the Duvaliers or the current military rulers, or perpetrated by the Dominican government and multinational companies via the exploitation of Haitian sugarcane workers in the canefields of the Dominican Republic. Peña Gómez is unabashedly pro-Aristide and enthusiastically supported the international economic blockade of the neighbor to the west as a means of forcing General Raoul Cédras to step down as head of the illegally constituted Haitian government. In the 1990 elections, even though the chief contenders for the presidency were Balaguer and Bosch, Peña Gómez was in third place with an impressive 23 percent of the votes.

Peña Gómez's primary opposition for the May 1994 contest was a former vice president, founder, and leader of the Partido Revolucionario Independiente (PRI), Jacobo Majluta. Majluta was unexpectedly propelled into the presidential seat upon the suicide in 1982 of Antonio Guzmán. As president of the Senate, Majluta had fought bitterly against many of Jorge Blanco's proposed legislative measures to legalize the entry of foreign aid into the country. Many critical observers still hold Majluta singularly responsible for blocking many development projects that many people felt might well have reinvigorated the depressive national economy during the mid-1980s. Other commentators have noted that during the 1994 elections, no one bothered to call special attention to the fact of Majluta's ethnicity or family origins—Lebanese, from the Middle East. Apparently, according to the ever-vigilant critics, ethnicity in the case of wealthy businessman Majluta was never an issue as it clearly was with *el haitiano.*

¿Va o No Va? (Is He Going to or Not?)

The question, asked throughout La República Dominicana and even appearing as the banner headline in several of the country's newspapers, referred to whether the octogenarian Dr. Joaquín Balaguer was going to declare himself a candidate or retire altogether from active participation (and domination) in the island's politics. He said publicly, on previous occasions and this time as well, that the 1994 elections would be the last in which he would actively participate, win or lose. In the 1990 campaign Balaguer won by twenty-four thousand votes against his seemingly perennial rival Professor Juan Bosch. This time

Balaguer withheld his decision to enter the presidential race until quite late, leading many Dominicans to believe that the battle would be fought between Peña Gómez and Majluta. It is no secret that many *reformistas* have for a long time perceived themselves as the true defenders of Dominican integrity. Some individuals, offering their own postelection commentary, have asserted that it was actually the *reformistas* who, at the height of election tension, created, nurtured, and circulated the notion that if *el haitiano* wins the presidency, he will carry to realization his long-sought-after goal of merging La República Dominicana with Haiti. More than one individual expressed the opinion that they would leave the country altogether if *el haitiano* won!

Nevertheless, some people saw a note of maturity just prior to the elections. All the candidates convened to sign a ceremonious El Pact de Civilidad (the Pact of Civility) in hopes of averting all conceivable fraud and violence associated with the electoral process. The international press corps was present, as were participating international election monitors. Everything appeared solidly in place to assure what Balaguer would afterwards say were the cleanest elections in Dominican history. Nevertheless, serious incidents of voting irregularities and fraud were recorded, especially into the nation's interior zones: Jánico, Navarrete, San Juan de las Matas, Mao, Villa González. Rumors of fraud inundated the organizational headquarters of all competing parties. No one was spared the taint of fraudulent behavior during the elections. There was one spectacular charge brought by the *reformistas* against the *perredistas:* supposedly, the *perredistas* had supplied official voter registration cards to some six thousand Haitians, therefore enabling them to vote in Dominican elections! Other minority parties also denounced the election results, charging that the *reformistas* had manipulated the elections in order to not recognize the will of the people. Without much doubt, the monumental issue of the electoral process of 1994 centered around the *listados de votantes* (the voter lists) throughout the island on the very day of the elections. Many valid names of currently registered voters simply disappeared. Even some congressional and municipal candidates were barred from voting because their name did not appear on official precinct lists. The outrage was quite predictable.

The principal candidates were as follows: Joaquín Balaguer and his selected vice president, Jacinto Peynado; and the opposing PRD candidates, José Francisco Peña Gómez and his running mate, Fernando

Alvarez Bogaert, who had been the *reformista* vice-presidential choice on the Balaguer ticket in 1978. Bogaert at the time (1978) became disenchanted with the *reformista* ideology. The PRS (Partido Reformista Social Cristiano) candidates won with 43.72 percent of the vote. The PRD (Partido Revolucionario Dominicano) won 40.47 percent of the vote. In third place with 12.85 percent was the PLD (Partido de la Liberación Dominicana) candidate Professor Juan Bosch, whose party exhibited jubilant satisfaction at having assisted in defeating PRD and Peña Gómez. Another presidential candidate, Father Antonio Reynoso (Padre Toño), was the leader of an organization called MIUCA, or Movimiento Independencia Unidad y Cambio (Independent Movement of Unity and Change). MIUCA ended with a 0.71 percent vote tally. Finally, receiving 2.22 percent was PRD's candidate Jacobo Majluta. Padre Toño severally criticized what he perceived to be Balaguer's attitude. He said that President Balaguer and his *reformistas,* by having committed evidenced election fraud, had made a mockery of the country's general electorate, the electoral process itself, as well as undermined the intent of El Pact de Civilidad that had been signed prior to the elections. He further warned that *el pueblo dominicano* were not in any condition to support new frustrations brought about by the lack of respect for the election results. Expressing indignation, Peña Gómez asserted that the Central Election Board itself had violated serious questions of ethics by not having submitted by the stipulated deadline all the voting registers, but instead had furnished different or false lists:

> El asunto de las listas falsas y otras irregularidades constituyen hechos bochornosos que ponen a la República Dominicana en peligro de convertirse en el hazmerreír de toda Latinoamérica.[10]

> (The question of false lists and other irregularities constitute shameful acts that put the Dominican Republic in danger of becoming the laughingstock of all Latin America.)

Despite strong protests from the opposition and the alleged foreign interference from the northern colossus, the eighty-eight-year-old Dr. Joaquín Balaguer assumed the presidency of La República Dominicana for a seventh time! Dr. Balaguer, now blinded by glaucoma and crippled by phlebitis, promised he would head what he personally called a government of transition. Balaguer was successful in gaining control of both houses of the Dominican Congress by forming an alliance with the party of former President Bosch, who finished third in the 1994 elections. Supporters of Balaguer's chief rival, Peña Gómez, boycotted both the National Assembly meeting and the official inauguration, charging that Balaguer reneged on an earlier agreement with Peña Gómez to shorten his term to just one and half years. Although the normal presidential term in the Dominican Republic is four years, Dr. Balaguer was sworn in for two. Reportedly, he agreed to a term reduction only after opposition politicians and influential international election observers accused him of election fraud. The Dominican Congress has voted to set Balaguer's term at two years, in addition to amending the constitution so that a president cannot succeed himself or herself. In a half-hour inauguration address, Balaguer offered to foster additional constitutional reforms. He added that "the most important construction that we have facing us is the maintenance of peace and harmony of the nation."[11] He also angrily criticized foreign interference in the internal affairs of La República Dominicana. Finally, the newly appointed United States ambassador to the island nation, Donna J. Hrinak, sent a letter to the Central Election Board following the May elections arguing that the election results were not legitimate because they did not address the findings of an international commission that found serious irregularities throughout the country. The Organization of American States (OAS), as well as United States Secretary of State Warren Christopher, also called for new elections to resolve the fraud allegations. As of this writing, new elections are scheduled for May 1996.

Perhaps in the final analysis, with the elections now over and a vote recount having been completed, with charges and countercharges of extensive and systematic fraud and gross irregularities in the voting process, with many individuals still unwilling to acknowledge defeat or the election results themselves, with some people asking of the election ¿Valió la pena? (Was it worth the trouble?), the fact remains that Dr. Joaquín Balaguer has been declared the winner. He again sits in the presidential chair at El Palacio Nacional, despite his advanced years or sight impairment. The entire Dominican community, whether in Santo Domingo, Barahona, Higüey, or Washington Heights in Upper Manhattan, New York, has to accept this reality and its inherent circumstances. Despite the vociferous claims of *dislocamientos de listados* (displaced or missing voter lists), or the hundreds of often disturbing rumors that circulated via *de radio bemba* (radio of the lips, or loose lips), or the stormy denouncements of the electoral commission, or the level of overall discontent on the part of the general electorate, the *pueblo dominicano* ultimately will have to determine to work as a cohesive, collective body in order to get on with the urgent task of pulling the nation out of the virtual economic paralysis in which it is presently submerged. The job will require spirited, sincere commitment from divergent segments of the populace so that meaningful results will benefit the entire nation.

Therefore, irrespective of the strident efforts of the United States Congress's Hispanic and Black Caucuses to have the Dominican elections investigated by official international agencies, for whatever motive, and notwithstanding the widely held view, especially outside the island, that the victory of one particular candidate over another might be a strategic plus for United States–Haiti relations at this moment in time, there exists one immediate reality. That reality is that only the Dominican people themselves can and must decide what issues and concerns are in their best interest. Around the island, a sizable number of political analysts and many ordinary citizens alike have remarked that it is without doubt that Dr. Balaguer most certainly did represent stability and security during these last four years (1990–1994); that he did maintain a certain degree of control over mounting inflation and held the reins on the balance of monetary changes. But by the same measure, there is absolutely no doubt that Peña Gómez represented the real possibility of change to something newer, something fresher, functional, and more openly democratic than the traditionally authoritative style and mentality *balaguerista*. Dominicans from across the full spectrum of ideological diversity in the island's society have justifiably called for revision of the country's entire electoral system.

Notes

1. There is a popular expression used in the island, *un fiel testaferro,* which means one who lends his name on a business contract that actually belongs to another person. Some commentators remark that appointments by Trujillo constituted *un fiel testaferro.* Classic *fiel testaferro* examples, as noted earlier, included Jacinto Peynado, Manuel Troncoso, Hector Trujillo, and Joaquín Balaguer.

2. Juan Manuel Garcia, *La Masacre de Palma Sola,* p. 27.

3. Juan Bosch, believing that the PRD had turned toward the conservative right, renounced the party altogether and later structured a new revolutionary

organization called Partido de la Liberación Dominicana (Party of Dominican Liberation, or PLD). Professor Bosch, of course, was correct in his observation that the old PRD had drifted into becoming a multiclass party of compromise. The PRD reorganized itself under the new leadership of its dynamic secretary general, Peña Gómez, and Senator Salvador Jorge Blanco.

4. One of Jorge Blanco's important political reforms centered around attempts to convert the country's traditional military forces into a modern, professional institution, thereby eliminating the antiquated Trujillo-style system of favoritism. This new element of professionalism would create a loyalty to civil authority, rather than to any particularly dominant, charismatic figure. Many of the upper-echelon career personnel lost long-held privileged status as a consequence. These embittered career officers would never forget or forgive this initiative by Blanco.

5. El Palacio Nacional (the National Palace) refers to the ornate building complex in the nation's capital that houses the official government offices, including the Executive Office Suite of the President.

6. In 1892, the government of Spain donated the elaborate tomb in the Catedral de Santa María la Menor (in Santo Domingo) where the remains of Christopher Columbus had long been housed. Upon completion of El Faro a Colón, the remains were ceremoniously removed from the cathedral and relocated in the new lighthouse.

7. *Yolas* is the local name describing the rickety, totally inadequate, and unsafe sailing vessels that are regularly and illegally chartered from the seacoast town of Miches, located on the northwest corner of the Dominican Republic, to cross the treacherous, shark-infested Mona Passage to nearby Puerto Rico.

8. *The New York Times,* May 20, 1994, p. 10.

9. *¿Y es fácil?* (And you think it's easy?) This is a frequently heard local expression, distinctly Dominican, used in conversation to imply the exact opposite—the actual difficulty, rather than the ease—of a given situation or circumstance.

10. Peña Gómez, in an article appearing in the island newspaper *Ultima Hora,* Santo Domingo, 17 Mayo 1994, p. 8.

11. Jaime A. Bautista, "Llegó la hora," newspaper article in *Hoy,* año XV, 10 de Junio de 1994, p. 14.

23

Conclusions

Dreaming Jointly in Defining Dominican Culture

Images in Retrospect

Someone whose name has long since been lost in time and space once referred to the island of Hispaniola as *La Isla Mágica* (The Magic Island). Quite a suitable description! The cultural matrix from which this truly magical island evolved reflects an interwoven pattern of diverse ethnicities in synthesis that indeed conjures up something magical. The mixture of cultures that unfolded in both Haytí and Quisqueya produced, among other significant aspects of what we call culture, a fusion of magical beliefs and spiritual traditions that frequently astounds, and usually confuses, the outsider not familiar or not genuinely comfortable with other belief systems. In Dominican culture, a triplex cultural fusion exerted a very profound impact upon the character and thought, as well as other distinctive features, of *el pueblo dominicano* that gives the nation its unique magical quality today.

First, Dominican culture is personified in the spirit of the valiant Taíno *cacique* Enriquillo, who led the first revolt against the invading Spaniards. Dominican culture is the realization, for instance, that the locally grown tuberous plant called *guáyiga* was used as a basic food staple in at least 1800 B.C. on the island. Along with *guáyiga*, other cultivated plants such as *yuca, maiz,* and *casabe* all continue to be essential items in the contemporary Dominican diet. The island's pre-Columbian Taíno culture is also responsible for the important sociohistorical occurrence of the *conuco* and the *bohío*, the former referring even today to the small plot of ground for cultivating subsistence food crops. The *bohío,* also discussed earlier in this work, describes the thatch-roof cabin made from wood, tree branches, or straw. In many rural zones of the island today, one frequently spots this traditional abode of the *campesino*. There is throughout Dominican society today an important psychosocial presence in the notion of the traditional *conuco*. Spiritually, the *conuco* symbolizes a measure of immediate independence for an individual and her family, allowing for that necessary sense of self-sufficiency. Historically, the *conuco* guaranteed the economic survival of the island society. Dominican culture displays rather proudly that spirit of survival. Although quite clearly there are no remaining indigenous Taíno living in *bohíos* and cultivating their individual *conucos* in scattered settlements around the island, the rich indigenous heritage nevertheless remains vibrantly intact and flourishing.

The Great Encounter

In the faces of the Dominican people, there are visible traces of cross-racial hybridization. Today one readily witnesses the society's amalgam of diverse skin hues, hair textures, and other distinctive racial-group characteristics. On any street corner in the nation's capital city of Santo Domingo, even the casual observer is struck by the human kaleidoscope of hues and tones that distinguishes the country's radiantly beautiful people. The second important element in the Dominican ethnic mosaic was immediately felt when the arriving Spanish conquistadors baptized the island with the name La Española, or Little Spain, on December 9, 1492, just four days after coming ashore. Instead of the delicate process of transculturation that ideally follows when two different cultures meet, in the case of the Spanish it was another scenario altogether. In this instance, the Great Encounter quickly turned into a process of exclusion, with the more powerful invading culture eventually destroying the indigenous, militarily weaker one. Spain transported to the New Territory just about everything it had to offer, and at first hastily superimposed its cultural priorities upon the more vulnerable aboriginal people before ultimately liquidating the remaining numbers.

The third major force in the Dominican cultural amalgam is the imported African heritage. However gingerly the issue is treated, almost apologetically at times, Dominican culture also holds with equal validity the realization that *la otra madre patria* (the other mother country) is Africa. Today's Dominican Republic most certainly does reflect the lusciousness of Afro-Hispanic culture, the impressive body of Afro-Hispanic literature and other creative arts, as well as the diverse contributions by Dominicans of African descent to the creation and development of the entire nation.

Determined Resistance

Dominican culture offers a legacy of celebrated chieftains of fugitive Blacks, runaway slaves called *cimarrones,* who were determined to resist fiercely the degradations and dehumanization of enslavement by the Spaniards. Lemba, Ocampo Vaquero, and Juan Criollo are prominent names of *cimarrón* leaders closely associated with the *manieles* of the Bahoruco in the remote southwest corner of La República Dominicana. Some of the historically important *manieles* were in and around such geographically diverse sites as Higüey, Azua, San Juan de la Maguana, La Vega, and Neiba. The African heritage is seen not only in terms of a physical legacy, readily exhibited by the myriad colors reflected among the crowds of *dominicanos* inspecting the goods for sale along Avenida Mella in Santo Domingo, but also in countless other ways. Certain vocabulary, an assortment of musical instruments, the rhythms and dances, certain basic foods and their distinctive preparation, some traditional festivals and celebrations are derived unmistakably from African roots.

Africa is present in the *toques de palos* (beating of the drums with sticks), for instance, at funerals or in the special *baquini* ceremony performed when an infant dies.[1] Likewise coming out of traditional Africa are the preference for so-called scandalously bold colors, the habit of some women of tying up or wrapping their hair with a kerchief or other length of brightly colored cloth, the very manner in which many *dominicanos* simply walk—the casually melodic, effortless, and rhapsodic body movements generally, the often robust display of an enjoyment of life itself. The African presence, however subtle and benign in character, is nevertheless very much in operation on many different levels of being Dominican.

Trio of Identity

One of the many noteworthy points of interest in the nation's capital is the stunningly beautiful Plaza de la Cultura, which consists of the ultramodern Teatro Nacional (National Theater), the Biblioteca Nacional (National Library), and the Museo del Hombre Dominicano (Museum of Dominican Man). Standing in the entrance patio of the museum are three imposing stone statues, sculptured lifelike, to introduce visitors to *la cultura dominicana:* Enriquillo, Bartolomé de las Casas, and Lemba. These three impressively large figures symbolize the fusion of the three interwoven legacies in the island's cultural evolution—the indigenous Taíno, the Spanish, the African. Together, not separately, this prominent trio of identity holds the nucleus of Dominican culture; these dramatically different, opposing historical references attest boldly to the ultimate process of arriving at a national identity. However arduous and painful that process proved to be in many cases, however antagonistic were some sectors of the emerging society to that inevitable process, the definitive conclusion struck the chords of unity and nation building. The subsequent cultural amalgam of the three initially divergent heritages led to the structuring of a formidable social conscience that, as a much needed psychological and ideological base, would indeed facilitate the formation of what we now know and recognize as *el pueblo dominicano.*

The Voices

Who can most accurately and most suitably define Dominican culture? Whose voice speaks most authentically for what constitutes Dominican culture? Many contemporary observers believe that, especially for many younger writers and other talented artists and creative thinkers in Quisqueya today, the graceful figure of the national poet, eighty-three-year-old Pedro Mir from the town of San Pedro de Macorís, is the exemplary embodiment of the island's culture. Pedro Mir's strident sociopolitical consciousness expressed in honest and intrepid poetic images stands solidly alongside the very best artistic voices that the

American continent has offered. Profoundly human and revolutionary in personal sentiment, Don Pedro is a genuine Caribbean voice in the distinct troubadour tradition of Nicolás Guillén, Jacques Roumain, René Marqués, Audre Lourde, and Derek Walcott. Pedro Mir possesses a fervent nationalism that easily far transcends the borders of his beloved Quisqueya in order to be able to incorporate all the wretched and exploited masses everywhere.

Nelson Mella, a seriously introspective young intellectual working diligently for national sociocultural reform and grassroots educational uplift for Quisqueya's disaffected sectors, views Dominican culture in terms of having a certain balance. This is a critical balance between the nation's historical reality and the women and men who live this reality on a daily basis. Mella says his ongoing, active objective is to reuse what he calls the *memoria histórica* (historical memory) found in the different neighborhoods of the capital city as well as in the small towns and hamlets throughout the island's rural zones. "Dominican culture oozes forth profusely from every corner and crack of Dominican consciousness—once that consciousness is unrestrained and liberated," asserts Mella.

Zeneida Severino considers herself a contemporary, practical, and open-minded young Dominican woman. She views Dominican culture from an all-encompassing, inclusive perspective that must recognize and defend uncompromisingly the legitimate identity of *la mujer dominicana* (the Dominican woman). Severino, as a young professional, affirms that "it is absolutely essential that we analyze what is expressed within the current cultural context as that expression functions on behalf of women." She believes that any efforts to arrive at conclusions about Dominican cultural identity will have to redefine the Dominican reality to incorporate honestly, perhaps for the first time historically, the active and meaningful presence of the Dominican woman—not her traditional and subordinate, submissive, and passive role in society.

For the spirited, creatively sensitive, and modern Julio Belén, Dominican culture is "the exceptionally delicate, and at the same time robust and agonizing process of promotion and revalorization of our sociocultural roots, especially the historical ethnic synthesis that produced Quisqueya la Bella." He sees the uniqueness in Dominican culture in terms of the multifaceted, multilayered Dominican personality that was forged from the rich blend of confluent cultures. Dominican culture for Belén is awakened each time the captivating rhythms of a merengue are sounded.

Dominican culture is embodied in an erudite and very amicable local historian, journalist, and serious collector of memorabilia housed at number fourteen on Calle Imbert in the town of Puerta Plata. Rafael Alberto Brugal Paiewonsky, known merely as Fifo, is the single individual, widely respected for his forthright and unfaltering embrace of Dominican culture, entrusted with the faithful rendering of the town's history. The *habitat de Fifo* (Fifo's abode) has as its objective documenting sociohistorical events, mainly those pertaining to Puerto Plata and the region, then providing free consultations and assistance to anyone conducting related research. Fifo exemplifies what is genuinely Dominican culture.

A thoroughly progressive, intellectually alert young Dominican woman, Milagos Holguín, speaks with easy eloquence and sincere conviction as she reflects thoughtfully upon the essential vitality of Dominican culture: the collective spirit and genuine expression of unadorned hospitality and warmth of *el pueblo dominicano*. Her hope, regularly presented over the local airwaves on her featured talk show, is to arrive at a national cultural identity by undergoing the process of self-discovery and strategizing a kind of unified purpose. At the same time, Holguín considers the urgent need to view Dominican culture in the larger context of embracing the entirety of Caribbean regional cultural connectedness and identity.

Eladio Regalado, a profoundly reflective thinker and genuinely warm human being, as well as Ramón Tejada Holguín, a dynamically brilliant and imaginative writer, are both young *dominicanos* with much in common. Both are keenly in touch with current issues and concerns within their country and beyond its borders. Both are quite impassioned, yet clear-focused and articulate as they address the urgency of the nation to reevaluate the question of Dominican identity in the process of defining Dominican culture. Regalado and Tejada Holguín avidly foster the restoration of the *mulataje* (African/European, mixed-race heritage) to its rightful place within the total scheme of the sociocultural genesis of Quisqueya.

Paulina Lantigua, the lovely, always exuberant and energetic *hospedera* (one who kindly receives guests and strangers), without question personifies the national quality of being what is referred to in the island as *hospitalaria* (hospitable). To Lantigua, Dominican culture means "all those beautiful and wonderful images that are so uniquely Dominican, from the delicately crafted ceramic faceless dolls to the mystical underground caves and springs at Tres Ojos."[2] Dominican culture for this unofficial Madame Ambassador awakens in every *dominicano* the authentic urge to share this exuberance about the splendors of Quisqueya, especially with anyone being introduced to the island for the first time.

Dominican culture is the master teacher himself, internationally renowned social anthropologist and folklorist extraordinaire Fradique Lizardo. In Professor Lizardo, whose tireless and valuable investigations have translated into glorious exposition the very soul of Quisqueya la Bella, we see genuine attempts to describe a national identity by way of the country's enormously rich folklore, its customs and traditions, and its ethnic origins. Whether tracing the origins and evolution of the merengue, *fiestas patronales* (festivals honoring patron saints), or indigenous musical instruments, popular games or *los palos* (drums played with sticks) of San Pedro de Macorís, Lizardo has dedicated his expansive erudition to rescuing popular Dominican culture from what he sees as the inevitable onslaught of the country's rapidly paced modernization. *El Maestro* reminds us further: *Quien no conoce la historia de su pueblo, mal puede quererlo.* (He who does not know his people's history cannot possibly love it.)

This poignant reminder seems to have been the driving theme behind the honest dedication to exploring and celebrating *la cultura dominicana* on the part of several premier, now legendary Dominican artists. Symbolizing Dominican culture in their collectively exquisite artistry and individual mastery are such towering figures as Casandra Damirón, who almost singlehandedly popularized and revitalized Barahona's music and dance tradition, *la mangulina;* Elenita Santos, who did the same for the traditional *salve;* master musical composer Rafael Solano; the incomparable Joseíto Mateo, one of the great pioneers of the merengue tradition; popular songstress Vickiana; and the indomitable *El Mayimbe* himself, the great voice of Fernandito Villalona.[3] Each of these artists and many others of celebrated status speak passionately in their distinctive mode about what Quisqueya la Bella means to them: the richness of its past, the moving vibrancy of its present, as well as the unlimited promise of its future.

Dreaming Jointly

Soñar solo es peligroso pero soñar juntos ha sido el comienzo de las grandes transformaciones de la historia. (To dream alone is dangerous, but to dream jointly has been the beginning of the greatest changes in history.) This was the principal theme behind the committed efforts of a group of disquieted, but determined young Dominican intellectuals during the difficult years of 1972–1973, as these young people grappled with seeking solutions to the serious internal crisis facing La República Dominicana. These activist thinkers were particularly disturbed by the existing state of national education. They felt that what was important for the nation's students was not necessarily formal academics, but rather the tortuous process of self-reassessment and rediscovery. These agitated young minds were engaged in an intensive search for national purpose and authentic commitment, solidarity of being, cultural connections, and, ultimately, the Dominican reality.[4] The strategy of learning how to dream jointly was perhaps the all-important linchpin in the conscious assessment of Dominican culture. Who are the Dominicans? What is Dominican culture? These agonizing efforts, then and today, involved the extremely delicate and pivotal task of analyzing the ever-changing circumstance of the people, purposely situating *el pueblo* in the role of active historical subject and protagonist.

The task of defining Dominican culture has always been long and painstaking. But perhaps this courageous group of committed young participants engaged in the search for hard answers determined the correct navigational strategy when they saw the necessity of collective dreaming for any workable definition. For them, it became a matter of real urgency that investigations and analyses focus upon the perception of Dominican identity. Accordingly, that identity must be treated as a confluence of an aggregate of Dominican identities, each legitimate in its own right, that have been evolving over the course of the island's long history. To speak of collective dreaming is to address all the divergent segments within the Dominican community in considering the social and historical, authentic and total Dominican reality. This process must be initiated to assist in finding solutions to the many serious problems facing the nation. One immediately noticeable facet of the Dominican character that may facilitate the task is the extraordinary spirit of *community,* in Spanish called *comunidad.* The concept is more frequently translated in the local idiom as *comunero.*

All the Right Ingredients

What are those seductively rich and savory ingredients in the recipe that give the Dominican cultural dish its special aromas, taste, and texture? The captivating hospitality of *los dominicanos* with their sincere warmth and merriment immediately enraptures every visitor to the island, seducing them into making repeat visits. Even the very sensual yet smooth and catchy national rhythm, *el merengue,* is considered by everybody—seasoned visitor and local resident alike—to be far more subtle and alluring than, say, salsa, souka, calypso, or reggae, which are other very popular and authentic Caribbean musical styles and rhythms.

From the top of the Torre del Homenaje, within the capital's walled colonial district, wave the flags of seven different nations that have governed the colony throughout its long history. The society has received a great many influences that drifted in and out, but through this cultural amalgam a clear and precise Dominican identity has emerged, one that is dynamic, solid, and secure. Perhaps the other national jewel among the many found in this historic treasure chest is the one that symbolically says it best: *sancocho dominicano.* Of the various delectable traditional stews prepared and enjoyed by Dominicans everywhere on the island, it is this one in particular, *sancocho,* that has become the undisputed national favorite. It is a very rich blend of various meats, to which is added an equally rich offering of locally grown vegetables and just the right sprinkling of spicy condiments, all simmering together slowly until reaching just the right tenderness and taste.

Mulatez: The Quality of Mulatto-ness

The visitor to Quisqueya is immediately struck by another indispensable ingredient in the cultural cauldron of the island. Totally disarmed and overwhelmed by the succulence of this unique element, the visitor is convinced that divine intervention must have had a major hand in selecting the right ingredients to complete the recipe. Like the culinary richness of the celebrated *sancocho dominicano,* the people themselves are the key to knowing more intimately the success of the recipe. Dominican culture owes its specific uniqueness to something called *mestizaje,* which roughly translates as mixed race or miscegenation.

However, the term most certainly does not carry the pejorative and hostile connotations of miscegenation often conveyed in the socio-historical context of the United States. It may be recalled that there was a period in the United States in the not-so-distant past, when many states, especially in the South, outlawed interracial sexual or marital unions. The practice of referring to an individual as half-caste or half-breed, with its accompanying stigma of mongrelization, is totally absent in Dominican society. In fact, it has been said that "la sociedad dominicana es una comunidad mulata única en el mundo."[5] (Dominican society is a unique mulatto community in the world.)

So unlike the United States, with its pervasive, emotionally charged preoccupation with matters of race, La República Dominicana approaches the question quite differently. For example, it frequently comes as a genuine shock when many a Dominican in the island described without hesitation as *mulato, indio claro, indio oscuro, mestizo,* or by any other color-coded designation, relocates to the States only to discover that she or he is simply *un negro,* or Black person. The fact is that many so-called Dominican Whites would readily be classified as "colored" even in post-apartheid South African society. In the United States context, clearly about 85 percent of the Dominican population would be designated and considered as Black.

Configurations of Color

Historically, a range of descriptive color configurations and classifications appeared quite early in the island. Investigations on the subject document such a system being practiced in the colony as early as 1549. During the colonial era the following terms were commonly used to classify individuals on the basis of color: *mulato* (mulatto), referring then as it does now to anyone who is racially mixed, Black and White; *blanco* (White), referring to any European/Caucasian individual; *negro* (Black), an individual who was 100 percent African; *mestizo* (mixed), an individual who was the offspring of an indigenous person and a Caucasian; *tercerón,* an offspring of a mulatto and a Caucasian, but with one-third African ancestry; *cuarterón,* called quadroon in the English-speaking Antilles, the offspring of a mulatto and a Caucasian, with one-fourth African ancestry.

There was even a classification described as *octerón* (octoroon), the offspring of a quadroon and a Caucasian, with just one-eighth African ancestry! Exactly how these quantitative fractions were gauged defies even the most bizarre imagination, of course. The conquistadors originated a despicably distasteful phrase relative to color gradations that became indicative of just how people were regarded socially. The phrase endured through time, becoming ingrained in the psyche of wider segments of the island's population. Although not heard with nearly the frequency these days that it was some decades ago, the phrase was more degrading to women, but most undeserving by all Dominicans: "Una blanca para el boato social; una negra para el servicio de la casa; y una mulata para la cama." (A White woman for social show [or marriage]; a Black woman for servicing or cleaning the house; and a mulatto woman for taking to bed.)

As cumbersome and perhaps a bit puzzling to the non-Dominican as the color configurations were, the system actually has expanded even more in attempts to codify skin color. Further complicating the matter has been the added notion of hair textures and distinctive racial features like the shape and size of the nose, lips, hips, and even buttocks. The standard Spanish word for hair, *pelo,* is no longer merely that in the island context. Now it becomes much more: it is either *pelo bueno* (good hair, like that of Caucasians) or *pelo malo* (bad hair, like that of Africans). Then there is *pelo lacio,* meaning straight, silky hair like that regularly associated with being *indio* (indigenous). Another example is seen in the standard Spanish word for lips, *labios.* In the Dominican idiom, lips become *bemba* or *bembón* to describe what are perceived as exceptionally thick or full lips—again, like those supposedly of Africans!

Within the indigenous category and encompassing other ethnicities, various sub-classifications have evolved that are currently used in La República Dominicana to designate every possible nuance of color:

- *grifo:* the offspring of a mulatto person and an indigenous person.
- *indio claro:* a light-complexioned indigenous person, usually tan in coloring or one who is Black/White mulatto with straight hair texture.
- *indio oscuro:* a dark-complexioned indigenous person, or one who is darker than the *indio claro,* but still with straight hair and slightly thinner lips than the person of African descent.
- *jabao:* yellowish in coloring with the characteristically descriptive African features in lips, nose, and hair texture.

- *zambo:* the offspring of an indigenous person and an individual of African descent.
- *negro lavao:* literally a "washed or cleaned-up" Black person; a Black individual with considerably thin lips, not-so-broad nose, perceived as being not so dark, but not altogether light-complexioned, with hair texture between straight and woolly.
- *blanco jipato:* a Caucasian with rather yellow complexion, resembling a light-skinned Black person in coloring and with kinky hair texture.

Finally, on an admittedly bizarre and often embarrassing note—according to many Dominicans themselves who are candid about the subject—there is a particularly unusual term of color configuration that still finds current favor along the northern coastal zones of the island. The term *cocolos* historically referred to immigrants of African descent, arriving from the English-speaking islands of the Caribbean.[6] *Cocolos* eventually designated all those Danish-speaking and Dutch-speaking Blacks from around the Antilles who landed at Puerto Plata and the Samaná Peninsula during the early 1870s as unskilled laborers, skilled craftsmen, and artisans.

> Historical records tell us that the term *cocolos* was used quite early, at least during the period of Boyer's regime. In about 1871 the community of established cocolos represented a significant 15¼ percent of the population in the town of Puerto Plata.[7]

Of course, Puerto Plata at this period in the history of La República Dominicana held the distinction, and justifiably so, of being the most cosmopolitan city in all the Republic. At least half of its total population was of foreign nationality. The city presents a true mosaic of ethnicities and languages, as Puerto Plata today still exudes a distinctive urbane flavor.

Viewing the social evolution of Quisqueya as a whole, the observer will readily note that except for that shameful episode during the Trujillo Era when the dictator was maniacally obsessed with notions of *blanqueando la nación* (whitening the nation), and thus orchestrated the monstrous campaign of genocide against resident Haitians (1937) and simultaneously the indiscriminate slaughter of Dominicans of clear African descent living among their Haitian brothers and sisters, there has been a noticeable absence of calculated acts of violence and brutality targeting *dominicanos* of African and/or Haitian origins. The whole of Dominican society, then, is a cornucopia of richly seasoned ingredients that blend marvelously to offer even the most demanding epicure a unique dish of cultural symbiosis. Each of the fundamentally different ethnic components—the indigenous, the European, the African—played significant and delicately interlaced roles in arriving at just the right consistency. The resultant exuberance and resilience ultimately formed the Dominican personality and spirit we know today. Of course, the aborigine component has disappeared, leaving the dominant strains of *padres españoles* and *madres africanas* to coalesce. The radiant beauty produced in its wake is what the visitor sees today in La República Dominicana. A traditional Dominican proverb reminds us that "Después que se apaga la luz, somos todos del mismo color." (After the light is turned out, we're all the same color.)

America's First City: Storehouse of Historical Treasures

To many Dominicans, the realities of a cultural interconnectedness and of community are most prominently illustrated by the network of the various towns throughout La República Dominicana. While each is certainly distinctive in flavor and character, these communities are nevertheless neatly interlocked by the presence of more than a conveniently engineered highway system. Dominican culture may quite possibly be defined by its many diverse, yet interconnected *pueblos,* a word interestingly enough meaning both *town* and/or *people.* An appropriate point of departure for an intimate excursion that will bring the reader closer to understanding and appreciating the essence of Dominican culture is the nation's historic capital city, Santo Domingo. A sensitively compiled poetic tome by Dr. Joaquín Balaguer—the sparkling poet this time, not the politician—*Guia Emocional de la Ciudad Romántica* (Emotional Guide to the Romantic City) is a most seductive personal reflection on the splendors of Santo Domingo, *la ciudad primada de América* (America's first city). With exquisite rhyme, meter, and resonance, the seasoned poetic voice of Balaguer offers a uniquely emotional tour, but with meticulous historical accuracy regarding the Republic's capital and chief seaport. Dominican culture, following the paths and incorporating the legacy of the early indigenous residents, begins in this settlement on the ancient banks of

Río Ozama. Santo Domingo de Guzmán was founded on August 4, 1496, by Columbus's brother Bartolomé. Noted chronicler of the colonial era Padre de las Casas affirmed that the city's founder wanted to call it Santo Domingo because he had the good fortune of arriving on a Sunday. Safe passage under the watchful protection of the saints prompted the navigator Bartolomé to name the settlement in honor of the "teaching apostle," Santo Domingo de Guzmán, who is credited with inventing the rosary. But historical accounts have conflicting versions of the precise circumstance surrounding the origin of the city's name. One popular version, attributed to Columbus's nephew, declares that the name was chosen simply to honor the memory of Christopher's and Bartolomé's father Dominico.

Whatever other accounts that may be floating about regarding how the city got its name, the solid fact of the city's uniqueness remains undisputed. For years this first capital in all the Americas was the strategic base for launching Spain's bold explorations and exploits of conquest of the hemisphere. It was from Santo Domingo that Juan Ponce de León set sail for Puerto Rico and Florida, that Hernán Cortés calculated his conquest of Mexico, that Balboa crossed the Isthmus of Panamá and reached the Pacific Ocean, and that Diego de Velásquez left to settle Cuba. This remarkably well-preserved city, in many instances the result of impressive restoration efforts, boasts historical treasures of monumental proportion. In 1990, the United Nations Educational, Scientific, and Cultural Organization (UNESCO) passed a resolution declaring Santo Domingo de Guzmán's colonial zone a World Heritage Site. Santo Domingo is without question America's First City.

The city is a striking cavalcade of firsts. The island of Hispaniola was, after all, where Europe's first sociopolitical, cultural, and economic undertakings in the New Territories occurred. The first female poets in America, Sister Leonor de Ovando and Doña Elvira de Mendoza, were born in Santo Domingo. Early in its history, the city earned the distinctive title *Atena del Nuevo Mundo* (Athens of the New World). Even earlier legends describe how Columbus, upon arriving upon the island, tied his three ships to the giant *ceiba* tree. That ancient tree, although now in a state of petrifaction, remains along the walled Avenida del Puerto, at the mouth of the Río Ozama. The poet Balaguer called the *ceiba* tree the humblest of all the city's many stately monuments.

Reminders of the Past

Also in the city's old quarter, on the west bank of the Ozama, are other prominent reminders of the architectural splendor of colonial Spain in Las Américas. Here in this area the visitor finds the first cathedral to be erected in the hemisphere, La Catedral de Santa María la Menor, whose first stone was laid by Diego Columbus, son of El Gran Almirante, in 1514; and the first military fortress in the Americas, the Torre del Homenaje (begun in 1503) inside Fortaleza Ozama. The grandeur of the era is likewise captured in the majestic structure that sits at the end of Calle las Damas, the Alcázar de Colón. For decades this building was the official seat of the Spanish Crown in the Americas. Built by Columbus's son Diego in 1510–1514, the Alcázar was the first residential house in the New Territories. Other historical treasures in the legendary settlement include the ruins of Monasterio de San Francisco, America's very first monastery. The Convento de los Dominicos, constructed in 1510, was the site of the founding of America's first university (1538). This venerable institution now bears the name Universidad Autónoma de Santo Domingo and has moved to another part of the city. The first European commercial center in the New Territories consisted of a cluster of eight buildings that served as the colony's vital storage warehouses and was also the site of the customs operations, the famous Casa de Contratación, sometimes called Las Atarazanas. The numerous old houses, churches, and chapels built during the colonial era are all dramatic monuments that offer testimony to the fervor of early settlement by the arriving Spaniards. This remarkable colonial architecture, above all else perhaps, preserves the authentic colonial spirit and tone of that daringly eventful era. Santo Domingo de Guzmán, capital de la Hispaniola, became the city from which would radiate the first sparks of light announcing the arrival of, as well as the point of departure for, Western European civilization throughout the newly encountered Americas.

To the East

Dominican culture is traveling perhaps twenty-five kilometers (fifteen and one half miles) east from the capital by way of the South Coast Highway, named Carretera Mella, and coming to the Playa Boca Chica, the capital area's main resort. The extremely popular beach is actually a reef-protected, shallow lagoon offering many kilometers of sparkling white sand. Especially on weekends, Boca Chica is inundated by a wave of residents fleeing the nearby metropolis, seeking respite from the pressures and tensions of the overcrowded capital. Local vendors are superaggressive in their efforts at selling the famous *yaniqueques* (johnnycakes). The country's other, equally popular beach lies a bit farther eastward, Playa Juan Dolio. One-third of the 1,566 kilometers (or 970 miles) of Dominican coastline is given over to gorgeous beaches.

Dominican culture is the town of San Pedro de Macorís, called La Sultana del Este (the Sultana of the East), the important seaport town resting on the banks of the Río Higuamo, or to use the indigenous name, Río Macorix. The birthplace of Quisqueya's national poet, Pedro Mir, and of noted historian and journalist Miguel Alfonso Mendoza, and the home of Doña América Bermúdez viuda del Risco (mother of deceased poet René del Risco Bermúdez), the town was once the reigning industrial capital of the entire island, with five operating *centrales azucareros* (central sugarmills). The local economy still is heavily dependent on the large sugar estates surrounding the town. For more than one hundred years, the name of Don Pedro Justo Carrión has been closely linked with the town's socioeconomic history by way of the lucrative rum industry and the nationally popular brand Ron Macorix.

Besides rum, there is the traditionally popular drink unique to San Pedro de Macorís, Guavaberi de Macorís, from the fruit of the same name. Drinking Guavaberi and watching the sun go down is a favorite pastime set to music by one of the country's top musical artists, Juan Luis Guerra. However, without the slightest doubt, one could not speak about San Pedro de Macorís without pausing to reflect on the town's truly unique status of being crowned the Legendary Birthplace of Many of the World's Best Baseball Players (Cuba notwithstanding!). Curiously enough, more United States major league baseball players of Hispanic origin come from this town than from any other single town in either La República Dominicana or the United States. Investigators suspect that the sociocultural dynamic operating here has to do, more than any other factor, with the lengthy United States military occupation of the whole country, and especially of the seaport areas such as San Pedro de Macorís during the period 1916–1924. That experience left many welcome and not-so-welcome North American cultural influences. The favorite American pastime, baseball, was one cultural element that really caught the attention of sports enthusiasts. Baseball quickly supplanted the *pelea de gallo* (cockfight) and *fútbol* (soccer) as traditional forms of popular sports entertainment.

Dominican culture continues eastward along the south coast, Carretera Mella, reaching La Romana. This is the site of the gigantic sugarmill operation Central Romana Inc., the island's largest. The mill's owners, the Gulf & Western conglomerate, are also responsible for the construction of the magnificent Casa de Campo, the nearby luxury tourist colony that features the renowned international artists' village, Altos de Chavón. The village is perched dramatically high upon the surrounding hilltop cliffs and is made to resemble an Italian Renaissance villa. Further eastward from La Romana is the town of Higüey. The definitive cultural significance of Higüey lies in the fact that here the traveler finds the famous Basílica de Nuestra Señora de la Altagracia, the revered patroness of La República Dominicana. On January 21 of each year, devout *dominicanos* from all points of the island make a solemn pilgrimage to the sacred shrine inside the ultramodern cathedral.

The road from here next turns northwesterly toward the picturesque town of El Seibo, before continuing onward to the northern coastal town of Miches. Sadly, the present-day notoriety of Miches results from the unfortunate circumstance that from this departure point increasing numbers of undocumented Dominicans launch their desperate and frequently ill-fated seaborne journeys. Aboard untrustworthy *yolas,* with the false hope of reaching an economically better life in nearby Puerto Rico, the fleeing voyagers often meet with a tragic end.

To the West

Traveling westward from Santo Domingo along the Carretera Sánchez, the visitor in search of Dominican culture will find it in the town of Haina. This is the country's most modern port facility, constructed to alleviate the heavily congested port at the capital. Continuing westward, the cultural journey's next stop is the town of San Cristóbal, the birthplace of Rafael Leonidas Trujillo. Perhaps in ironic contrast, here also was the site where the nation's first constitution was signed (in the Palacio del Ayuntamiento). At the nearby Santa María caves, the African-derived *festivals de los palos* (stick and drum festivals) are traditionally held. Baní is the next town reached upon traveling still westward. There is a fascinating biographical note associated with this town. One of Latin America's noblest patriots, Máximo Gómez, was born here in Baní. Even many Cubans do not realize that the great nineteenth-century liberation fighter for Cuban independence was actually born on Dominican soil. On the outskirts of the town is the village of Paya, which produces what is regarded throughout the island as the best goat's milk cheese to be found anywhere.

To the South and Southwest

From Baní, La Carretera Sánchez carries us on to the town of Azua, whose complete name is Azua de Compostela. The town is quite ancient and overflowing in rich history. Founded as an early strategic garrison town in 1504 under the colony's aggressively ambitious governor Nicolás de Ovando, Azua was later the site of an important fugitive slave *maniel.* In the whole of the southwestern zone, a region occupying approximately 30 percent of Dominican territory, but constituting a mere 13 percent of the nation's population, the lush and fertile Valle del San Juan boasts two dynamic commercial centers: Azua and San Juan de la Maguana, as the latter was known in earlier times. Popular folklore recalls the fierce rivalry that existed between the two towns during the colonial era. The competition for socioeconomic dominance in the valley grew so intense that in Azua, the older of the two settlements, the citizenry referred mockingly to the more recently prosperous *sanjuaneros* (residents of San Juan) as *barriga verde,* meaning green bellies. The insult derived from the practice of the *sanjuaneros* of wearing buttonless shirts, thereby exposing their green stomachs (*barriga verde*)—a practice considered quite unsophisticated and brutish.

The next stop along our cultural quest, still in the mainly dry and arid southwest, is Barahona. It is here, as many Dominicans will affirm, where the island's best coffee, plantains, and bananas are cultivated, despite the region's characteristically uninviting climate. Barahona is the principal city of the southern zone and offers a wealth of natural attractions, beautiful beaches, and exciting ecology. Located not far from town is the spectacular Lago Enriquillo, abundant in crocodiles, iguanas, and flamingos. A salt-water lake, Enriquillo holds the distinctive title of being the largest lake in the entire Antilles, measuring almost two hundred kilometers (or seventy-eight square miles) in length and lying forty-four meters (144 feet) below sea level. The Isla Cabritos, where the crocodile colony is located, lies in the very center of the lake. Also in this region is a magnetic phenomenon, a topographical slope that gives the impression that a person is ascending, when in fact the individual is descending.

To the Frontier Zone

The journey that is destined to arrive somehow at a clearer definition of Dominican culture, although now held up in the far western provinces along the Dominican-Haitian border (called *la zona frontera,* or the frontier zone), certainly does not end here at that border. From the town of Pedernales, the Republic's most westerly town, to the other towns along the way, Duvergé, Jimaní, Elías Piña, to Bánica and Bajabón, what emerges quite noticeably in all the towns of *la frontera* is a Dominican culture that undergoes a marked transformation consistent with the general pattern of so-called border zones around the globe. Everywhere throughout the zone are checkpoints set up adjacent to roadside military installations, staffed largely by underpaid, routinely morose and lonely *militares* (soldiers) who must wonder daily *¿Por qué yo?* (Why me?) for this desolate, unglamorous assignment. Why not the international airport at Puerto Plata or La Romana? First of all, as with most border zones worldwide, there is an often ambiguous feeling or even contradictory ambience about the area generally. Sometimes there is unmistakable tension and heavy scrutiny, but at other times there is a kind of laissez-faire attitude in operation. Soldiers on duty, for instance, may often look the other way, or seem not overly enthusiastic or vigilant about the petty contraband trafficking (except, of course, in the case of illegal drug trafficking, which is most seriously monitored and interdicted by government troops).

Here, there is most commonly a flurry of activity, mainly commercial, throughout the zone as anxious Haitian merchants, artisans, traders, and vendors pass through laden with every conceivable kind of housewares, clothing goods, foodstuffs, and indescribable sundries. These items are destined for sale in the principal Dominican towns along *la frontera* like Elías Piña, Dajabón, or Pederanles. There are often regularly scheduled market days authorized by the Dominican government, a schedule that may or may not be necessarily adhered to by attendant militaries. Human traffic is usually voluminous, with merchants of both sexes, children often in tow, having walked from within the Haitian interior for a few days just to reach the border in time for the market days. There is a narrow skirt of territory separating the two sister republics—called *la tierra de nadie* (no man's land)—and is a kind of outdoor waiting room for this mass of humans who must then individually negotiate their actual crossing. Usually there will be a shallow stream or river to cross, but not presenting much of a problem. Transport is normally by foot, but also by pack mules and donkeys, or mopeds and *motoconchos* (motorcycles) operated by enterprising Haitian youths.

La frontera between Haiti and La República Dominicana, not at all unlike border areas universally and throughout the ages, reflects certain cultural patterns that are not nearly as static and resistant as those patterns found in the more protected interior zones. Here along the border there is general receptiveness to cultural modes of an interchangeable nature. There is a ready fluidity and seeming ease with social interactions, including exchange of language (Haitian Kryol and Spanish). Many individuals, Haitians and Dominicans alike, speak the language of the other with effective results. Even the currency, the Haitian *gourd* (not accepted anywhere else in Dominican territory) and the Dominican peso, are interchangeable here in the border zone without hesitation. Also, there is a greater instance of interethnic marriage, more prevalent among Haitian women and Dominican males than vice versa, in *la zona frontera* than elsewhere in the island. What we see here is a marked cultural blending or fusion into a kind of frontier homogenization, but without the cream separating.

Here in *la frontera,* there are no squalid *bateys* for migrant workers, which readily account for the resultant exclusion and separateness of the workers and their families from mainstream sociocivic intercourse with the surrounding larger community in the traditional sugarcane zones of the country. The character of the border zone practically rules out marginalized segments of the populace. The huge market at Elías Piña, for example, conveys a definite air of being more in Haiti than in La República Dominicana, with its colorful assortment of merchandise, aromas, rhythms, and especially the staccato-like sounds of Kryol, the predominant language in use here. One witnesses with fascination all manner of intensive human activity, almost frenetically engaged in what is really quite ordinary social interaction with other human beings. The government-authorized market days, after all, are of very limited duration. Everyone consumes wisely and fully every authorized minute.

To the North

The cultural axis linking Santo Domingo with the northern zones, piercing the island's heartland of El Cibao, is the highway called Carretera Duarte. This modern highway travels through the heavenly beautiful and luxuriant valley of La Vega Real (the Royal Plain), often called the Garden of the Antilles. This boastful title, totally deserved in every regard, comes by virtue of the fact that the valley is endowed with the Caribbean region's richest alluvial soils. The valley proper, El Valle del Cibao, is watered by the numerous tributaries flowing from both the Northern and Central Cordillera, and generously supplied with rainfall. Here is the Republic's granary, its fruit and vegetable baskets, as well as abundant sugarcane. Brugal, a rival rum distillery to the southern zone's dominant Macorix and Barceló, is headquartered here. The Carretera Duarte passes leisurely through the towns of Bonao and La Vega, allowing for meandering links with the hillside towns of Jarabacoa and Constanza, actually in the foothills of the Cordillera Central mountain range. Military personnel stationed here for the first time recount later to their disbelieving families, without exaggeration, how temperatures in winter at Constanza easily drop sharply to zero, and how even frosts often occur. Directly in the Cordillera Central, quite near to Jarabaoa and Constanza, is the majestic Pico Duarte, the Caribbean's highest peak, rising to a spectacular 3,175 meters (10,414 feet). The climb by pack mule takes a full two days.

Secondary roads branching off from the scenic Carretera Duarte, once winding around to the east, lead into the towns of Cotuí, San Francisco de Macorís, and Moca, the latter serving as an important coffee and cacao center, contributing heavily to the overall economic wealth of this northern region. The village of El Higuerito, just minutes outside Moca, captures the artistic soul of *la cultura dominicana* in the form of the world-renowned faceless ceramic dolls that are hand-crafted here by local traditional artisans. The town of Tamboril is the next approach, just outside the stately city of Santiago. In the smaller of the two municipal parks located in the center of Tamboril, the almost legendary folk character of Don Viga Pichardo, to whom nearly everyone refers affectionately as *el alcalde del parque* (the mayor of the park), holds court daily from sunrise until sundown. Mayor Viga is like a venerable jumble of traditional West African cultures: a master storyteller, a humorist, a walking reservoir of anecdotes and local social history—sometimes invented, sometimes subjected to personal interpretation. Tamboril is also the town that boasts the island's best version of the traditional *sancocho dominicano,* as prepared by Doña Gudelia, who insists upon using only locally raised chicken (i.e., raised in the town itself, not imported from Santo Domingo or New York!) in her jealously guarded recipe.

Nearby Santiago de los Caballeros (founded in 1500) is the second largest city in La República Dominicana, and rivals the capital in both economic and cultural sophistication. The city is proud of its equally impressive history that dates back to its initial establishment as a fort under the direct orders of El Gran Almirante himself, Christopher Columbus. Santiago, situated on a high bluff on the Río Yaque del Norte, has long been the agricultural nucleus of El Cibao, and is today the region's center for rum and tobacco production. Leading the journey out from Santiago, the Carretera Duarte continues as the principal conduit through the whole of this northern zone. The north coast, bathed by the warm waters of the Atlantic Ocean, is known more popularly as the Amber Coast because it happens to be the site of the most abundant amber mines in the entire world. Although classified as semiprecious, amber is actually tree sap that fossilized some forty-eight million years ago, trapping numerous particles of plant and insect life. Gem connoisseurs, who often pay thousands of dollars for a single piece, report that the unique Dominican amber is known to be the most transparent in the world and also contains the highest concentration of insect inclusion. An impressive collection of rare Dominican amber is on permanent display at the Amber Museum in the town of Puerta Plata.

Founded in 1502 by El Gran Almirante, Puerta Plata, with its ambitious, ongoing restoration projects of exquisite colonial architecture seemingly on every corner, is the chief town on the Amber Coast. The colonial Fortaleza de San Felipe is the oldest in the Americas. Just outside town a *teleférico* (cable car) shuttles passengers to the summit of Loma Isabel de Torres, which has an elevation of about 793 meters (2,601 feet). From on high, a statue of Christ looks out over the sweeping panorama below. The luxury tourist complex of Playa Dorada, lying just east of Puerta Plata, is fast becoming the pleasure favorite of international visitors to the island. Thanks largely to the country's expanding and aggressive tourist industry, the entire Amber Coast is rivaling the southern coast in attracting both investment—domestic and international—and visitors from different parts of the globe.

Since the mid-1800s, the steady influx of Europeans, in addition to considerable numbers of Scandinavians, Eastern Mediterranean groups, Sephardic Jews, Afro-Antilleans (mainly from the English-speaking Caribbean, and referred to as *cocolos*), North Americans, Cubans, Puerto Ricans, Chinese, and Filipinos have together provided this northern coastal zone with its tradition of being quite urbane and cosmopolitan. Consequently, the cuisine is especially varied here. The ethnic and linguistic mosaic is immediately discernible in the profusion of non-Hispanic family names now quite commonplace (e.g., Paiewonsky) in the area today. Not far from Puerta Plata is the town of Sosúa. This is a town that began its socioeconomic rise with the hasty, government-fostered settlement of Jewish refugees arriving from Nazi-infested Europe during the 1940s. The successful local dairy indus-try—including the kosher cheeses produced here—serves the entire island. The main street in town is named Main Street, rather than the standard Spanish, *Calle Principal.* About twelve kilometers east of Sosúa is the seaside town of Cabarete, currently the undisputed windsurf mecca of the resort world. International championship tour-naments are hosted here annually in June. Río San Juan, Cabrera, Nagua—which is more correctly a fishing village on the shores of the Bahía Escocesa—and Sánchez are towns that contribute enormously to the scenic wonders along the length of the coastal road leading to historic Samaná. Sánchez was once a considerably prosperous seaport, boasting at the time the country's only railway, which used to run to San Francisco de Macorís and La Vega.

The Samaná Peninsula, for a long time the coveted territorial prize of foreign (mainly North American) annexationists with imperialist designs, is strategically situated in the extreme east of the Cibao. When Columbus arrived at the peninsula on January 12, 1493, he and his soldiers were so fiercely repelled by the indigenous Ciguayo people that he named the bay the *Golfo de las Flechas* (Gulf of Arrows). Now called Samaná Bay, the area is absolutely stunning in scenic splendor, completely fringed with coconut palms and dotted almost everywhere with islets. On the peninsula is the city of the same name, Samaná. The city was established in the mid-1750s as part of an aggressive scheme by the colonial authorities to attract families from the Spanish Canary islands. In stark contrast to the more widely practiced Catholicism through La República Dominicana generally, Protestantism flourishes in this region. The proliferation of the Protestant church is due in large measure to the influx of English-speaking immigrants into the peninsula. In fact, the Protestant church here, locally called *la churcha* rather than the standard Spanish word *la iglesia,* physically dominates its Catholic sister in the number of actual houses of worship as well as in structural height. Also, the idea of an informal, usually boisterous party is frequently called a *churcha*—throughout the island.

On the north coast of the peninsula is Los Terrenos, featuring some of the finest beaches in the whole of La República Dominicana. Truly glorious are the coral reefs, underwater grottoes, and an abundance of sea life. Out from the peninsula are several enchanting offshore islands. On the south coast of Samaná Bay is a region known as Los Haitises, a government-protected coastal zone. This rare environment of humid tropical forest and seascape of mangrove swamps, caves, and most unusual rock formations emerging abruptly from beneath the sea, called *magotes* locally, is not seen anywhere else on the island.

Returning to the Sosúa locality, if the traveler ventures in the opposite direction along the Amber Coast, heading toward the Haitian border, she or he approaches the towns of Luperón, La Isabela, and finally Monti Cristi at the extreme western end of the coast. The historic town of La Isabela, where Columbus built the first European settlement in the Americas (1493)—remember that Santo Domingo was not founded until 1496 and by Columbus's brother Bartolomé—was also the site of the first Catholic mass said on American soil (January 6, 1494). The first city hall, called *El Ayuntamiento* as are all such municipal complexes throughout the country, and court were established here as well (April 24, 1494).

Beyond Tourist Souvenirs

In the island's widely circulated, glossy tourist magazine *Bohío,* the minister of state tourism regularly extends a cordial welcome to visitors to La República Dominicana. He genuinely invites them to "Descubra los colores y sienta el ritmo dominicano." (Discover the colors and feel the Dominican rhythm.) The minister's invitation is absolutely sincere, as the visitor discovers immediately the truly hospitable personality of the Dominican people. The enjoyment of

Quisqueya's stunningly beautiful hills and mountains, the sunny white and golden beaches fanned by shady tropical palms are certain to be placed high on the list of pleasant memories of a luscious Caribbean vacation. The tourist minister may well wish that indelible cultural images will be etched profoundly upon the consciousness of every person fortunate enough to have experienced this delectably seductive island called Quisqueya la Bella. To actually experience the distinctively Dominican culture is to savor every delicate morsel, with its unique blend of ingredients. Only in this way will the sojourner depart the island with something far beyond the usual tourist souvenirs and often gaudy trinkets tucked away in her luggage.

Dominican culture, it can be said correctly, is an eclectic assemblage of images that collectively reveal the essential *alma,* or soul and spirit, of all that is Dominican. That diverse assemblage manifests itself in the land, with its contrasting topography—from the elevated northern Cordilleras to the humid Azua lowlands in the south, or the arid southwestern Bahoruco; in the numerous rivers and their sometimes forgotten tributaries, nearly all of which still carry their indigenous name from an ancient, almost mystical past; in the resilient and physically beautiful people themselves with their rich legacy of an ethnic kaleidoscope that readily defies any sensible cataloguing; in the cities, small towns, villages, and hamlets sprinkled alongside meandering roads and dotting spectacular natural landscapes and coastlines; in the agonizing and action-packed history of relentless struggle—even when it meant ugly and brutal civil war—toward efforts to determine and forge a common destiny for the entire island; in the combined traditions and customs of a trifold heritage, the food, the music and dance, the games, the laughter and merriment—in all those things that surround the people daily, constituting and defining exactly who are *los dominicanos.* This is what the lucky visitor must discover and feel when participating in any authentic Dominican cultural experience. In conclusion, Dominican culture embraces the historical reality and glorious rebirth of an optimistic vision, a pure and unwavering faith in the strength of the Dominican character, a strengthened self-confidence in the people's collective capacity to transform the nation into a thoroughly modern, effectively productive, and responsive democracy for all its citizens. Dominican culture is the realization of an arduous process by which a seemingly defeated community managed to summon the will to resist any manner of defeat. The lengthy history of Quisqueya la Bella, of the Dominican people, has seen the nation subjected to a continuous series of often brutalizing shocks, jolts, and tremors, which together gradually revived the people. These shocks have been the necessary catalysts that have reawakened the spirit of *comunero,* or community, that has long been the keystone in the character of *los quisqueyanos.*

In retrospect, Dominican culture is:

- Dancing the merengue along the Malecón in Santo Domingo at the National Merengue Festival held annually during the last week of July through the first week of August.
- Walking the steps to the top of the monument to *Los Héroes de la Restauración,* the city's highest point, in Santiago de los Caballeros.
- Visiting some of the deserted beaches on the exotic offshore islands of Samaná.
- Taking a leisurely ride in a horse-drawn carriage around El Ciabo's premier city, Santiago.
- Browsing through the booths at the traders' market at Elías Piña.
- Celebrating Independence Day, 27 *de febrero,* with Dominican friends.
- Playing a lively game of sandlot *béisbol* with a group of youngsters of San Pedro de Macorís.
- Wading across any of the shallow streams along the border zone into *la tierra de nadie* that separates Haiti and the Dominican Republic.
- Shopping for local crafts at El Mercado Modelo on Avenida Mella in the nation's capital.
- Swimming in any of the cool, hillside *balnearios* (swimming holes) nestled among the hills around Jarabacoa or San José de las Matas.
- Meditating in the solemn quietness of the Basílica de Altagracia in the town of Higüey.
- Visiting a *batey* on the outskirts of either Barahona in the southwest or near the town of Ramón Santana in the southeast.
- Boldly venturing a ride in a *carro público* (public taxi) or a *motoconcho* (motorcycle) through the streets of Santo Domingo.
- Strolling among the midday throngs along Calle Conde in the capital.
- Eating a freshly made *chimichurri* sandwich from any of the vendors along the capital's Malecón.
- Sitting for about an hour in the central plaza of any small town,

chatting idly with the local elders who are there regularly every day.

- Tasting a plate of *mondongo* in San Pedro de Macorís.
- Playing a fast-paced game of *dominó* (dominoes) at a table set up along the sidewalk, well into the evening hours, with a group of locals in San Juan.
- Listening to traditional *perico ripiao* music played artistically anywhere throughout El Cibao.
- Eating a bowl of *sancocho* prepared the old-fashioned way in a traditional Dominican kitchen.
- Sitting late into the night with Ramón and Zeneida in their apartment, discussing all the current sociopolitical and cultural issues facing the country.
- Gazing up at the spectacular Monument of Fray Montesinos in the capital.
- Being fortunate enough to eat succulent *lambí* as prepared in Josefina's ample kitchen in Azua.
- Going bargain hunting among the unimaginable assortment of merchandise from sidewalk vendors along Avenida Mella or Calle Duarte in the nation's capital.
- Sipping Guavaberi with Juan Luis Guerra, watching the sun go down in San Pedro de Macorís.
- Spending a romantic, tropical moonlit night on the beach at Boca Chica.
- Becoming completed enraptured by the delightfully sweet sound of the lovely Olga Lara as she sings the ballad "La Revancha."
- Participating in any of the annual *fiestas patronales* (Festivals to the Patron Saint), held in small towns throughout the island— every town has its traditional festival.
- Dancing to the rhythms of the World Ambassador of the Merengue, the incomparable Johnny Ventura.
- Walking across El Puente Mella from Calle Prolongación Méjico into Villa Duarte—everybody calls the bridge *la bicicleta* (the bicycle) because it is so narrow.
- Dancing the *bambulá,* one of the traditional dances commonly performed at local festivals around the Samaná Peninsula.
- Taking the long, leisurely bus ride along the scenic route from Santo Domingo to Puerto Plata; although the bus is equipped with a mounted color TV, everybody seems mesmerized by the breathtak-

ing landscape as the bus slowly penetrates deeper into El Cibao.
- Listening to the haunting melodies of classic Dominican songs as interpreted by the sultry voice of Maridalia Hernández in her collection *Dulce Recuerdo,* compositions by her grandfather.
- Buying locally published books on every conceivable subject at the very popular *Librería La Trinitaria,* at the corner of Arzo. Nouel and Calle J. Reyes in the capital.
- Watching Doña Fela create a pastry masterpiece with her home-baked birthday cakes—later tasting a slice is heavenly.
- Being totally overwhelmed by the magnitude of El Faro a Colón.
- Eating the famous local dish, *pasteles en hojas* (made from *plátano,* minced meat, and other spicy ingredients) in the town of San Cristóbal.
- Watching the skill of Milagritos as she haggles with the astute Haitian market women at Elías Piña.
- Listening with awe as the master folklorist Fradique Lizardo reminds us of the glory of *la cultura dominicana.*
- Reading with measured intensity the poetic lyricism and intellectual commentary of Doña Aida Cartagena, Pedro Mir, and Blas Jiménez, for a pure taste of Dominican reality!

¿Y es fácil?

Notes

1. *Baquiní* (or *baquiné* in Puerto Rico): derived from a West African (Yoruba of coastal Nigeria) religious ceremony that celebrates the joyous departure (i.e., death) of an infant from the horrors of the earthly world, so that she might join the ancestors in the more harmonious spiritual world. The child is dressed completely in white lace, and special chanting and drumming mark the musical farewell.

2. Tres Ojos (Three Eyes) refers to three ancient underground caverns featuring an intricate network of freshwater springs, located near the modern Santo Domingo International Airport.

3. El Mayimbe: of rural Afro-Cuban origins, the term means the undisputed leader of the village or head of the household.

4. *Hoja Cedee.* Centro Dominicano de Estudios de la Educación, año vi, no. 13, pp. 15–17.

5. Interview with Rafael A. Iberto Brugal Paiewonsky, June 1993 in Habitat Fifo, Puerta Plata.

6. Ibid.

7. Ibid.

Appendix A

What Makes the Language of Quisqueya Different?

A somewhat cursory inspection of the language of Quisqueya is of special note because of, once again, the interlacing patterns of ethnic diversity enhancing the nation's basic cultural fabric. Again, there is a unique Dominican nature in the evolution of the linguistic kaleidoscope that marks the island's colorful and unquestionably vibrant language. To begin with a very important observation, one must be aware of the fact that the Spanish language in the Americas is distributed geographically among roughly five linguistic zones. These zones are (1) the Río de la Plata region, the most populous areas of Argentina and all of Uruguay; (2) Paraguay, where Spanish has become practically overshadowed by the more widely spoken indigenous language Guaraní, thus justifying in part a totally separate linguistic zone; (3) the Andean region, encompassing the whole of the imperial territory of the ancient Inca culture, the major portion of Colombia and parts of Venezuela; (4) Mexico, the Yucatán, and Central America; and finally (5) the Caribbean, with the three Spanish Antilles islands of Cuba, La República Dominicana, and Puerto Rico—plus a large segment of Venezuela and the Caribbean coast of Colombia.

Linguistic Evolution

The Spanish that is spoken in Quisqueya, like language in any other nation, is the result of a lengthy and rather complex evolutionary process. That process is necessarily complex because language does not simply march forward on its own accord, nor does it proceed at random. Rather, language is most inextricably woven, impelled, or sometimes even obstructed by the peculiarities and dynamics of a country's political, social, and cultural circumstances. Adding to Quisqueya's already present indigenous foundation, Spanish and African linguistic elements factored considerably into the vernacular that would ultimately evolve into an exceptionally rich quality and style of expressiveness in the island's speech. Historically, the island of Hispaniola, like the rest of the Spanish-speaking Caribbean, is characterized linguistically by a very strong *castellano* (Castillean) flavor in its vocabulary, syntax, and phonetic quality. As we know, the Iberian Peninsula in its entirety was fully represented by the diverse geopolitical and cultural regions of Spain from which the successive waves of fortune-seeking adventurers, soldiers, settlers, and other early arrivals came. However, the predominance of the peninsula's southernmost zones, mainly Extremadura and Andalucia, accounted for the principal makeup of the populations destined for the new territory of Hispaniola.

Therefore, when the various language patterns merged, there was a noticeable speech inflection, together with other significant language components, that resembled more the speech of Spain's southern provinces than that of the central plateau region, the locale of *castellano*. The bulk of the early arrivals to the Spanish Caribbean was comprised of landless peasants, agricultural workers, military personnel, artisans, and numerous other folk of humble origins. In large measure, the speech of this particular segment of Iberian society would reflect the precise sociocultural circumstance and status as this European population nucleus was being formed. The formation took place during the initial period of settlement, ten to fifteen years immediately following the Great Encounter of 1492. It was at this juncture that the island's linguistic base was likewise being established. The speech pattern, including matters such as lexicon, syntax, and pronunciation, would feature many archaic linguistic elements, even obsolete traditional forms of Spanish that were descriptive of this group of the Iberian society. Of course, the contemporary speech/vocabulary of La República Dominicana does not reveal any particularly close relationship to any given province of Iberia. There are, nevertheless, any number of image-laden, playfully colorful, and inventive dominicanisms that evoke the archaic vocabulary and syntax of the variant of Spanish that has been spoken in traditional fashion for many generations throughout the rural southern Iberian provinces. Add to that distinctive character some significant contributions of the indigenous Taíno and several West African language variants, especially in terms of vocabulary and morphology, and what results is Spanish as spoken in La República Dominicana.

Linguistic Divisions

Finally, the territory of contemporary Quisqueya is divided into regions, each with its own distinct linguistic character, however minor or subtle. Mostly, the speech patterns of the large, major urban center are quite uniform throughout the island. On the other hand, the speech of the rural zones, which constitute the major portion of Dominican territory, is divided in a manner that parallels closely the established geopolitical and traditional economic zones of the nation. These divisions evolved similarly along cultural lines as well. The southwest, including the Distrito Nacional eastward to incorporate the provinces of San Pedro de Macorís, La Romana, El Seibo, and La Altagracia; the Cibao region, encompassing the whole northern coastal tier from Monti Cristi to Samaná; and the southwest from Azua to Pedernales are the major zones. Without the slightest debate, it is the northern region of El Cibao, more than the other regions of the island, that presents a very special case for the country's linguistic anomaly and other outstanding speech irregularities. Such variants do not, of course, exert such a strong influence along the northern coastal areas, where the dominant element is either Haitian Kryol in the *zona frontera* toward the west, or a kind of pidgin English toward the east of Samaná.

It is here in the Cibao—and more precisely within the internal localities of this zone, between the Cordillera Central and the Cordillera Septentrional—where we hear the distinctive language variant. Here quite pronounced archaic forms in speech are common. Most characteristic and identifiable, for example, is the phonetic vocalization of the final syllabic "r" and "l" transforming to "i": *comer* = to eat → *comei; papel* = paper → *papei; capital* = capital → *capitei*. A *dominicano* from this region of El Cibao, called *un cibaeño,* reveals his or her regional origins immediately upon merely opening his or her mouth.

There are also some rather unusual linguistic occurrences in syntax and vocabulary, again exhibiting strong archaic remnants from traditional southern Iberia. What follows is a sample glossary of personally selected dominicanisms that, while commonly heard throughout the country today, crossing nearly all the island's socioeconomic strata and political ideology, are nevertheless strictly confined within the borders of Quisqueya and understood solely by *quisqueyanos*.

Glossary of Frequently Used Dominicanisms

A

Abejón colorado: Mulato de pelo rojizo (a mulatto with reddish-colored hair).
A calito me: A horcajadas sobre la espalda de uno (Get up on my shoulders).
Acotegar: Acomodar; arreglar (to satisfy).
Agallú: Hombre de muchas agallas (an ambitious individual).
Aigullo: Orgullo (pride).
Amemao: Tímido (a very timid individual).
Angurria: Ambición de quererlo todo para sí (obsession to want everything for one's self).

B

Bachata: Fiesta popular (traditional music of the rural zones).
Balsa: Gran cantidad (a crowd of people).
Bandera nacional: Bandera nacional (national flag). This is a very common, very basic meal consisting of rice and beans, plantain, and a piece of meat of any variety.
Batey: The word, of indigenous origin, referred to the area where men regularly played a kind of handball. Today, the *batey* is the usually squalid residential compound of migrant Haitian cane workers.
Bembe: Of West African origin; Labio grueso (fleshy lips).
Boche: Reprimenda de palabra (a verbal reprimand).
Bochinche: Desorden (scandal or confusion).

C

Caballada: Disparate (talking nonsense).
Cacarear: Repetir mucho una cosa (repetitious).

Cachivache: Cosa en desuso, sin valor (junk).
Can: A party or merriment.
Carabiné: A popular dance. This was an early form of the merengue made popular during the 1916–1924 United States military occupation. The dance form was so named because North American soldiers, who normally carried a carbine rifle strapped to the leg, could consequently only dance stiff-legged fashion.
Carrancho: An old-model car.
Cocotazo: Refers to a knock or blow to the head.
Cocotú Rico: Rich and wealthy individual.
Concho: An interjection conveying the idea "Don't bother me, dammit!"

CH

Chamuchina: Gente de barrio pobre (residents of a poor neighborhood).
Chimichurri: A kind of hamburger, only spicier, with lettuce, tomato, and onions, and normally sold by pushcart vendors on the streets.
Chele: Un centavo (one penny, one cent).
Chepa: Casualidad grande (serious accident).
Chévere: Bonito (beautiful).
Chin: Muy poquito (a very little amount).
Churcha: Of North American origin, the term is an Americanization of the word *church*. It refers to a boisterous crowd of people intent upon having fun and a good time.

D

Dar carpeta: Molestar; fastidiar (to annoy).
De carambola: Por casualidad (by accident).
Definfarrar: Destruir (to destroy).
De orilla: Persona plebeya (individual of very humble origins).
De pe a pa: From top to bottom.
Desguabinado: Debil (weak).

E

Ecolecuá: Of Italian origin; estar de acuerdo (to agree).
Embromar la paciencia: Bromear (to joke).
Enjé: We'll see about that; implying disbelief.

En la bajada te espero: I'll wait for you outside; implying a threat.
Entrote: Used in the Cibao region (to be in love with someone).

F

Farjarse: Trabajar (to work).
Fantoche: Fanfarrón (boastful).
Flaquindé: Flaco (skinny).
Fuá: An interjection used when the lights suddenly go out.
Fucú: To do something that makes people laugh.

G

Gabear: To climb a tree.
Gallareta: Refers to a very talkative person.
Gancho: Estafa; fraude (fraud; a dishonest scheme).
Guagua: Autobús (public bus).
Guapo: To be angry.

H

Hacer lun serrucho: To take up a monetary collection to defray cost.
Hacer el chivo loco: To play the part of the fool in order to gain one's personal goal.
Hereméutica: Truco (a trick or deceitful act).

I

Inforforarse: Estar muy incómodo (to be very uncomfortable).
Inglés: An Englishman (a bill collector).

J

Jabao: Term describing a light-complexioned Black person; yellowish in color, but with characteristically African features in lips, nose, hair texture.
Jacha: Dientes grandes (very large teeth).
Jarina: Llovizna (a very light rain; a drizzle).
Jipato: Term describing a very pale Caucasian individual, almost resembling a jabao in other physical features.

Joderse: Fastidiarse (to be very worrisome).
Juum: Onomatopoeic utterance meaning yes; also implies a threat.

K

Kaki: Caqui (popular, yellowish-colored cloth).

L

Labioso: Charlatán (a smooth talker).
Lamber: Comer (to eat).
Latoso: Charlador (very talkative; being long-winded).
Lote: A group of various unimportant items.
Lunático: Moody or changeable character.

M

Mabí: A popular local beverage made with fermented cane juice.
Ma-Chepa: Hijo de Ma-Chepa (a nobody; of little social importance).
Machucar: Pulverizar (to pulverize).
Mangú: A local porridge made with mashed plantain, garlic, olive oil, and salt.
Mojiganga: Ridículo (ridiculous; object of ridicule).

N

Na: Nada (nothing).
Ni así, ni asao: De ningún modo (by no means).

Ñ

Ñeco: To be without arms; amputated arms.
Ñoñería: Extreme immaturity.
Ñoño: A spoiled individual, in the manner of an infant.

O

Ofrézcome: Un susto (sudden fear).
Oye eso: Eschuche (listen to that).

P

Pai: Papá, padre (daddy).
Pariguayo: Idiota (idiot).
Pendenciar: Vigilar (to watch carefully; to be vigilant).
Pique: Slight irritation.

Q

Quema: Borrachera (a drunken stupor).
¡Qué vaina!: What a mess! Totally unnecessary.

R

Rebú: Disorder or confusion.
Rullir: Roer (to gnaw or to destroy gradually).

S

Salado: Mortal (fatal; mortal).
Salapatroso: Muy sucio (very dirty).

T

Tabaná: A tap on the head.
Tacaño: A very cheap person.
Tajalán: A very tall, skinny person.
Trancar: Cerrar con llave (to lock up).
Trica: Refers to making fun of someone behind the person's back.
Truño: Cara triste (to be sad-faced).

U

Una añada: Muchos años (many years).
Unjú: Sí (yes).

V

Vejigazo: Knocks or blows to a person's stomach.
Ventanero: An individual who has the habit of spending a lot of time

leaning out the window. From *ventana* (window).

¡Virgen Santísima!: Holy Virgin Mary!; an exclamation of disbelief.

Volcarse: Equivocarse (to make a mistake).

Y

Yaguazo: Refers to hitting someone.

Yelo: Cold. A variant of the word *hielo* (ice).

Yico: A person who lacks elegance.

Z

¡Zafa!: Exclamation used to shoo a person away.

Zafacón: Trash and garbage receptacle; a person of very low character.

Zapatazo: A forceful kick; from the word *zapato* (shoe).

The Human Body

The local vernacular of Quisqueya, especially in the rural zones, becomes decidedly colorful, at times even playful, when references are made to the human anatomy. The words used are by no means reflective of any intent on the part of the speaker to be vulgar or obscene, or disrespectful. The listing that follows is a sampling the words that one hears in ordinary conversations with individuals from various rural zones around the island.

Standard Usage	Dominicanism
boca (mouth)	hocio
cabello (hair)	grenas, pelo trenzas, risos, pasas
cabeza (head)	testa, caco, coco
cara (face)	facha, cacheta
cuello (neck)	pezcuezo, galillo, cocote
dientes, muelas (teeth)	hachas
espinazo (spine)	rabadilla
excremento (excrement)	sica, mierda, pupú, caca
intenstinos (intestines)	tripas
labios (lips)	bembe, chemba

lengua (tongue)	la colorá
mandíbula (jaw)	quijada
mejillas (cheeks)	buches, mofletudo
naríz (nose)	nata
ojos (eyes)	usually described in some distinctive manner: ojos de gatos: (cat's eyes); ojos bizcos (cross-eyed).
oreja (ears)	guataca
orina (urine)	miáo, pipí
piernas (legs)	canillas
pies (feet)	patas

Popular Dominican Sayings

Throughout La República Dominicana much of daily conversation, even that of a serious nature, is readily sprinkled with a savory dose of popular phrases and witticisms, converted into local proverbs. A sampling follows:

1. *Llevar los pantalones.*
To wear the pants = the man of the house.

2. *Duro de pelar.*
Hard to peel = a stubborn individual.

3. *Viejo pero no pendejo.*
I'm old, but I'm nobody's fool.

4. *Dios le da barba al que no tiene quijada.*
God gives a beard to him who has no jaw = Fortune comes to those who least deserve it.

5. *Se ahoga en vaso de agua.*
You can drown in a glass of water = You're not resourceful enough to solve even your simplest problems.

6. *La semana de los tres jueves.*
The week of three Thursdays = It will never happen.

7. *Hacerse el que no tumba una paja.*
To make oneself (appear) as one who doesn't even drop a straw = He wouldn't hurt even a fly; looks are deceiving.

8. *De noche todos los gatos son prietos.*
   At night, all cats are black. (Behind closed doors, everybody is the same.)

9. *No hay mal que por bien no venga.*
   There's always a brighter day ahead.

10. *Mientras el perro es más flaco más pulgas tiene.*
    The skinniest dog carries the most fleas.

11. *Tardío, pero seguro.*
    Late, but sure. I may be late, but at least I'm here.

12. *Se salió del tiesto.*
    You finally left your cage. (Implying a state of personal independence.)

13. *Los hombres son como el alacrán, que esperan la noche para hacer su can.*
    Men are like scorpions; they wait for nightfall in order to raise hell.

Appendix B
National Treasures

In La República Dominicana there are two indomitable symbols that, more than any other images, are totally unyielding in their representation of the spirit and flavor of *la cultura dominicana*. In fact, so thoroughly etched into the soul of the nation, so deeply revered by the people of the island are these two icons that they have attained the stature of safely enshrined national treasures. Quite irrespective of other barriers of socioeconomic circumstance, or political ideology, educational level, or regional competition, these national treasures bear unfaltering prominence in the national psyche. *El sancocho dominicano* and the *merengue* have been, and continue to be, the two precious gems of immeasurable value and esteem to the nation. Without question, these treasures are the two images that correctly evoke the true meaning of Dominican culture.

El Sancocho Dominicano

The reader must understand from the outset that there exists an infinite variety of this tremendously popular local dish, with individual cooks using jealously guarded family recipes that have been passed down through generations of family cooks. Here is but one such secret: Doña Paulina's recipe is enough for ten to twelve servings.

Use choice cuts:
½ lb. pork shoulder
10 cups water
1 lb. flank beef steak

2 chopped onions
2 lbs. chicken, cut up
2½ chopped tomatoes
½ lb. pork
2 chopped hot peppers (ajíes)
1 lb. ham shank (bone in)
2 ears green corn, cut into 1 inch slices
2 sprigs cilantro
1 tbsp. salt

Traditional island seasoning herbs, including: *adobo* mix, *sazón* (with *achiote*), *sofrito* sauce. Locally grown (tropical) vegetables, cut into 1½-inch cubes or slices:

½ lb. *yautía*, ½ lb. *yautía amarilla*, ½ lb. *yautía blanca*, ½ lb. *yuca*, ½ lb. *ñame*, 2 or 3 *plátanos*, ½ lb. *aullama*, ½ lb. *malanga*

Cut meats into one-inch cubes; season well. Sauté meat cubes in small amount of olive oil. Add chopped onion, parsley, chopped tomatoes, chopped peppers. Sprinkle on some of the seasoning herbs and salt to taste. Cook in 10 cups water at simmering temperature until meats are tender. Remove meat from stewing pot and set aside. Bring broth to boil. Add a bit of cilantro, onion, and red peppers. Now add all vegetables: *yuca, yautía, yautía amarilla, yautía blanca, ñame, malanga, plátano, aullama.* Then add remaining seasonings. Cook slowly until all vegetables are tender. Return cooked meats to mixture. Add bits of *naranja agria* (sour orange) for final touch of flavor.

El Merengue

Without exception, this is the singular national rhythm of La República Dominicana. It is undisputedly the country's most popular dance and dominates the musical life of the entire island. To mention merengue is to mention La República Dominicana. Exhaustive investigations (most especially by Fradique Lizardi) into the subject of the origins of this traditional music/dance have produced substantial evidence to support the claim that the form itself comes from African/Haitian sources. Most research affirms, however, that the merengue seems to have evolved in conjunction with the founding of the First Republic in 1844. The rhythm was executed initially with the use of the drum, the güira (made from a dried gourd, with deeply cut ridges along one side, then scraped briskly with a steel comb-like pluck), and the guitar. This was the early period of the merengue, more than one hundred fifty years ago, when it was commonly known as the *Perico Ripiao,* or *merengue típico.*

Since the beginning of its enormous popularity, the merengue has been identified with the common folk—much like the early tango in Argentina, the plena in Puerto Rico, the rumba in Cuba, reggae in Jamaica, and calypso in Trinidad. Moreover, like these other distinctively national rhythms, merengue in the Dominican Republic was quickly declared *vulgar y obsceno* (vulgar and obscene) by the upper echelons of island society. Organized campaigns launched vicious attacks against this music and its accompanying dance form. There were even cries by some politicians and intellectuals to expel from the country all the *merengueros* (musicians who play or sing this music). Much later, during the rise to power of Trujillo, merengue symbolized something more. After becoming Padre del País, Trujillo used the merengue as a form of his personal, sardonic revenge against so-called high society. This was the same socioeconomic elite that had rebuffed his earlier, obsessive efforts to gain entry into their social ranks, especially upon a particular occasion regarding an exclusive social club in El Cibao's premier city, Santiago de los Caballeros. Trujillo therefore was instrumental in forcing the vulgar and obscene music to be played and danced at the country's most socially prominent salons. And instead of the humble grouping of drum, güira, guitar, and the additional accordion, the music now featured full orchestral arrangements. Don Luis Albertí is generally considered El Padre del Merengue in this regard.

The highly sophisticated, rather sedate merengue of the Trujillo Era gave way to the greater freedom of a seductive exuberance upon the assassination of the dictator. The size of the orchestra, for example, diminished, and the musicians themselves, who formerly remained seated in rather stiff regimented positions, now all took standing positions, swaying with the rhythms they executed. One phenomenal musician more than any other was responsible for the dramatically bold transformation of the merengue during this post-Trujillo period: the innovative World Ambassador of the Merengue, Johnny Ventura. The historical leaders of the *merengue dominicano* since the 1960s would have to be Ventura, Wilfredo Vargas, and Juan Luis Guerra. But by far the most charismatic, almost mythical, and certainly the most popular interpreter of this eminently national music has been El Mayimbe himself, Fernandito Villalona.

Appendix C
The Dominican Flag

The official flag of La República Dominicana is divided into four squares, two red and two blue, separated by a white cross. The color red symbolizes the blood shed by the patriots who fought so valiantly for their country's liberation. Blue represents the peace desired by *el pueblo dominicano*. The white cross is in remembrance of Christ, who died for the salvation of mankind. The Dominican coat of arms, located at the center of the flag, bears the same tricolor pattern as the flag. In the center, the Holy Bible and the cross are surrounded by lances and flags that symbolize the patriotic spirit of the Dominican people. At one side of the red and blue square is a laurel branch—indicating immortality and triumph. Standing along the other side is a palm branch for freedom. Together, the laurel and the palm represent heaven. Floating above the coat of arms is a sash on which are written the words *Dios, Patria y Libertad* (God, Country and Liberty). The sash at the bottom displays the name of the country, República Dominicana.

The Dominican National Anthem

The country's melodic national anthem was written in 1883 by the famous Dominican poet Emilio Prud'Homme, with accompanying music composed by José Reyes. The hymn's lyrics reveal a great deal about the historic and noble sentiment of the Dominican people. Even earlier, on February 27, 1844, a single rallying call for independence issued the significant proclamation insisting upon *la libertad de los ciudadanos, aboliendo para siempre la esclavitud* (the liberty of citizens, abolishing slavery forever).

El Himno Nacional Dominicano

I

Quisqueyanos valiente, alcemos	Brave Quisqueyanos, let us raise up
Nuestro canto con viva emoción	Our song with enlivened emotion,
Y del mundo a la faz ostentemos	And let us show the world the face of
Nuestro invicto, glorioso pendón	Our invincible, glorious banner.
¡Salve! al pueblo que, intrépido	Hail to the people who, fearless and
y fuerte,	strong,
A la guerra a morir se lanzó,	Threw themselves into battle, prepared to die,
Cuando en bélico reto de muerte	When in the warlike defiance of death,
Sus cadenas de esclavo rompió.	They broke their chains of slavery.

II

Ningún pueblo ser libre merece	No people deserve to be free if
Si es esclavo, indolente y servil;	They are indolent and submissive slaves;
Si en su pecho la llama no crece	If in their heart there does not rise
Qué templo el heroísmo viríl,	The flame that tempered virile heroism,
Más Quisqueya la indóminto y brava	But the brave and indomitable Quisqueya
Siempre altiva la frente alzará;	Will always raise its lofty head;
Que si fuere mil veces esclava	That if it were enslaved a thousand times,
Otras tantas ser libre sabrá.	As many others shall know how to be free.

Bibliography

The following general reference list is designed to be of maximum assistance in introducing both the student and the general reader to the material on the Dominican Republic. Emphasis is placed on sources readily available in English, although many entries in Spanish are cited. Many more exceptionally fine works on Dominican history written in Spanish are accessible on the island.

Alavarez, Julia. *How the García Girls Lost Their Accents*. Chapel Hill, NC: Algonquin Books, 1991.
———. *In The Time of the Butterflies*. Chapel Hill, NC: Algonquin Books, 1995.
Balaguer, Joaquín. *Colección Discursos*. Títulos publicados, viii tomos. Santo Domingo: Editora Corripio, 1983.
———. *Guía Emocial de la Ciudad Romántica*. Barcelona: Los Telleres Sirven, 1978.
———. *La Isla Alrevés: Haití y el Destino Dominicano*. Santo Domingo: Editora Corripio, Librería Dominicana, 1984.
———. *Los Próceres Escritores*. 2a edición. Buenos Aires: Rafael Calzada, 1971.
———. *La Venda Transparente*. Madrid: Impresos y Revistas, 1987.
Barnet, Miguel. *Biografía de un Cimarrón*. La Habana: Academia de Ciencias de Cuba, 1966.
Bautista, Jaime A. "Llegó la hora," in *Hoy,* xv, 10 de Junio de 1994, Santo Domingo.
Black, Jan Knippers. *The Dominican Republic: Politics and Development in an Unsovereign State*. Boston: Allen & Unwin, 1986.
Bosch, Juan. *Breve Historia de la Oligarquía*. Santo Domingo: Impresora Arte y Cine, 1971.
———. *Composición Social Dominicana: Historia e Interpretación*. 17a edición. Santo Domingo: Alfa y Omega, 1991.
———. *De Cristóbal Colón a Fidel Castro: El Caribe, Frontera Imperial*. Barcelona: Editora Alafaguara, 1970.

Calder, Bruce J. *The Impact of Intervention: The Dominican Republic During the North American Operation of 1916–1924.* Austin: University of Texas Press, 1984.

Campbell, Mavis. *The Maroons of Jamaica, 1655–1796.* Granby, MA.: Bergin & Garvey Publishers, 1988.

Cassá, Roberto. *Historia Social y Económica de la República Dominicana.* 2 tomos. Santo Domingo: Editora Alfa y Omega, 1989.

———. *Los Taínos de la Española.* Santo Domingo: Universidad Autónoma de Santo Domingo, 1974.

Centro Dominicano de Estudios de la Educación (CEDEE). *Escarbando las Raíces de la Explotación.* No. 1. Santo Domingo: Ediciones Cedee, 1987.

Cordero Michel, Emilio. *Historia Económica, Social y Política de Santo Domingo.* Tema viii. Santo Domingo: UASD, Facultad de Ciencas Económicas y Sociales, 1970.

———. *La Revolución Haitiana y Santo Domingo.* Santo Domingo: Editora Taller, 1974.

Caswell, Robert D. *Trujillo: Life and Times of a Caribbean Dictator.* New York: Macmillan, 1966.

Deive, Carlos Estéban. *Los Cimarrónes del Maniel de Neiba: Historia y Etnografía.* Santo Domingo: Banco Central de La República Dominicana, 1985.

Diop, Chekh Anta. *The African Origins of Civilization.* Westport, CT: Lawrence Hill, 1984.

Dobal, Carlos. "Herencia Española en la Cultura Dominicana de Hoy." In *Ensayos Sobre Cultura Dominicana.* 3a edición. Santo Domingo: Fundación Cultura Dominicana, 1990.

Drake, St. Clair. *Black Folks Here and There: Essays in History and Anthropology.* 2 vols. Los Angeles: Center for African American Studies, UCLA, 1990.

Fage, J. D. *A History of West Africa.* New York: Cambridge University Press, 1989.

Ferguson, James. *The Dominican Republic: Beyond the Lighthouse.* London: Monthly Review Press, Latin American Bureau, 1992.

Fernandez de Oviedo, Gonzalo. "Historia General y Natural de las Indias." In Herrera Miniño 1979.

Franco, Franklyn J. *Los Negros, Los Mulatos y La Nación Dominicana.* 8a edición. Santo Domingo: Editora Nacional, 1989.

García Manuel, Juan. *La Masacre de Palma Sola: Partidos, Lucha Política y el Asesinato del General: 1961–1963.* Santo Domingo: Editora Alfa y Omega, 1986.

Gleijeses, Piero. *The Dominican Crisis: The 1965 Constitutionalist Revolt and the American Intervention.* Baltimore: Johns Hopkins University Press, 1978.

Hall, Gwendolyn M. *Social Control in Slave-Plantation Societies: A Comparison of Saint-Domingue and Cuba.* Baltimore: Johns Hopkins University Press, 1971.

Heinl, Robert, and Nancy Heinl. *Written in Blood: The Story of the Haitian People, 1492–1971.* Boston: Houghton Mifflin, 1978.

Henríquez Ureña, Pedro. *El Español en Santo Domingo.* 4a edición. Santo Domingo: Editora Taller, 1982.

Herrera Miniño, Francisco R. "Raíces, Motivaciones y Fundamentos de la Raza Dominicana." *Ultima Hora* xix (22 de Marzo de 1979), Santo Domingo.

Hoetink, Harry. *El Pueblo Dominicano: 1850–1900, Apuntes para su Sociología Histórica.* Santiago de los Caballeros: Universidad Católica Madre y Maestra, 1985.

Holly, James T., and J. Dennis Harris. *Black Separatism and the Caribbean, 1860.* Ann Arbor, MI: University of Michigan Press, 1971.

James, C. L. R. *The Black Jacobins.* New York: Random House, 1963.

Jimenes Grullón, Juan Isidro. *La América Latina y La Revolución Socialista.* Santo Domingo: Editora Cultural Dominicana, 1971.

Jiménez, Blas. *Caribe Africano en Despertar.* Colección Cimarrónes. Santo Domingo: Nuevas Rutas, 1984.

Larrazábal Blanco, Carlos. *Los Negros y La Esclavitud en Santo Domingo.* Colección Pensamiento Dominicano. Santo Domingo: Julio D. Postigo e Hijos Editores, 1967.

Lawrence, Harold G. "African Explorers of the New World." *The Crisis* (June–July 1962).

Lemoine, Maurice. *Azúcar Amargo: Hay Esclavos en el Caribe.* 2a edición. Santo Domingo: Ediciones, CEPAE, 1987.

Lizardo, Fradique. *Danzas y Bailes Folklóricos Dominicanos.* Ediciones Fundación García Arévalo y Museo del Hombre Dominicano. Santo Domingo: Editora Taller, 1975.

———. *El Folklore: Problemas, Métodos y Prioridades en la Antropología en La República Dominicana, Una Evaluación.* Santo Domingo: Fondo para el Avance de las Ciencas Sociales, 1978.

———. *Instrumentos Musicales Folklóricos Dominicanos.* Santo Domingo: Editorial Santo Domingo, 1988.

Marrero Aristy, Ramón. *Over.* 15a edición. Colección Pensamiento Dominicano, Santo Domingo: Biblioteca Taller No. 4, 1992.

Mella, Nelson. "Balance Critico de una Práctica Cultural," *Hoja Cedee.* Centro Dominicano de Estudios de la Educación, año vii, no. 13, Santo Domingo, June 1993.

Mir, Pedro. *Hay un País en el Mundo y Otros Poemas de Pedro Mir.* Biblioteca Taller No. 81. Santo Domingo: Ediciones de Taller, 1994.

———. *El Gran Incendio: Los Balbuceos Americanos del Capitalismo Mundial.* Santo Domingo: UASD, Colección Historia y Sociedad, Editora del Caribe, 1970.

———. *Tres Leyendas de Colores.* Santo Domingo: Editora Nacional, 1969.

Moya Pons, Frank. *Manual de Historia Dominicana.* 5a edición. Santiago de los Caballeros: Universidad Católica Madre y Maestra, 1980.

Murray, R. N. *West Indian History.* London: Thomas Nelson & Sons, Ltd., 1987.

Paquin, Lyonel. *The Haitians: Class and Color Politics.* Brooklyn: Multi-Type Press, 1983.

Peña Gómez, José Francisco. *Diez Discursos.* Ediciones de la Secretaria General del Partido Revolucionario Dominicano. Santo Domingo, 1989.

Pequero, Valentina, and Danilo de los Santos. *Visión General de la Historia Dominicana.* Santo Domingo: Editoria Taller, 1981.

Price-Mars, Jean. *La República de Haiti y la República Dominicana.* Port-au-

Prince: Colección de tercer Cincuentenario de Haiti, 1953.

Remigio Pichardo, Diomedes. *Peña Gómez: Su Pensamiento Político.* Santo Domingo: Editora Victorama, 1994.

Rodríguez Demorizi, Emilio. *Cancionero de Lilís,* Santo Domingo: Editora del Caribe, 1962.

Salmador, Victor. *José Francisco Peña Gómez.* Madrid: Edición No Venal, 1990.

Sherlock, Sir Philip. *A History of The West Indies.* London: Nelson Press, Ltd., 1983.

Silié, Rubén. *Economia, Esclavitud y Población.* Santo Domingo: UASD, 1976.

———. "El Hato y El Conuco: Contexto para el Surgimiento de la Cultura Criolla." In *Ensayos de Cultura Dominicana.* Santo Domingo: Fundación Cultura Dominicana, 1988.

Tamayo García, E. "Familia y Economía Campesina en la Frontera Dominicana." In *Revistas Sociales,* año xii, no. 48, Octubre–Diciembre, Santiago: UCMM, 1979.

Tolentino Dipp, Hugo. *Raza e Historia en Santo Domingo: Los orígines del prejuicio racial en América.* 2a edición. Santo Domingo: Fundación Cultura Dominicana, 1992.

Torres, Alfonso. "Primero la Gente," *Ulitma Hora,* 17 de May de 1994, Santo Domingo.

Van Sertima, Ivan. *Blacks in Science: Ancient and Modern.* 11th ed. New Brunswick, NJ: Transaction Books, 1991.

———. *They Came Before Columbus: The African Presence in Ancient America.* New York: Random House, 1991.

Vega, Bernardo. "La Herencia Indígena en la Cultura Dominicana de Hoy." In *Ensayos Sobre Cultura Dominicana.* Santo Domingo: Fundación Cultural Dominicana / Museo del Hombre Dominicano, 3a edición.

Wilentz, Amy. *The Rainy Season: Haiti Since Duvalier.* New York: Simon & Schuster, 1989.

Williams, Sir Eric. *Capitalism & Slavery.* Sixth Printing. New York: Capricorn Books, 1966.

Index

Wheel, 33
Wilson, Woodrow, 163*n*.5, 167

Y

Yague del Norte River, 23
Yaque del Sur River, 24

Yuna River, 23

Z

Zaire, 81
Zulu, 81

Alan Cambeira teaches at Clark Atlanta University and DeKalb College. A native of the Caribbean, the author was trained in Latin American Literature and Culture at Pennsylvania State University, Brooklyn College, and the City University of New York. Recipient of an NEH Fellowship to investigate the culture of the Dominican Republic, he continues to conduct seminars and workshops on building greater awareness of Caribbean and Hispanic cultures.